SUBDUED FIRES

FIRES

An Intimate Portrait of Pope Benedict XVI

Garry O'Connor

D1465031

The History Press

Truth doesn't drip oil onto wounds to stop the burning pain, or sit you on a donkey to be led through the streets. Truth must be hurtful, must hide.

Karol Wojtyla, John Paul II, *Gospel*

This book is dedicated to Harry Kit, my grandson, born on 6 March 2013, the same day I delivered the manuscript of *Subdued Fires* to The History Press.

Front cover: Pope Benedict XVI leads his first *Via Crucis*, way of the Cross, in Easter Holy Week at the Roman Colosseum, April 14, 2006. (Alessandra Benedetti/Corbis)

Back cover: Joseph Ratzinger as a young boy of perhaps six or seven.

First published 2013

The History Press
The Mill, Brimscombe Port
Stroud, Gloucestershire, GL5 2QG
www.thehistorypress.co.uk

British Library Cataloguing in Publication Data.
A catalogue record for this book is available from the British Library.

ISBN 978 0 7524 9897 3

Contents

PART II

THE COVERED-UP CHURCH

About the Author

Garry O'Connor worked in the theatre as a director for ten years, after which he became a theatre critic for the *Financial Times*, then a full-time, award-winning author of biographies, plays and novels. Recent publications include the novel *Chaucer's Triumph,* a joint biography of Cherie and Tony Blair, *The Darlings of Downing Street*, and the acclaimed *Universal Father*, the life of John Paul II. Garry O'Connor is married and has six children and four grandchildren. For The History Press he is the author of *The 1st Household Cavalry 1943–44: In the Shadow of Monte Amaro* and *The Butcher of Poland*, a life of Hitler's lawyer, Hans Frank, to be published in autumn 2013.

Praise for Garry O'Connor's *Universal Father; A Life of Pope John Paul II*:

An artistic achievement in its own right. None of O'Connor's predecessors has matched his exposition of the literary, philo-sophical and dramatic resources of John Paul's pontificate, or his nimble untangling of the strands of theological argument. (*Daily Telegraph*)

A distinctive, insightful and enjoyable book. (*Independent*)

A fine, enduring biography. (*Glasgow Herald*)

Also by Garry O'Connor

FICTION

Author Garry O'Connor meets Pope John Paul II.

DRAMA

Different Circumstances
Dialogue Between Friends
Debussy Was My Grandfather, Two Plays

THEATRE AND CINEMA STUDIES

Le Théâtre en Grande-Bretagne
French Theatre Today
The Mahabharata: Peter Brook's Epic in the Making

Foreword

6 June 2004

Omaha Beach, Normandy, scene of the first landings of the Allied invasion of mainland Europe in 1944, which is to lead, together with Russia's advance from the East, to the overthrow of Adolf Hitler and the Third Reich. Steven Spielberg has replicated with graphic impact the carnage unleashed on the beachheads in his film *Saving Private Ryan*.

The Vatican delegation, sent by John Paul II to commemorate the invasion, is headed by Joseph Ratzinger, an alleged former Nazi youth who, while resident in Rome for the previous 23 years as Prefect for the Congregation of the Faith (CDF, formerly the Holy Office, formerly the Inquisition), is known generally in the media as 'The Panzer Cardinal', or 'God's Rottweiler'.

This is the German sheepdog breed which goes back to Roman times, famed for its savagery, brutality and ugliness, but today in Ratzinger's native state of Bavaria legally subject to muzzle and leash control.

The 77-year old, white-haired cardinal, small in build, stooped, gracious and mild in manner, hardly lives up to this description. For many years, since 1981, he has been the papal enforcer of worldwide Church discipline, often at the cost of outrage and hostility, and the Pope's closest colleague.

Ratzinger is in Normandy from his own choice, and while ever the patriotic German, he finds his presence here painful.

Born in Upper Bavaria, near to the border with Austria, he looks more to the old cosmopolitan Austro-Hungarian Empire, with its former border only a few miles away from his home, than to the narrowly nationalistic Prussia of Frederick the Great.

As a gesture of reconciliation he has insisted on being at the scene of the Allied landings, symbolic of the beginning of the end of Hitler's power.

What does Ratzinger, standing in that beach-hood ceremony in Normandy, remember from his own childhood – passed often in mortal peril in the darkest years of his country's history?

He believes, and has said, that it is crucial to remember the past. He *remembers*, and as such is an apt testifier to the Greek word for truth, which is *aletheia** – literally 'not-forgetting'.

His own memories are of a rich and warm childhood in a pious, respectable, even rigid household. A safe childhood. But there are significant omissions which were to have an important effect on the future, both his own and the world's.

† † †

The life story of Joseph Ratzinger, Pope Benedict XVI (April 2005–February 2013), is a supreme example of the evolution of an outstanding intellect, combined with an unusual power of survival and the ability to reach the very pinnacle of achievement at the age of 78.

Here was an extraordinarily person of mature belief, who recognised and attempted consistently to apply in all his written works, speeches and actions the values of objective and clear thought, and of the careful use of evidence, maintaining these as the outstanding and lasting qualities of what it meant to be human.

Yet it cannot be denied that he has sometimes shown prejudice and even irrationality, indicating something unresolved and hidden in his character; when checked and aware of how he has caused outrage he has carefully tried to adjust and adapt, even backtrack on it. Ninety per cent of the time he applied his thinking dispassionately to the problems of living faith, as well as the

---

* From the root 'Lethe' meaning forgetting, as in the mythological river in Hades; aletheia, with its prefix a–, means 'against' or 'not' forgetting.

eschatology, of mankind, and much of what he said, and some of his Church reforms, have been apt and effective. But over them there has always been a shadow cast – that of the past.

Did he as a man, during his reign as pontiff and one of the most important figures on earth, stand as an example, not only for Catholics everywhere, and for adherents of other faiths – but also for the majority of secular and scientific non-believers in Western Europe, and the United States? This is one question I will attempt to answer.

† † †

For a long time Ratzinger was, as Prefect for the CDF, in the shadow of Pope John Paul II. He and the former Pope did not always see eye to eye – for instance he declined to endorse the Pope's view of the Third Millennium as 'a spring of the human spirit'. He opposed the 1986 World Day of Peace: 'This cannot be the model,' he commented. He said the restrictive side of his job was to help the Pope with the necessary '"Nos" when the Pope [John Paul II] had a natural inclination to say "Yes".' This prompted the Pope to respond, 'Maybe I should have been more assertive.'

When Ratzinger became Pope Benedict he remained ambiguous and mystifying, except in theological matters of faith, and never showed the world who he was until that turning point of his pontificate in 2010 when the sexual abuse crisis threatened to overwhelm the Church. Like his predecessor, he admitted to and underlined the fact that everyone has a good side and a bad side, but on the whole – except for occasional mishaps and unconscious, or unintended, lowering of his guard – the range and many-sidedness of his character never emerged in daylight.

He always refused requests for interviews, including my own, and he has only opened up to one journalist, after a tryout with John Paul's Italian chronicler, Vittorrio Messori, namely his fellow Bavarian Peter Seewald, suggesting he had a need to control what emerged in his own words in the way of personal confession, keeping it very much to the minimum, while the exchange of more general views are almost on a fifty–fifty basis with his interrogator.

I take one word from him, his excellent and humble description of his Jesus of Nazareth – as a part guide to what I am attempting – a 'proposal' for looking into the inner man, who may be divided into three: Joseph; Ratzinger; and Pope Benedict.

Perhaps ultimately there was always some residual fear in him, which again makes it important to show or try to examine where it came from, and how it influenced him: 'What is this need to see a person?' wrote Pope Paul VI when he became pope. When evaluating a pope's thought and influence just as a pastor and teacher it is perhaps not so important, but attempting a portrait of a figure on the world stage whose public utterances influence millions, and can cause both disasters and unexpected miracles, one cannot but look closely at the person.

Benedict pointed again to the contradiction in every human being in 2009 when he said in his book *Paul of Tarsus* that the inner contradiction of our being is not a theory. 'As a consequence of this evil power in our souls, a murky river developed in history which poisons the geography of human history... Blaise Pascal, the great French thinker, spoke of a "second nature" which superimposes our original good nature' – and Benedict concluded that 'the power of evil in the human heart is an undeniable fact.'

This 'second nature' has, to a debateable degree, been evident in the Vatican during the 32 years that Ratzinger has been there, first as cardinal then as Pope Benedict. The question to be asked is: to what extent has he stopped the Vatican encroaching upon the power of the good, or encouraged the good that would check and dispel it? Given the recent scandals and disclosure of thefts, sexual impropriety, corruption, the tendency of the Vatican to operate like a royal court, with all the ensuing gossip, bitchery, vanity and secrecy that goes with it – it might be thought the overall spectacle (in spite of the many good men) has changed little since the time when Cardinal Newman described Rome: clear from the top of the hill – down below full of malaria and swamps. Will the river of faith in global consciousness, if not to many millions of devout followers who don't want to notice it, always have a constant murky streak?

I am not going to presume to say what should be done by his successor, now that Benedict has so bravely stepped down.

It is not for nothing Benedict has earned his title of 'the Pope of Surprises'.

† † †

Those critical of Benedict have tended to overlook the fact that the man is primarily an intellectual visionary and idealist, and as such a great inspiration to the body of the Church as its teacher and mentor, rather than to the world outside. This visionary aspect of his character, as deep and many-layered as that of some of the great visionaries of mankind, has been ignored. It has flowered late in life.

Perhaps we should look to literature and art for similar late flowerings of vision, to the example of Sophocles, in Greek theatre, writing *Oedipus Rex* at a comparable age – not only a great play and the first example of detective fiction, but a seminal work for Freud and modern psychology – and leaving its sequel unfinished when he died at the age of ninety; or to Rome and the world of Italian Renaissance art, in which Michelangelo worked in his eighties designing St Peter's Basilica.

Ratzinger's own vision has been much quieter and more restrained than either of these – less a heaven 'full of the sound of clashing swords' in W.B. Yeats's trenchant phrase, rather the muted harmonies of a pretty Bavarian landscape. It is expressed through the carefully chosen words and concepts of an intellectual. Some critics wrongly claim that this, strictly speaking, is not a vision at all, or if so, hardly realised; and it is too soon to assess how much, or the degree to which it holds together consistently, or will last as a positive influence.

Yet whether it came in written form, simplified in his many lucidly simple homilies and encyclicals, or through measures, less convincingly, attempted in governance of the Catholic Church, there was still an aspiration to transcendental scale and cosmic relevance. It is far too early to ask, 'Was this the right vision for the Catholic Church?' My intention is to show as far as I can how that vision came about, and what it did or did not reflect of the inner man.

† † †

No one can deny that largely, even with the new advances of globalisation, we live in an age of double standards and precarious peace. The disrepute into which the Catholic Church fell as a result of increasing public knowledge of abuse cases from 2010 onwards, which began and even were evident much earlier, reduced trust and prestige to their lowest ebb. Tens of thousands left the Church, numerically compensated by new members joining mainly through the increasing birth-rates in Africa and South America, so the Church could save face in the statistics but not cover the decline in morale, especially in Europe and North America.

First I have to return to that earlier period of his past when similar double standards in much more extreme operation were the rule rather than – as some apologists of the flagrant abuses and present dark trends maintain – a series of unrelated episodes and unhappy exceptions.

Unlikely Bankroller

... Our natures do pursue
Like rats that ravine down their proper bane
A thirsty evil, and when we drink, we die.
William Shakespeare, *Measure for Measure*, I, ii

Spring 1919. In the late-eighteenth century, neo-Roman nuncia-ture or embassy of the Roman Catholic Church in Munich the stick-thin archbishop, the Vatican's legate or nuncio, to all observ-ers gentle and pious, knelt at prayer in the chapel.

Aged 43, six feet tall, with beautiful tapering hands, large and luminous dark eyes, the pallor of his skin had an eerie transpar-ent effect, as if projecting from the inside a cold, white flame. A Roman by birth, from a family of Church lawyers, he had arrived in Munich two years earlier, and impressed the war-weary Bavarians with his vigorous efforts to organise relief.

But now the city was in turmoil. Law and order had broken down. Left-wing mobs were on the rampage in the fashionable districts. The rump *Reichswehr*, the regular force allowed by the Versailles peace treaty, stayed in their barracks. The 20,000 strong newly recruited Free Corps, a right-wing, paramilitary force of mainly demobbed soldiers, had not yet arrived on the scene, to restore order and carry out savage reprisal.

There was an unholy banging on the embassy door. On the steps outside stood a bloodthirsty, armed contingent of Red revo-lutionaries. They had already killed those who resisted, and had taken aristocrats from the racialist Aryan Thule Society as hostages.

Eugenio Pacelli, the papal ambassador, rose to his feet. He had a lavish domestic entourage, but no security guards. Sister Pasqualina Lehnert, a beautiful South German nun, accompanied him everywhere. Later to be known as *La Popessa* (the popess) when Pacelli became Pope Pius XII, the wartime pope, it was Pasqualina who opened up the door.

The revolutionaries stormed into the embassy. Some demanded car keys and straight away stole the official vehicle.

Pacelli stood his ground and confronted the invaders. Haughty and dignified, he spoke with calmness and courage, telling them they had broken diplomatic law. The leader stepped forward and pressed the barrel of a rifle against his chest. Pacelli reeled. He tottered on his feet. Pasquelina ran to his aid, shouting at the insurgents to leave him alone.

Ultimately the Communists left him unhurt, but he suffered a terrible collapse, the first of many nervous collapses. A later generation, when psychological terms became current, would call it a trauma, and say that what he had suffered from was post-traumatic stress disorder, or PTSD. The invasion of his sanctuary and psyche by a Jewish-led Bolshevist mob produced a psychological wound from which he never fully recovered. It gave rise to bloodcurdling nightmares from which, it was alleged, he would awake screaming for the rest of his life.

† † †

Enter Kurt Eisner, a middle-class Jewish theatre critic from Munich's bohemian Schwabing district. Short of stature, small, wire-rimmed spectacles perched on his nose, he sported a heavy grey beard, a black cloak, and huge broad-brimmed black felt hat in the style of Lenin. Eisner had brought mayhem to Munich the previous November, 1918. Released from Cell 70 in Stadelheim gaol after a sentence for organising strikes to end the war, Eisner sneered at political convention.

Eisner wasn't exactly a Marxist but a way-out Democrat given to theatrical gestures. When immediate social breakdown and anarchy threatened the Social Democratic Party's control of Munich he organised a brass band and banners, summoned a crowd, exhorted it to occupy the army barracks and seize the Bavarian State Parliament.

He met no resistance from the diminished defence force allowed by the Versailles treaty, and was endorsed both by the revolutionary 'Workers' and the 'Soldiers' Councils'. Then, as leader, calling himself an Independent Social Democrat, and supported by the Majority and Independent Social Democrats, he proclaimed the Bavarian kingdom a Republic, the 'People's State'.

All sides condemned Eisner as a pacifist agitator, a Jew, a journalist, a bohemian and, worst of all – as they were in Bavaria – a Berliner. He had, even more nefariously and treacherously, published the secret and incriminating documents, collected by Felix Feuenbach who was his secretary, blaming the Germans for starting the war. Food supplies dwindled because the Bavarian peasantry withheld their support. Eisner's 'government' quickly foundered, while the Allied powers requisitioned the trains.

On 21 February 1919, Count Anton von Arco-Valley, an aristocrat and 19-year- old Munich student, shot Eisner twice at point-blank range in the street, killing him instantly. Murder and recrimination followed, with huge demonstrations at Eisner's funeral. Munich sank more and more into unregulated mob rule.

While on paper there was a legitimate Bavarian government of Majority Social Democrats, it couldn't command authority. The Workers and Soldiers' Councils distributed arms, and then a Soviet-style putsch seemed in the offing. Writers such as the playwright Ernst Toller – 'coffee house anarchists' – proclaimed Munich University open to all applicants except those who would study history!

Armed clashes between the 'Red Army' and Social Democrats became frequent. More militant Communists squashed the airy-fairy idealists to proclaim a Bolshevik Bavaria. They contacted Lenin in Moscow. 'Have you nationalised the banks yet?' enquired Lenin politely (and astutely). They followed his advice, and took hostages from the aristocracy and middle class.

The 'Goddess Reason' reigned in Munich's Catholic churches; radical priests of a persuasion that would later be termed 'Liberation Theology' joined the insurrection. Soon they were training a 'Red Army' of 20,000; many were boarded in churches and monasteries, where weapons were stored. It seemed Bavaria was about to spearhead the Bolshevisation of Europe.

Pacelli had, before his shocking experience, already visited a leading Bolshevik faction which had supported Eisner's seizure of power and made their headquarters in the former Bavarian royal palace. He wrote to his Vatican superior, in order to keep the Pope in Rome informed, that what he found was 'chaotic, the filth completely nauseating...' Once the home of a king, it resounded 'with screams, vile language, profanities... An army of employees was dashing to and fro, waving bits of paper, and in the midst of all this, a gang of young women, of dubious appearance, Jews like all the rest of them, hanging around in all the offices with provocative behaviour and suggestive smiles...'

This female gang's boss was their leader, Levine's, mistress, a young Russian woman, a Jew and a divorcee, while Levine, aged about 30 or 35, was also 'Russian and a Jew, Pale, dirty, with vacant eyes, hoarse voice, vulgar, repulsive, with a face that is both intelligent and sly.' In this and from other statements and actions Pacelli displayed a physical repulsion which reinforced an inherited anti-Judaism present in his heart and in his theological conditioning. It was to pave the way for his reluctance in the future to denounce – or even allow through his silence – the persecution of, and the atrocities committed against, Jewish people.

When he had recovered from his nervous collapse Pacelli quickly took a hand in helping to reassert full Catholic and legitimate democratic authority in the Bavarian capital.

† † †

There was an even stranger and darker sequel to the break-in at his embassy.

Some weeks later, unannounced, an unknown young man rang the embassy door bell and asked to see the papal legate. He had, he told the gatekeeper Pasqualina, a letter of introduction from no less a personage than General Erich Ludendorff, a hero of the Great War. He was admitted at once.

Pasqualina ushered the respectably dressed young man into Pacelli's study, and stood outside to listen to what followed. He told Pacelli he was an Austrian by birth who had fought in a Bavarian regiment and been decorated for bravery. Recently he had served as a *Bundingsoffizier*, an instructor to combat dangerous ideas among the rank and file. And now he was forming a new party called the *Deutsche Arbeiter Partei* (German worker's party), or DAP. They badly needed money.

Pasqualina heard him say (as she wrote in her 1959 autobiography, which was not allowed to be published until 1983) that he was a Catholic and his new party were determined to stop the spread of atheistic Communism. 'Munich has been good to me, so has Germany,' he told Pacelli. 'I pray to Almighty God that this land remains a Holy Land, in the hands of our Lord, and free of Communism.'

While Pasqualina listened to the young man's impassioned words, what she did not see in her listening post was the mesmeric effect of his deep blue eyes and hypnotic personality.

These, as a later supporter wrote, transfixed you and pierced right into your very soul. Another disciple, Julius Streicher, editor of the Munich *Der Stürmer*, said of his own first encounter with this charismatic figure: 'I had never seen the man before. And there I sat, an unknown among unknowns. I saw this man shortly before midnight, after he had spoken for three hours, drenched in perspiration, radiant. My neighbour said he thought he saw a halo round his head, and I experienced something which transcended the commonplace.'

The spell he cast was spiritual, the power that of an evangelist. Pacelli, who was hardly in the first flush of youth, allegedly fell entirely under the spell too, and was to remain so for many years. As Adolf Hitler left, Pasqualina saw Pacelli hand over a considerable sum of Vatican money.

'Go quell the devil's works,' Pacelli told him. 'For the love of Almighty God!'

Was this the start of an emotional subservience, almost a co-dependency – or at least a compliant response – by the high-ranking Catholic cleric to the future dictator of Germany?

Why this should ever be so was a mystery. Although in the words of one of his cardinals when he was pope, Pacelli was 'weak and rather timid. He was not born with the temper of a fighter,' this was by no means the whole story.

It was to have catastrophic consequences for the Catholic Church in Germany and for the whole world.

PART ONE

THE BOY FROM BAVARIA

What is the story of mankind?
What are good and evil?
What awaits us at the end
of our earthly existence?
Benedict XVI

An undated photograph of the Ratzinger family; Maria, Georg, Maria mère, Joseph, Joseph père.

1

Shadowland
or Fairyland?

'Co-operators in the truth.'
Ratzinger's motto when consecrated bishop

A plaque on the wall of number 11 Markltplatz, Marktl am Inn, near the Austrian border, where on the other side of the River Inn, just less than forty years earlier, Hitler had been born, marks the birthplace of Joseph Ratzinger on Easter Saturday, 16 April, 1927.

That he was baptised on Easter Sunday with fresh holy water blessed the night before, which gave the child special protection, sets a tone which permeates most accounts, including Ratzinger's own, of the very Christian atmosphere of his birth and early years. 'I love the beauty of our country, and I like walking. I am a Bavarian patriot; I particularly like Bavaria, our history, and of course our art. Music. That is a part of life I cannot imagine myself without.'

Joseph Ratzinger, the future Pope Benedict XVI, exactly repeats the sentiments and hobbies of many Bavarians who enthuse about, and are very proud of, their homeland. For example, the 18-year-old Hans Frank, later the first Nazi Bavarian Minister of Justice, wrote in his diary on 6 April 1918, 'We Bavarians, members of a genuine Germanic race, have been armed with a powerful sense of free will; only with the greatest reluctance and under duress do we tolerate this Prussian military dominance. It is this fact above all that constantly renews for us the symbol of the great, unbridgeable dividing line made by the mighty Main River, which separates South Germany from the North. To our way of thinking, the Prussian is a greater enemy than the Frenchman.'

'We remain anchored in our own Bavarian spirit because it is our cultural identity,' wrote Ratzinger in similar terms, in his memoir, *Milestones*. 'Our experience during childhood and youth inform the lives of each one of us. These are the true riches which we draw on for the rest of our lives.'

The Pope's Bavarian background has been highly and romantically idealised by both he himself and commentators on his life. The Italian writer Alessandra Borghese calls him 'the happy produce [*sic*] of a land such as Bavaria: Catholic from the start, firm in her faith, serious in her ways, but also warm in her feelings, fond of good music and thus of harmony, and always giving such colourful expression to life.'

Borghese rejoices in the link between Bavaria and her native city, Rome: 'happiness and openness, love of conviviality are shared qualities... Benedict is often told Munich is Italy,' she asserts.

Joseph's parents by chance (or 'providence') were named Joseph and Maria (Mary in German and Italian). His mother, a miller's daughter, the eldest of eight who had a tough upbringing, worked as a hotel pastry cook in Munich, while his father, from a slightly higher social bracket, came from an old family of poor Lower Bavarian farmers.

Joseph senior served two years in the Royal Bavarian Army before training for the police during the First World War at Ingolstadt. We learn nothing about this. He and his son would often go hiking when he was 'on extended sick leave', when he would tell Joseph 'stories of his early life', although Joseph does not tell us in *Milestones* what these were. He worked as a constable, or inspector, or commissioner (he is referred to as all three).

Joseph's parents met through an announcement in the press that he was looking for a wife. Forty-three-year-old Joseph, in March 1920 – calling himself 'a low-level civil servant', according to Bavarian State archives – placed an advertisement in a Catholic newspaper for a wife, a girl who knew how 'to cook and also sews a bit', and who shared his faith. Today he would presumably have had to go through a dating agency, or post his details on the Internet.

As a policemen with poor pay he added that he would not 'be displeased if she had some money of her own'. At the age of over forty, advanced in those days, he then wrote to his superior officers requesting permission to marry.

It would seem from the first he was unable to support fully a wife and family, similar to many a policeman today. Maria, still unmarried at the age of 37, came forward.

This was four months after the first advert, when, with little or no success, he had upgraded his CV to 'mid-ranking civil servant'. This is not mentioned in *Milestones* as an important milestone, but in the Bavarian State archive. She had no money of her own but she did work. They married on 9 November 1920.

Joseph senior was grey-haired with a moustache, not a handsome man but rather scraggly-looking, and tenacious; he was, Joseph said with hindsight, 'very strict, perhaps too strict'. He thought differently from the way one was supposed to think, and with a 'sovereign superiority'.

Maria, on the other hand, was from all accounts cheerful and good-natured. She sang hymns to the Virgin Mary while washing up, which incurred her husband's disapproval. His parents had 'two very different temperaments... a difference which made them complimentary'. Both valued thrift, honour, and led a life of frugality, which enabled Joseph senior to put money aside and save for a home for his retirement.

Up until that time when they owned a house they lived in local constabularies manned by Joseph senior – 'above the shop', as had happened with Margaret Thatcher, although in Ratzinger's case, and as the father was an important local functionary, the 'copshop' was a grander if more decaying establishment.

† † †

Karol Wojtyla, Pope John Paul II, mentioned that his birth sign, Taurus, was indicative of his personality. Joseph's birth sign was that of Aries, the Ram, representing in its symbolic aspect sacrifice. The popular trait of this star sign promises a gradual and deliberate rather than a spontaneous rise in life, but also a potential leadership complex, which has to be reined in. The combination of an Arien and Taurean, John Paul II, who later became Pope Ratzinger's close colleague, made for an excellent match. At the same time, interpreters of the sign warn of a tendency to temperamental outbursts much to be avoided (or not shown).

Joseph's uncle Georg, Joseph's great-uncle, had been a priest and theologian, a Reichstag deputy and member of the Bavarian parliament. He championed the rights of peasants, and, noted for his richness of thought and animated exposition, and frequent changes of political allegiance, he had once written attacking the political economy of Adam Swift.

Georg was also fiercely anti-Semitic in his writings and thought, blaming Jewish financial power for undermining traditional German values of discipline, modesty, family integrity and the Christian faith. (This is not mentioned in Joseph's memoir, *Milestones*, published in 1998, nor in Peter Seewald's biography, *Benedict XVI*.)

'Jews were part of the alien world of Munich rather than rural society,' writes Nicholas Boyle. 'Georg's long and severe involvement with urban and economic affairs must have made him a somewhat suspect character... If Josef is said to have had "no friends as a boy" it must in part have been because he was repeatedly uprooted and learned to put his trust in no one but the family and the church.'

To have had an avowed intellectual anti-Semite in the family presumably, too, was not a bad credential for survival in the Nazi era, for if necessary, Nazi investigators dug deep into family history. Not that there was any need for or use made of this.

Cultivating an uncritical, detached picture of Joseph's early life runs the risk of being accused of concealing other sides of the story by not bringing attention to them. Today's world is curious and questioning. In 1996, as cardinal, he praised Georg's work supporting peasant rights, and against child labour. 'His achievements and his political standing also made everyone proud of him,' Ratzinger told Seewald. But from what he tells us and what we know we can never properly form a picture of the father and the family, as we can do in the case of Karol Wojtyla. He tells us what he feels he ought to tell us, in view of his position, to form the correct idea of him that we should have.

Just before Joseph was two, his father was posted to Tittmoning, a small and picturesque baroque town that bordered Austria. Joseph had only just survived an attack of diphtheria, which made him unable to eat. They lived once more in the town square, in what was formerly the seat of the town provost. A proud house, Joseph recalled, 'from my childhood land of dreams', although the reality was more often than not that of his aged mother hauling up coal and wood two flights in a dilapidated dwelling with crumbling walls and peeling paint.

On 15 March 1929 Hitler launched an impassioned appeal for the German Army to think again about its rejection of National Socialism, and its support of the Weimar Republic. Even so, the Nazis still floundered – until the Germany economy suddenly collapsed.

The Wall Street Crash of 1929 changed Hitler's fortunes. Then, and only then, did Nazism seriously begin to catch fire in the hearts and minds of the German people.

In 1931 Cardinal Michael Faulhaber visited the town to confirm some children. According to legend, Joseph, who welcomed the cardinal with other children by singing songs, was so enamoured of the blood red of the cardinal's cassock, and his black, chauffeur-driven Mercedes limousine that he shouted, 'One day I will be a cardinal too!'

Georg, his elder brother, calmed him down by saying, 'I thought you said you wanted to be a house painter.' He had already expressed this desire – perhaps from consideration of the state of the Tittmoning house's interior decoration.

The dwelling also housed a special holding cell for prisoners, who were fed from the frugal family table. On the other hand, Joseph senior's uniform was not exactly short on ceremonial flourish. He wore, for formal parades, not only his green uniform, polished belt and buckle, sabre and revolver, but also the distinct and rather comical Bavarian policeman's helmet.

Whenever the father went out on night patrols, Maria prayed with her children that their father would come home safely. During his day duty on the beat Maria used to man the telephone in the office. It was a very ordered, institutional life from which, in some form or other, the children were never to deviate in the future.

By the end of 1932 his father had been posted again, this time to the less idyllic village of Aschau, where the authorities rented for him and his family part of a pretty farm house a local farmer had built for himself. They lived in second-floor rooms and had running water but no bath. In front of the house stood a roadside cross, and in the garden there was a pond into which one day Joseph fell and almost drowned, leaving him with a lifelong fear of drowning.

The ground floor was occupied by the office and an auxiliary policeman, an ardent atheist and Nazi, who outside in the garden performed military exercises with his wife. This policeman attended Catholic Mass to spy on the priest and make notes on the sermon with a view to inform, in case it was seditious. To do this he had to genuflect before the Stations of the Cross, which caused some merriment in the family.

Joseph, who had attended kindergarten, began primary school in Aschau. He noticed how his father more frequently, as time went on, had to 'intervene' at public meetings in disturbances caused by the violence of the Nazis. As usual, he does not say what actually happened, and what form his father's intervention took. When he became an altar boy, he witnessed the Nazis beat up his parish priest. Again, there was no resistance in the Ratzinger family.

It was during this time Jews began to leave, or were driven out of their homes and businesses. Or maybe it was the Communists who suffered. Erich Röhm's Brown Shirts, the SA or *Sturmabteilung* (Storm Detachment or Assault Division), were now a self-proclaimed, auxiliary police force.

We take Ratzinger's word for it that from the start his family were conscientious objectors to Nazism, although there is no other proof of this than his word. But at heart, while unwilling to conform, they were quietists rather than active or clandestine opponents during the rise of Nazism, and later against the Reich.

On Sunday Joseph senior smoked a Virginia cigarette and read the anti-Nazi *Gerade Weg*. The parents never discussed the declining political situation, as they did not want, so Joseph later wrote, to involve the children. Yet to think of the many millions of children who were to perish later, as a result of the acquiescent attitude of many millions of Germans, is mind-boggling.

'Man lives on the basis of his own experiences,' said the Polish John Paul II, who was Ratzinger's direct predecessor in the papacy. Joseph's experience in childhood was that you didn't discuss such matters. Joseph senior and Maria weren't people who came forward to assert their views. They were Mr and Mrs Bavarian Everyman. They didn't discuss politics, certainly not in front of the family. They questioned a bit, but not too much. Their religion gave them faith in modest circumstances and they took heart and found security in finding them similar to those of their saviour. Obedient to the Catholic catechism, they surrounded their family with an atmosphere of love and attention. The two boys were intellectually very able and academically very clever, so the daughter took on a subsidiary role as they did everything they could to further the boys' education, trying to make sure nothing would get in their way.

This was the early stage, when and where the resistance *was* needed. As the Lutheran pastor Martin Niemöller wrote in a poem which became world-famous:

When the Nazis came for the Communists
I was silent.
I wasn't a Communist.
When the Nazis came for the Social Democrats
I was silent.
I wasn't a Social Democrat.
When the Nazis came for the Trades Unionists
I was silent.
I wasn't a Trade Unionist.
When the Nazis came for the Jews
I was silent.
I wasn't a Jew.
When the Nazis came for me
There was no one left
To protest.

From early on in his life, the colouring of Joseph's speech probably came from his mother's South Tyrolese idiom, which 'mixed with the dialect of Upper Bavaria and the accented colouration of the vowels, later became virtually his trademark'. The accent was provincial. The mindset of his early years, too, was markedly Bavarian, by which I mean baroque. This cultural influence over his thought and character went deep, but more important was the unconditional love of his parents and the refuge his family supplied.

With his Bavarian background, and first eighteen years spent in Nazi Germany, he shared a culture with Hans Frank which had a very different outcome, yet still exerted a deep influence over his thought and character.

The 'true riches' of his childhood and youth had a dark side, and it could possibly be that, in the future, sometimes in drawing on that past he lacked sufficient self- knowledge to be clear what exactly he was drawing on.

2

The Pied Piper of Lower Bavaria

Unfortunately, the narcissistic personality ... formed in the earliest years is heavily endorsed by our society with its emphasis on *imagining ourselves*. The vast, technically empowered world of advertising stresses day and night the importance of being with the 'right' people, in the 'right' clothes, in the 'right' car, in the 'right' job etc. I must be forever improving my image, learning more and more to see myself in the image of the good life.

Sebastian Moore, *Must I Tell You Who I Am?*

Four years before Joseph was born, in 1923, when his older brother Georg was in early infancy, there happened in Bavarian history an extremely important event, which must have involved Joseph senior, as a Bavarian state policeman, in some way, possibly a very personal way – although we have no record of this. The momentous event took place in Munich, which was not very far away.

It would serve, even at this early time, to bolster up for the family and for the future Pope, the Catholic Church, both as a symbol and as a shelter and insulation from the traumatic experiences of their fellow Germans.

In the long term how strong and secure it would prove to be was another consideration.

In *Milestones* Ratzinger distances himself from most of the fear and misery of the Third Reich, and avoids blaming the Germans. He blames the rise of Nazism and the Third Reich on non-Bavarian factors, such as Austrian decadence: 'The poisonous seeds of Nazism are not the fruit of Austrian and Southern German Catholicism, but rather of the decadent cosmopolitan atmosphere of Vienna at the end of the monarchy.'

Unfortunately, and I am sure unintentionally, this patriotic statement is distressingly similar to the one Adolf Hitler gave for leaving Vienna and settling in Munich. Twenty years old, twice decorated for bravery (the second time for capturing fifteen English soldiers single-handed), in October 1918, and after being gassed in the last battle of Ypres, he found himself blinded and in an army hospital.

The news of the German Army's surrender in November brought on a sickening sense, as he later described it in *Mein Kampf*, of sell-out, of a stab in the back that was for him both a personal and national sense of utter collapse. He suffered a total despair, which led to the visionary or hallucinatory summons, a Damascene moment, to free Germany from bondage. Up to then there had been nothing to mark him out as unusual, but this spiritual shock and re-orientation was of such enormous proportions it arguably transformed his whole personality.

Hysterical blindness and autism may have contributed to his certainty that 'Providence' had chosen him to perform the mission of liberation, with him as its leader. He was, from now on, to be guided 'with the certainty of a sleepwalker along the path laid out for me by Providence'. His sight, or so he claimed, came back next day.

Hitler left Pasewalk Hospital on 11 November 1918. For him the Amnesty was a betrayal, a stab in the back for Germany, engineered by cowardly military leaders colluding with a weak Republican regime which had replaced the rule of the Kaiser. 'The more,' he wrote, 'I tried to achieve clarity on the monstrous event in this hour, the more the shame and indignation and disgrace bashed my brow. What was the pain in my eyes compared to this misery?'

The depth of Hitler's suffering, which propelled him into politics in his adopted hometown of Munich was, by any standards, immeasurable. He hated Vienna, where he had been stung by rejection as a struggling, untalented artist, living below the poverty line in soup kitchens and workers' hostels, hawking his tepid canvasses for small sums of money. Studying intensely the machinations of the three main political parties, which battled for hegemony in the multicultural and multiracial morass of the Austro-Hungarian Empire, repelled him.

'The conglomeration,' he wrote, 'of Czechs, Poles, Hungarians, Ruthenians, Serbs, and Croats, and everywhere the eternal mushroom of humanity – Jews and more Jews. To me the city seemed the embodiment of racial desecration.'

He promised he would cleanse Munich of similar contamination: he told Josef Hell, editor of *Der Gerade Weg*, a Catholic magazine and the favourite reading of Joseph Ratzinger senior until it was shut down, 'As soon as I have the power to do it I shall, for example, have erected in the Marienplatz in Munich gallows and more gallows, as many as can be fitted in without stopping the traffic. Then the Jews will be hanged, one after another, and they will stay hanging, until they stink. They will hang as long as the principles of hygiene permit. As soon as they have been taken down, the next ones will be strung up, and this will continue until the last Jew in Munich is destroyed.'

One might almost see the papal legate Pacelli reading this and, like so many Germans, feeling a twinge of sympathy while not believing it literally and really taking Hitler seriously. Yet it was as crude an enactment of the racial scapegoat principle as that in the popular Passion plays performed every Easter in Germany and Poland, which Joseph, although he never mentions them, presumably attended as a child (as did Karol Wojtyla, who as a child numbered Jews among his friends).

These portrayed the Jews, often in monstrous caricature, as killers of Christ. They hardly touched on and far from underlined the fact that Jesus was also a Jew and a rabbi, and that the reason he was crucified was for his belief that he was, while following many Jewish practices and principles, fulfilling the predictions of Old Testament prophets, as the Son of God.

In any case, to identify all, or even most, Palestinian Jews as prosecutors and persecutors of Christ and Christians was equally as false as saying all British citizens supported and support Blair's invasion of Iraq.

† † †

In Vienna Hitler had nevertheless discovered his true genius, a political acuity formed from study and judgment of the strengths and weakness of the three main political parties, the Social Democrats, the Christian Socialists, and the Pan-German Nationalists. He perceived with masterly clarity that the success of the Social Democrats lay in their manipulation of the crowd through propaganda, 'the gigantic human dragon', and the value they attached to what he called 'spiritual and physical terror', or in twenty-first century jargon, 'spin' – unleashing a 'veritable barrage of lies and slanders against whatever adversary seems most dangerous, until the nerves of the attacked person break down... This is a tactic based on precise calculation of all human weaknesses, and its results will lead to success with almost mathematical certainty.'

Above all, he understood the appeal of using the anti-Semitic ticket, even though he numbered Jews among his mentors, friends and those he admired, such as the composer and conductor Gustav Mahler.

Hitler developed also, before he had arrived in Munich, an equal understanding of how actual physical terror towards the individual and masses could achieve political aims – 'While in ranks of their supporters the victory achieved seems a triumph of their own cause, the defeated adversary in most cases despairs of the success of any further resistance.'

Hitler's astuteness had impelled him back to Munich, yet he had the same impotent feelings of many young German males, almost using the same words one of them wrote: 'For days I wondered what could be done, but at the very end of every meditation was the sober realisation that, nameless as I was, I did not possess the least basis for any useful action.' (So wrote in his diary Hans Frank, later to become the Third Reich's leading lawyer.)

Following the events of late 1918 and early 1919, and using the frame of reference of pre-war Vienna, he saw the main chance to become an influence on the right – among the disaffected monarchists, whose Wittelsbach King Ludwig III had abdicated. His battalion, he found, had joined the left-wing Soldiers' Council, so he resolved to leave, but he spent the winter on guard duty in a prisoner-of-war camp at Traunstein, the future home town of the Ratzingers, where Joseph passed the years from ten to twenty.

Back in Munich, in the spring, he avoided arrest by what he called left-wing scoundrels, and had begun political activity as an investigator, and researched for his infantry battalion into the causes of the brief 'Red' regime. He then built up his political base, expanding the DAP into the fledgling NSDAP or Nazi Party, forming the paramilitary and 'protection' army of the Brown Shirts or SA under Erich Röhm, a former army captain, until he too made a bid by force to seize power in Munich.

The failure of the *Bürgerbräuhaus Keller Putsch,* the 'Beerhouse Putsch' of 8 November 1923, was Hitler's first serious setback. Since September 1923, in campaigning for his own party, Hitler had begun by holding fourteen mass meetings over Bavaria, stirring the authorities into declaring a state of emergency. While Hitler's strategy of creating a vanguard-elite party on a mass working men's base followed Lenin's model, the actual seizure of power in his eyes had to come from a paramilitary coup.

In autumn 1922, Benito Mussolini, with his army of 40,000 raggedly armed Black Shirts, had marched on Rome, and taken over Italy. The German currency collapsed in 1923, with farcical, runaway inflation and banks charging 35 per cent interest a day (tips in restaurants were 400 million marks). The poorer off lost everything in these circumstances, and were starving, while the winners were the landowners and the industrialists. This fermented unrest and blame centred on the Versailles Treaty and Jewish speculation. These factors, and Mussolini's success, encouraged Hitler to believe his hour had come.

By now he had adopted a folksy, Bavarian persona. He planned with High Court Judge Theodor von der Pfordten, an undercover supporter of the Nazis, and General Erich Ludendorff, a provisional constitution for a national dictatorship of Hitler and Ludendorff.

An uprising by Communists in Saxony added further stimulus to Hitler to march at 2045 hrs, on the cold night of 8 November, on the *Bürgerbräu Keller* with a detachment of steel-helmeted SA men under Röhm. Here a mass political meeting was being held, and with von Kahr, the Bavarian Premier, on the rostrum were Police Chief Rutter von Seisser, and General Otto von Lossow, head of the German defence force permitted by the *Diktat* of Versailles. While the SA set up a machine gun in the gallery Hitler stormed into the *Keller* and up to the rostrum, pushed the pale and confused von Kahr aside, and shouted:

'The national revolution has broken out! The hall is filled with six hundred men. Nobody is allowed to leave. The Bavarian government and the government in Berlin are deposed. A new government will be formed at once.'

This time the Bavarian government defeated Hitler. The march on the Munich state buildings next day was met by reso-lute Bavarian state policemen, colleagues of Ratzinger senior, who exchanged fired with Hitler and his Nazi followers, some of whom were killed, and others, like Hitler and Hermann Göring, wounded before they fled.

† † †

The primate of Bavaria, Cardinal Michael von Faulhaber, who was Archbishop of Munich for thirty years, and who visited Joseph in Tittmoning when he was four, and ordained him in 1951, also effectively opposed, together with the Christian Democratic lead-ers and Centre Party, Hitler's failed Beer Hall Putsch in 1923.

A staunchly conservative Catholic, Faulhaber was dining with Franz Matt, vice-premier of Bavaria, and Pacelli, when news came of the putsch. As the army and government reasserted its control Faulhaber played an important part in preserving the status quo. He even promised Catholic support when Matt, not counting on the Catholic premier von Kahr's decisive action, started to plan to set up a rump government in exile in Regensburg.

The Church's influence was powerful in Bavarian politics. It was immensely rich, and in Germany as a whole there were 23 million Catholics. The Catholic Centre Party was so powerful it could well have been, ten years later, the decisive factor in stop-ping Hitler's rise to power.

Göring escaped to Sweden, but Hitler was arrested and convicted of treason, and sent to Landsdorf fortress where he was kept in style, and his five-year sentence reduced to six months during which he began tapping out *Mein Kampf* with two fingers on an ancient typewriter.

He soon stopped, as he preferred ranting it out loud to a succession of copyists, and he had just the right amount of time to finish it before his release. Thus was germinated and born one of the most horrifically influential, ideological tracts in world history.

During his last days in prison, now armed with his notorious text, which was edited and corrected by a Catholic monk, Hitler designed a 'people's car' – a *Volkswagen* (literal translation), manufactured to drive on specially designed scenic roads or *autobahns.* On his release just before Christmas 1924 he dashed off first to the house of Ernst Hanfstaengl where, with extreme hunger pains from Wagner starvation, he commanded, 'Play the *Liebestod.*' Next morning he purchased a Mercedes, and, as his valet Otto Dietrich asserted, overtook every other driver on the road.

During his jail sentence a new German in charge of the Reichsbank, by ceasing to print money and slashing government expenditure, had stabilised the currency. For a short period of years, during which all three Ratzinger children were born, peace and prosperity reigned – and support fell away from Nazism.

In 1928 the Nazi Party polled only two and a half per cent of the National vote, but with proportional representation twelve deputies were elected to the Reichstag. But Hitler kept alive the fanatic spirit of the Party nucleus and its 'old fighters'. The four dead policemen who had resisted Hitler belonged to the same Bavarian police force as Joseph's father. They became in Nazi eyes the execrable villains.

3

Hiding in Cassocks from the Long Knives

Thus conscience does make cowards of us all,
And thus the native hue of resolution
Is sicklied o'er with the pale cast of thought.
William Shakespeare, *Hamlet*, III, iv

Ratzinger was nearly six years old when Adolf Hitler was appointed Chancellor on 30 January 1933. Only on 25 February 1932, eleven months earlier, had Hitler became a German citizen; on 10 April 1932 Hitler polled 37 per cent of the popular vote; on 6 November 1932 the Nazi Party returned in the Reichstag elections 196 Reichstag deputies, 33 per cent of the vote. After a secret meeting between Alfred von Papen, Reich Chancellor and Hitler on 4 January 1933 – present at which were Rudolf Hess and Heinrich Himmler, now head of Hitler's SS – von Papen moved over.

Just over a month after von Papen appointed Hitler Chancellor Nazi agents planned to set fire to the Reichstag, and blame it on the Communists. By chance , if this disputed fact is true, one of the latter did carry this out. The reign of terror against Communists could begin again, with the excuse of the fire.

30 January 1933, a monumentally important date in the history of mankind, may have been a cold grey Sunday, but Berlin became a 'seething, red, clear burning sea of torches' as thousands chanted '*Sieg Heil*', a 'compound of triumph, aggression and strange exultant relief'.

Worship of Hitler was now a religion, a spreading, evangelising movement engendered in the red-hot gospelling of the quasi-divine leader, and his disciples. It was infectious, and not primarily instilled by fear, but spread with hubristic and dynamic enthusiasm. One morning – as Claus Hant, a contemporary German writer, told me in 2010 – 'Your postman, delivering the letters, instead of just dropping them through the box, would greet you with "*Heil Hitler!*" Everyone, kids, grannies, the young and the old wanted to go to the rallies, to join dazzle and spendour.'

Where was the opposition? Where was the Bavarian Catholic Church? 'At last we are saved,' Hitler said in his first broadcast. He promised to preserve basic principles: 'Christianity as the foundation of our national morality, and the family as the basis of national life.' Church belfries were adorned with swastikas, crosses draped with Nazi flags. There would be a new priesthood, 'storm troopers of Jesus'; racial purity and holy martyrdom were one and the same.

By the end of 1933 so complete had the seduction and coercion of the German people become that 92 of the 96 per cent of registered voters cast their ballots for the single Nazi list for the Reichstag, while 95 per cent endorsed German repudiation of the peace treaty. Were Ratzinger senior and his wife two of these? Like many millions of others, they could have done this without becoming Nazi supporters, yet there is no record of what they did. 'History has sufficiently demonstrated how destructive majorities can be,' commented Benedict in 2010, without mentioning the context of such destruction.

'On the eleventh of November [meaning the Armistice of 1919] the German people formerly lost its honour,' ranted Hitler in an election speech at Breslau; 'fifteen years later came a twelfth November and then the German people restored its honour to itself.' The *Diktat* of Versailles was dead. The Germans could re-arm.

For had not the Treaty of Versailles robbed Germany of its decisive character, denied the activities that were its very life-blood, Hitler would never have come to power:

> The exercises, the receiving and passing on of orders, became something which [Germans] had to procure for themselves

at all costs, [wrote Elias Canetti, the British Nobel Prize-winning author].The prohibition on universal military service was the *birth* of National Socialism… The party came to the rescue of the army, and the party had no limits set to its recruitment from within the nation. Every single German – man, woman, or child, soldier or civilian – could become a National Socialist. He was probably even more anxious to become one if he had not been a soldier before, because, by so doing, he achieved participation in activities hitherto denied him. (Canetti, 1952)

'The most dangerous moment,' declared Napoleon, 'comes with victory.' Hitler shrewdly realised that while the Party had ben-efited and relied on the brutality and sadism of the SA, from which in public as a natural leader Hitler could dissociate himself, claiming he had no control over it, and was not responsible for its warring factions, its notorious homosexual feuds and sexual jealousies, now was the moment to ditch it.

While making use of their support, he disliked brawling homosexuals like Edward Heines, leader of the Munich SA, who was a convicted murderer. His own murderers, ideally, were faithful married men with families, if possible abstemious and nicotine-free.

He had appointed the eminently respectable – at least out-wardly – loyal and meticulous Himmler to form and lead the Schnitzstaffel, the SS, and ultimately the Gestapo and police.

Mild-mannered, and with the air of a self-deprecating oddball, and much involved in esoteric cults, Himmler, another Bavarian, bred chickens in a village near Munich. As his loyalty and dedi-cation to Hitler were rock solid, Hitler had made an important decision: to purge Röhm, who had been instrumental in his rise, but who now, according to Hitler's instantly summonable para-noia, had 'begun preparations to eliminate me personally'.

Hitler manoeuvred masterly, wheeling and dealing, and play-ing every trick in the book in those crucial weeks of 1933 to make sure his takeover as sole dictator of Germany became com-plete and triumphant. Realising Napoleon's *obiter dictum* that the most dangerous moment comes with victory, he also practised

Machiavelli's even cleverer *dictum*, namely that the first thing you do when you achieve power is to remove those who helped you to it – you need obedient subordinates, no longer unruly rebels who destroy the old order. And so he planned his next move.

He had the German Army on his side; he had the daily more powerful SS; and he had the German people. One may wonder eternally how so utterly intolerant a man could have countenanced in the first place so many reprobates and frankly immoral scum to help him achieve power. But it was power, political power, that was going to help him achieve his mission.

Not only did blackmailers, pimps, embezzlers, murderers, alcoholics (and 'sexual deviants', in that age's homophobic terminology) find in Nazi Germany their Utopia, but the prim and respectable also did too. Albert Speer acutely observed of the Führer that his temper tantrums, his rantings, were always under his control in this period, and that his decisions, while all around him were in turmoil, came from ice-cool judgment. He staged his hysterical outbursts carefully, Speer said, while his pretended fits of passion forced others to yield. 'In general, self-control was one of Hitler's more striking characteristics.'

Hitler honed to perfection the facets of the demotic 'people person', ahead of his time, and the prototype, late twentieth- and early twenty-first-century popular politician. He lived modestly, was a vegetarian, didn't smoke or drink, patted children, and loved dogs. His self-imaging was perfect and he did all the right things. His one personal luxury was the latest supermodel car, always a Mercedes-Benz.

His followers were unaware of his many faces, and saw only the façade which he presented to them at any one time. He permitted each individual to project upon him that type of personality which that individual most respected and admired. With Göring he was friendly, outspoken and blunt; with Dönitz he was simple, intellectual, and quiet; with Baldur von Schirach he was a dominating authority; and with Ribbentrop a father and a master.

With Hans Frank, now made Bavarian Minister of Justice, he was Messiah-like and affectionate, talked philosophy and music, and played the gentle and forgiving guru to his deferential disciple.

In addition to these personality assets, Hitler's eyes, which almost everyone spoke of as having a hypnotic effect, cast their *Walpürgisnacht* spell. He had learned the knack of actually staring down opposition. On women he lavished 'southern' charm and friendliness, while he mentally seduced men with his 'knowledge', namely a spectacular display of superficial information and astonishing photographic memory feats which they interpreted these as true education and brilliance.

Frank, a popular member of Hitler's entourage, flattered and aped his master, and found himself and his wife Brigitte included in the intimate cultural circle. Brigitte reports an occasion when she had the honour of sitting or standing next to 'Herr Hitler' at Bayreuth. She dropped her programme.

'Just imagine! Herr Hitler bent over and picked up the programme, kept it for himself, and gave me his own to keep. The Führer was such a gentleman!'

† † †

During these years of turmoil and rapid change the Ratzinger family had grown fond of Tittmoning, but apparently Joseph senior had spoken out too much against the Brown Shirts, so he was demoted. They moved on to Aschau, where the buildings were plainer and the 'dialect a bit coarser'.

On the day Hitler became Chancellor, Georg and Maria had to perform a march through the village which, because it was so rainy, turned into a tramp through mud and slush. But now the hitherto secret Nazis in Aschau brought out their brown uniforms to show they were in the SA. They had received their validation, so spying and informing were on the up.

Like Eugenio Pacelli as a child, from an early age, and with his brother and sister Maria, Joseph acted out the ritual of the liturgy. Like Pacelli he had a gift for languages and a prodigious memory. He was an extraordinarily pretty boy, small of stature, lightweight, shy, absorbed in his books and his dreams. Like Pacelli he was not cut out to be a fighter, but a contemplative, a child of peace.

Even though the rise of Hitler dominated German life, Ratzinger never – as far as I can discover – asked himself why the rise of Nazism should have happened specifically in his heartland of Bavaria centred round Munich, whose archbishop he was to become. It was not only a hefty percentage of the leaders, but it seems, as in the towns and cities, the ordinary folk in little villages like Aschau who carried the torch for Nazism's growth – although, as Ratzinger says, the transformation took place more slowly.

Could it be that he would reveal later, in the biographies of Jesus and St Paul he was to write later, his attitude to growing up – in describing those of his subjects? Or would it be, that by skirting round certain uncomfortable issues, he would tell us something important about himself?

† † †

There were disquieting signs in his locality. An anti-aircraft tower with searchlights was erected near Aschau, and following this, in a nearby forest, a new munitions plant. Social unrest and political upheaval spilled out from Munich into the villages and small towns of Bavaria.

The old liturgical year was broken up by one gifted young teacher who erected a Maypole as a symbol of the pagan life force. While in parochial schools there was conflict between preserving the provisions of the Catholic faith and the Führer's ideology, the latter made increasing headway. Every German family was sucked into, or to some extent or another caught up in, Nazism, and even if hostile to it shared a common patriotic Germanic spirit, inexplicable to the world outside.

As Hitler centralised government, stripping Bavaria of its autonomy, Ratzinger senior, a lover of his Free State traditions and its cultural heritage, felt the urge to apply for early retirement. Sensing that war was coming, he wanted to find a house of their own.

In this crucial year, 1933, he bought for 5,500 Reichsmarks an alpine-style dwelling, which had an orchard and barns, just outside Traunstein in a picturesque hamlet called Hufschlag. Although the roof leaked, and the water came from a pump, it represented a foreseeable future in a grim epoch.

Joseph senior was still serving as a Bavarian State policeman, a member of that fiercely independent force which had fired on and killed Communist demonstrators in Munich, when arms for left-wing insurrection were stored in churches and monasteries, and later, during the 'Beer Hall Putsch', which wounded Hitler and Göring, and killed 18 prominent 'martyrs' of the fledgling Nazi party. As noted already, the four Bavarian State policemen who died were not honoured. They were not popular in Nazi folklore. Soon Nazi personnel and leaders infiltrated this police force to bring it in line with Hitler rule.

Yet to most Germans Hitler's appointment as Chancellor in 1933 was not in any way a disaster, but the beginning of Germany's restoration to former greatness, and the creation of a prosperity up to now unknown. This, while there was still peace, was shared almost universally by the population with the notable exceptions. If pride was stirred in every young German Aryan's heart, the means were much overlooked, for the excuse was that the aspirations were as much culture-driven and visionary, as political and violent.

As the drive to enrol young Catholics into Hitler Youth widened and deepened it became clear to the Ratzinger family that their cherished religious identity was under threat.

In 1934 Baldur von Schirach, the aristocrat youth leader appointed by Hitler, started to encourage Hitler Youth units to pick fights with rival Catholic youth groups. During the Night of the Long Knives, in which Röhm's SA and the leader himself were eliminated, the SS shot dead Erich Klausener, General Secretary of Catholic Action in his Berlin office, and Adalbert Probst, head of the Catholic Youth Sports Association. Nearer to home they also shot dead Fritz Gerlich, the editor of Joseph senior's favourite weekly, *Der gerade Weg*, which was based in Munich.

None of this seemed to be spoken of, or lamented, in the Ratzinger apolitical home. On Ratzinger the influence of music and literature, when he began to read and play the piano, was very great. The Ratzinger family was bound up in music. The musical orientation was especially strong and potent. He was, as he says, very much under the influence of Salzburg.

How could it be good for some and bad for others? Salzburg, Bayreuth, were music festivals constantly visited and loved by the Nazi leaders too. Some, perhaps most, would argue that music was neutral in its political and cultural significance. Notably one great German writer would devote years to showing this was not the truth.

Thomas Mann, yet another Bavarian, who left Germany as an exile in 1933, depicts in his last great novel *Doctor Faustus* Nazism as primarily a cultural, artistic phenomenon. His Faust, Adrian Leverkuhn, a composer, when he contracts syphilis from a whore, is led by his diseased hubris into madness and self-destruction. As Mann described it when writing this novel, the history of Germany under Nazism showed a desire to 'escape from everything bourgeois, moderate, classical, sober, industrious and dependable into a world of drunken release, a life of Dionysiac genius, beyond society, indeed superhuman – above all, subjectively, an experience and drunken intensification of the self, regardless of whether the world outside can go along with it'. (It sounds rather terrifyingly like present times.)

Mann identifies Nazism closely with the world of German music. Looking at the beginnings in Munich University, in the beer cellars, the cabarets and cafés, the crumbling army barracks, and with characters such as Eckhart, Röhm, Drexler and Harrer, and with Hitler's intoxication with Wagner, and his involvement with the Pan-German Thule Society, one appreciates the force of Mann's analysis, and his choice of the symbolic composer.

Rather like some members of the British parliamentary class Hitler was an out-and-out elitist who believed that the public at large could be manipulated:

For myself, [said Hitler about Wagner] I have the most intimate familiarity with Wagner's mental processes. At every stage in my life I come back to him. Only a new nobility can introduce the new civilisation for us. If we strip *Parsifal* of every poetic element, we learn from it that selection and renewal are possible only amid the continuous tension of a lasting struggle. A world-wide process of segregation is going on before our eyes. Those who see in struggle the meaning of life, gradually

mount the steps of a new nobility. Those who are in search
of peace and order through dependence, sink, whatever their
origin, to the inert masses. The masses, however, are doomed
to decay and self-destruction. In our world-revolutionary
turning-point the masses are the sum total of the sinking civilisation and its dying representatives. We must allow then to
die with their kings, like Amfortas. (*Hitler Speaks*, 1940)

Music was, from the beginning, an important theme, too, in the
life of Joseph Ratzinger and his older brother Georg (though
Joseph never appears to mention Wagner) and although as a
human being Mozart hardly came up to the Catholic ideal, for
Joseph he was the supreme composer. Unlike Hitler, who identified with Wagner to the extent of writing the draft of an opera
libretto, Ratzinger identified with the executants and interpreters of music, and the works themselves, more than the creative
spirits themselves. For him, God was not so much a creator but
more a gifted theologian, an interpreter, for this was how God
made Ratzinger. His concern was more with hitting the right
note and avoiding cacophony.

4

The Dying Fall: Kirchenkampf

We are the jolly Hitler Youth,
We don't need any Christian truth
For our Leader Adolf Hitler, our Leader
Always is our interceder.

Whatever the Papist priests may try,
We're Hitler's children until we die;
We follow not Christ but Horst Wessel.
Away with incense and holy water vessel!

As sons of our forebears from times gone by
We march as we sing with banners held high.
I'm not a Christian, nor a Catholic,
I go with the SA through thin and thick.

In the crucial 1930s years of Nazi growth the Catholic Church and some of the other Christian churches potentially offered the strongest and toughest ideological opposition to Nazi principles. It was not quite the same for the Lutheran churches of Germany. They slipped up badly in failing to show right at the very beginning uncompromising hostility to the Reich on more than a narrowly religious front, which for the most part could be ignored by the Nazis.

In fact many fanatical Lutherans supported the Nazi doctrines, and their leader Ludwig Müller, Hitler's friend, later became, backed by SA and Gestapo intimidation, the first 'Reich Bishop', with dictatorial power to unite all Protestants in one great Reich Church.

The Catholic Church, and even the majority of moderate Protestants, both conservative in politics, not only for a long time had a tradition of anti-Semitism. It blundered from the start by seeing in Nazism a protection against Bolshevism and the Soviets. Hitler could see that Catholicism and the other churches were prone to, even riddled with, fear and superstition, and were in awe of magic and hidden forces.

Because of their doctrinal differences they failed to unite. While uneasy and defiant they could be lulled, manoeuvred and forced into substituting the ideology of the Nazi German state which 'would last a thousand years', for the Christian belief in the immortality of the soul. Hitler knew that to win the battle against the churches would be to confer unanimous Nazi-hood on the German people.

Massacres of priests in the Spanish Civil War by the Falangists were also to be widely reported, so, as well as the guarantee of physical security; here was support for the Nazi strict morality on cultural decadence, support of the family, public order, cleanliness and so on:

'Wherever you drove you saw perfect order. The people were clean and appeared well fed; they were polite and friendly – in short, it was a charming country, a pleasure to visit, and how was anybody to credit these horror tales? Irma was in a continual struggle between what she wanted to believe and what was being forced upon her reluctant mind.' (Sinclair, 1941)

Nazi Germany promised safety and security, and under its paternalistic Führer comfortable, unquestioning dependence. It was a society scrutinised and overseen by Dr Joseph Goebbels, Hitler's Minister of Propaganda, the new master of Germany's intellectual life. His word could make or break anyone in any profession; an invitation to his home was at once a command and the highest of opportunities. Men bowed and fawned, women smiled and flattered – and at the same time they watched warily, for it was a perilous world, in which your place was held only by sleepless vigilance. Jungle cats, all in one cage, circling one another warily, keeping a careful distance; the leopard and the jaguar would have tangled, had not both been afraid of the tiger.

> But they were civilised cats, which had learned manners, and applied psychology, pretending to be gentle and harmless, even amiable. The deadliest killers wore the most cordial smiles; the most cunning were the most dignified, and the most exalted. They had a great cause, a historic destiny, a patriotic duty, an inspired leader. They said, 'We are building a new Germany,' and at the same time they thought: 'How can I cut out this fellow's guts?' They said: 'Good evening, *Parteigenosse*,' and thought: '*Schwarer Lump*, I know what lies you have been whispering!' (Sinclair, 1941)

Still up until mid 1932, the Catholic Church had presented an unshakeable and united front to the NSDAP. There were 400 daily Catholic newspapers, accounting for one sixth of total circulation, two news channels and feature services, hundreds of periodicals of which 30 had circulations of over 100,000.

Thanks to the Centre Party Catholicism was flourishing politically as well as numerically. During the 1920s the clergy increased from 19,000 to 21,000, those in religious orders from 7,000 to 14,000, while male monastic foundations increased from 366 in number to 640.

The first test of the Christian Churches' attitude towards the Jews, the 1933 boycott of Jewish businesses, evinced no religious response from either bishops or synods. Further, the Premier of Bavaria reported on 24 April 1933 to Hans Frank, Minister of Justice, and other ministers, 'Cardinal Faulhaber had issued an order to the clergy to support the new regime, in which he (Faulhaber) had confidence' [parenthesis in original].

Faulhaber further pronounced in a letter addressed to Cardinal Pacelli, now promoted from Germany's nuncio to the Vatican's Secretary of State: 'We bishops are being asked why the Catholic Church, as often in its history, does not intervene on behalf of the Jews. This is not possible at this time because the struggle against the Jews would then, at the same time, become a struggle against the Catholics, and because the Jews can help themselves, as the sudden end of the boycott shows.'

Faulhaber has been lavishly portrayed as a famous and fearless opponent of the Nazis, and an icon of inspiration both by, and for, the future Pope Benedict. 'The grand and venerable figure of Cardinal Faulhaber impressed me greatly,' wrote Ratzinger. 'You could practically touch the burden of sufferings he had to bear during the Nazi period, which now enveloped him with an aura of dignity. In him we were not looking for "an accessible bishop"; rather what moved me deeply about him was the awe-inspiring grandeur of his mission, with which he had become fully identified.' (Seewald, 2008)

Considering how in Bavaria the Church was now to become weakened and marginalised, and looking more closely at the statements he made and the events which reduced the Church's influence, it becomes questionable how accurate Ratzinger is overall.

† † †

'The Church which is married to the Spirit of the Age will be a widow in the next.' Dean Inge's judgement is often quoted today in support of Catholic traditional values. In many disastrous ways the Catholic Church in the late 1920s and throughout the 1930s was indissolubly married to the 'Spirit of the Age'. Pacelli was from the time he became the Vatican's best diplomat, and for all his delicate sensibility and fastidious piety, dedicated to the absolute leadership principle which swept Europe in the 1930s.

His ideology was based on an autocratic papal control and the dictatorial authority he later assumed when he became Pope. He loved, as did the monarchs and the dictators, the luxuries he could enjoy with his position, which included, when he travelled first to Germany as Papal Nuncio, a private rail compartment and 'a wagon with 60 cases of special foods for his delicate stomach' – shocking the reigning Pope Benedict XV with his extravagance.

Moreover like many millions of German and Polish Catholics, he continued to show, in the spirit of the age, his antipathy towards the Jewish race. There was a huge discrepancy between Pacelli's attitude and the 'providential' circumstances not only of Jesus of Nazareth but also those of Karol Wojtyla, John Paul II, who was born in a Jewish-owned flat for which his father paid rent, and who once played goalkeeper for a Jewish boys' football team.

Whatever the reasons for, or advantages which accrued from, the Lateran Treaty and the Italian Concordat, negotiated by Pacelli's brother, a canon lawyer, for the independence and power of the Italian Catholic Church, which also conferred statehood on the Vatican, its sinister provisions (bishops taking an oath of allegiance to the Mussolini dictatorship, the order to clergy not to oppose or harm it, the dissolution of the Catholic Party) their terms delighted Hitler, who wrote, 'The fact that the Curia is now making its peace with Fascism, shows the Vatican trusts the new political realities far more than it did the former liberal democracy...' (*Volkischer Beobachter*, 22 February 1929). Fascism was 'justifiable for the faithful and compatible with the Catholic faith'. The Vatican, with its new power as an independent state, helped Fascism in Italy in the same way it was to help Hitler.

The Concordat which Pacelli was negotiating in 1933 between the Vatican and the Third Reich hardly differed from that signed with Mussolini. The German Church, deliberately excluded by Pacelli in the diplomacy, had no say in the matter. Pacelli lied over and over again to Faulhaber, when he had agreed to conditions, saying it was still at a talk stage. Some bishops such as Cardinal Bertram vehemently tried to oppose certain aspects of the treaty when they were known, but they were ignored.

Just before its signature, on 26 April 1933, Hitler met the Catholic bishops and declared his undying support for Christianity, and asserted how much Germany needed its religious and moral foundation. He pointed out that National Socialism and Catholicism had fundamental agreement on the Jewish question, as the Church had always regarded Jews as parasites and banished them into the ghetto.

His outright lies were swallowed by the bishops, the pro-Nazi Bishop Wilhelm Berning of Osnabruck in particular, who reporting him as saying, 'We need soldiers, devout soldiers. Devout soldiers are the most valuable, for they risk all. Therefore we shall keep the parochial schools in order to bring up believers.'

Hitler could and did boast privately he had tapped the deep well of Catholic anti-Semitism. For a long time there had been ambivalence, a source of impulses among people to protect as well as respect Jews, but now bishops had to swear loyalty to the Reich and the state, and there would be no more safeguards.

Moral ambivalence, and its relation to music, is a theme Mann also explores in his depiction of German cultural hubris. 'Music turns the equivocal into a system,' says the composer Adrian Leverkuhn in *Doktor Faustus*: 'Take this or that note. You can understand it so or respectively so. You can think of it as sharpened or flattened, and you can, if you are clever, take advantage of the double sense as much as you like.'

The Concordat was signed between Hitler and the Vatican on 20 July 1933. Hitler more than tripled the subsidy he paid the Catholic Church between 1933 and 1938, which might literally be called blood money, as it bought silence concerning the increasing climate of atrocity. He left the Roman Church the richest landowner in south and west Germany. He demanded of France, Britain and America, 'What was your subsidy to the Churches?'

In that same summer of 1933 Faulhaber sent Hitler a handwritten note: 'What the old parliaments and parties did not accomplish in sixty years, your statesmanlike foresight has achieved in six months. For Germany's prestige in East and West... this handshake with the papacy, the greatest moral power in the history of the world, is a feat of immeasurable blessing.'

† † †

In his account of his family, his early years and the German Church of that time Ratzinger hardly makes mention of the scandalous Concordat. Again, perhaps as often in his accounts of childhood, his disarming understatement is one of a cultivated omission. There is perhaps a good reason for this, which we will come to: certain provisions that were to work in favour of the Ratzinger brothers as they grew up.

It was not long before Article 31 (Protection of Catholic organisations and freedom of religious practice) and Article 32

(Clerics may not be members of or be active for political parties) were flagrantly abused. The schools started to be targeted to de-Christianise young children. Mandatory prayer was stopped from 1935 on, while from 1940 religious education for the 14–15 year olds was eliminated.

Now any cleric criticising the Reich or Hitler could be accused of breaking Article 32, for from now on any Catholic who opposed Hitler was committing a sin, while every war the Reich fought would be a just and holy war. Catholics flooded to join the Nazi Party, as they believed it had the support of the Church, and German Catholic democrats had their voice and leadership silenced. The Centre Party, the powerful Catholic party of middle-class democratic Germany, voluntarily 'disbanded' itself.

The paradox of all this was that the wily Hitler continued to fear the power Pacelli, the Church's representative, could wield, yet all the time Pacelli acted as if Hitler held all the power and leverage, and he had none. Pacelli seemed doubly culpable as he had so sedulously wooed Hitler to achieve his delusion of a great Vatican triumph, yet Hitler made his signature dependent on the Centre Party's voting for the Enabling Act, the legal means which gave him a dictator's power to muzzle Catholic resistance, to dissolve the Centre Party, and grant him a free hand to persecute and finally liquidate the Jewish race.

The Concordat, designed by Cardinal Pacelli to strengthen the Church, had the opposite effect. Perhaps unintentionally, or even intentionally, he wanted this to happen. He was, some say, in Hitler's power, and that from their first meeting when he gave Hitler money he remained a pawn. 'This was the reality of the moral abyss into which Pacelli the future Pontiff had led the once great and proud German Catholic Church,' commented a well-known Catholic writer.

That Pacelli temporised and capitulated can be confirmed in his comments. At one stage he felt a pistol had been held to his head, and he was 'negotiating with the devil himself'. He claimed, as he thought (either the claim was false or his thinking was erroneous), that he had to choose between 'an agreement and the virtual elimination of the Catholic Church in the Reich'. But, to be sure, the point is that the Church doesn't, or mustn't, negotiate with what it sees as the devil. Anyway, the devil won hands down.

Just after the Concordat, and during the Röhm purge, the Vatican did not protest over the murder of Catholic leaders and intellectuals which became part of the package. The comment of the anonymous priest who wrote later during the Second World War to Cardinal Magline may serve as an accurate judgement on the Church's behaviour during the whole Third Reich period:

'I wonder just which bishops have asked the Holy Father to remain silent. According to your Eminence, they did so out of fear of aggravating the persecution. But the facts prove that with the Pope being silent, each day sees the persecution becoming more cruel.'

There was no doubt Pacelli, like the British prime minister Neville Chamberlain at Munich, had fallen under Hitler's spell. He believed that by making concessions, by severing the links between Church and the Centrist Party, he would increase the Church's influence with Hitler. Even, in the previous month when Catholic youths at a Munich rally were attacked by SA thugs, beaten up and chased off the street, and the planned open-air Mass was cancelled, he failed to see that by surrendering Catholic political power he would be playing right into Hitler's hands, and thereby committing German Catholics to obey the Nazis.

In line with Pacelli, Cardinal Faulhaber imposed a ban on youth organisations and muzzled his priests from speaking out or engaging in political activity. Pacelli thought he was centralising power in the Papacy; in effect he was giving the green light to the Gestapo and SS to crack down on the Church, the Bavarian People's Party, and then to subsequent murder or arrest, and deportation to concentration camps, of those Catholics, especially clerics, who did not fall in with the terms of the Concordat as interpreted by the Nazis.

From 20 July 1933 newspapers were forbidden to call themselves Catholic any longer, while from September in Bavaria the State police under their Chief of Police Himmler, and approved by Hans Frank, banned all activities of Catholic organisations with the exception of youth groups, charities asking for money, and church choirs holding rehearsals. Protests were made, but the inaction generally spelled out one word: appeasement. It was quite likely that Joseph senior, about whom we hear nothing at this time, found himself enforcing legal measures he found abhorrent.

In October 1933 Archbishop Gröber in Freiburg said, 'I am placing myself completely behind the new government and the New Reich.' The latter selected a few notable Catholics here and there to be murdered, but on the whole, Himmler's 'softly softly' approach was, not unlike that of England's Elizabeth I toward Catholics, to spread fear, not take draconian action. The weak Catholic leadership fell in with this tactic, believing it could lessen the harm done to the Church by cooperation with the Nazis.

Cardinal Faulhaber did sometimes counterattack the Nazi position; for example, without being explicit, in his popular Advent sermons of 1933: 'It is my conviction that a defence of Christianity is also a defence of Germany. An apostasy from Christianity, a relapse into paganism, would be the beginning of the end of the German nation.'

He drew a vivid picture of life in Germany in a pamphlet before the advent of Christianity. Taken from the Roman historian Tacitus, 'early German gods, fashioned after the likeness of men, were idealised portraits of what a German hero or housewife were conceived to be. They offered human sacrifice to the Gods; they indulged in savage superstition as well as savage warfare; they practiced vendettas as a moral duty. They had slaves, whom they put to death at will; they drank heavily and became murderous... They were loyal to their comrades, monogamous and faithful...'

Nobody much seemed to get the picture. It was too late. The words of Faulhaber's, which anyway could be read two ways, became more a prediction than a warning. Faulhaber did make other speeches and sermons criticising the Nazis from 1933 onwards; in 1935 some Nazis called in an open meeting for Faulhaber to be killed, while gunmen fired two shots into his house.

But these were mere gestures. On the persecution of Jews and the political violence, the Catholic Church, with exceptions, remained tragically silent; only the Jehovah's Witnesses were firm in their hostility, begging to be martyred themselves. Himmler was so impressed by their fanaticism he held it up to his SS men as an example.

† † †

When Pope Benedict was nine years old, and now attending school, the following incident took place. It could even have been in Ratzinger's own class.

'Watching a young Hitler Youth member enter a classroom in August 1936, Friedrich Reck-Malleczewen observed how his glance fell on the crucifix hanging behind the teacher's desk, how in an instant his young and still soft face contorted in fury, how he ripped this symbol, to which the cathedrals of Germany, and the ringing progressions of the *St Matthew Passion* are consecrated, off the wall and threw it out of the window into the street... With the cry: "Lie there, you dirty Jew!"'

These episodes and other like them were not raised to self-awareness in the mature Ratzinger contemplating the past, so he could be forever on his guard against similar events.

For Himmler, who had the personality and conviction of a religious fanatic, the Swastika was redemption on earth. As his SS plan put it in 1937: 'We live in an age of the final confrontation with Christianity. It is part of the mission of the SS to give to the German people over the next fifty years the non-Christian ideological foundations for a way of life appropriate to their own character.'

Particularly sinister was the Nazi reaction when, after too long a silence, out of fear, it seemed, and in spite of Pacelli, his predecessor as Pope, prompted by five German cardinals and bishops who had broken ranks, Pius XI issued his fiery encyclical, *Mit brennender Sorge* ('With burning concern') in March 1937.

This brave encyclical excoriated Nazi hatred and calumny of the Church. But even in the encyclical there featured no explicit condemnation of anti-Semitism. Göring fulminated and vowed reprisal, but under Pacelli's influence the impact was played down, and most Catholic bishops softened in their support of the encyclical.

By this time it was too late. The Catholic hierarchy in Bavaria had allowed Hitler to insert the thin end of the wedge, while German Catholic independence had been paralysed.

In response to the encyclical Goebbels intensified propaganda against the Church. Fifteen monks were arrested and tried, accused of sexual abuse of minors and currency misdemeanours. Probably there was outrage among Catholics like Ratzinger senior over this pure persecution and victimisation (a foretaste here, too, of the future). And still Faulhaber unctuously continued the official Catholic approval of Hitler:

'The Führer commands the diplomatic and social forms better than a born sovereign... Without doubt the Chancellor lives in faith in God. He recognises Christianity as the foundation of Western culture... Just as clear is his conception of the Catholic Church as a God-established institution.'

5

The Traunstein Idyll

In 1937 Joseph Ratzinger's father, aged 60, retired from the Bavarian police. He had taken plenty of sick leave before then, an opportunity for father and son to spend time together. In April they moved to the house they had bought earlier, No. 10 Eichenweg, Hufschlag, just outside Traunstein.

'We arrived in the car of our landlady in Aschau,' Joseph reports, 'and the first thing we saw was the meadow, strewn with primroses.'

He walked to school locally at first in Traunstein, then boarded in the nearest *Gymnasium* – all three Ratzinger children were sent away to board at school. During this period he must have absorbed his country's history, and his own family's special circumstances. What did his family think?

The pressure on most parents to make their children join in one of the youth movements was extreme. Joseph was ten and saw everywhere the rise of Nazism, to which his own family, as devout Roman Catholics, were opposed. Even so, after the frequent moves of the previous years, settling down in Traunstein made him very happy. Nazi indoctrination and von Shirach's Hitler Youth threatened. As a peaceful and happy boy, secure in the love of his parents, he dealt with this by ignoring it, as any child of comparable age would, turning a blind eye, rather than expressing or feeling any kind of deep revolt. German had rearmed. Virtually the whole nation was in uniform and mobilised for war. Soldiers in uniform were everywhere: boys love this. One cannot feel there was anything wrong in this attitude of Joseph.

In this new idyllic setting Joseph reports that he turned his thoughts to the beautiful mountain views, the local Hochfellen and Hochgern, the flowers and the fruit trees, and his dreams. Even when they played in the barns the three children were strictly pious. Ratzinger told Seewald later, 'Cigarettes were secretly snatched, and they played at being priest with almost inexhaustible zeal. Uncle Benno, the rake from Rimsting, donated a little altar for this. Aunts lovingly stitched albs, stoles, and vestments. For Mass chalices they used miniature vessels of pewter. The children would go up in procession to their holy altar, and... it sometimes happened that their sister's braids got singed by one of the candles.'

From an early age Joseph loved ceremonial, loved dressing up, a passion for which was to remain with him. It was, for example, hardly surprising to hear that as pope he reinstalled the practice of bishops kissing the pope's ring when received into his presence. This was to shock a bishop who had not been told of the change.

† † †

On 6 September 1938, Pius XI, who was a Hebrew scholar, again denounced anti-Semitism in an angry informal outburst before Belgian pilgrims: 'It is not possible for Christians to participate in anti-Semitism. Spiritually we are Semites!'

It was *Krystallnacht,* in early November 1938, when Joseph was eleven: the murder, arson and pillage of Jewish people and property all over Germany, that followed hard on this denunciation. Here, for once, Faulhaber condemned the racism.

The Bavarian Interior Minister attacked Catholics as allies of the Jews, and a mob broke the windows of Faulhaber's episcopal palace (but it did not, as Ratzinger claimed in *The Salt of the Earth*, storm it).

The mob's slogan was, said Ratzinger, 'After the Jews, the Jew-lovers.' Ratzinger did not mention that the Jews in Traunstein were also attacked on *Krystallnacht*, nor that there was now an outer camp of Dachau in Trostberg, only 20 kilometres from

Traunstein. Any resistance to Nazism was impossible, he stressed. But was it?

One local man, Rupert Berger, Mayor of Traunstein in the 1930s, was sent to Dachau as early as 1933 for his democratic and Catholic views. Joseph senior confined his to reading anti-Nazi newspapers and resigning from the police.

Ratzinger raises a wider issue when, questioned by Seewald, he mentioned *Krystallnacht*. 'The fact that Hitler's annihilation of the Jews also had a consciously anti-Christian character is important and must not be passed over in silence.' This is true to the extent that Hitler meant that after the Jews he would eliminate the Catholics. But it gives added force to the argument that earlier and stronger resistance should have been put up. It is hard to believe Hitler seriously thought that Catholicism, as Ratzinger also maintained, was trying to 'judaise' the Germanic race.

Hitler simply wanted any religion out of the way that would jeopardise his own manic vision. He thought of Christianity as feeble and easy to dominate (as it so proved). The German writer, Claus Hant, to whom I talked, convincingly shows in *Young Hitler* (2010) that Hitler was not especially anti-Semitic to begin with, but adopted the policy for purely political ends to gain power: it was a creed primarily, the creed of racial purity that came to obsess him, with himself as its messiah, to which all other religions were rivals and had to be crushed. This was confirmed by another source, Hans Frank, who wrote in similar terms.

There was but one small jump from the Hitler Führer principle, or *Führer Prinzip*, that 'the law is the will of the Führer', to the belief that God has willed someone to do something, and that therefore in obeying God's will he was sanctioned in putting into force what he believed was true, because it had come from God – or that God would agree it was the right course.

Hitler believed the spiritual power which drove him came from God, from providence, from destiny. He attributed to these various powers the great inner force that impelled him from the time he experienced his 'conversion' from a rather pathetic down-and-out and failed artist, to an imperious leader of total self-belief, able to exercise power and wreak destruction at will. Most demonise this power as one-off pure evil or mental imbalance, or derived from social or historical causes, all of which played their part, but his many millions of followers believed him and followed him to the death because the power first of all came from the spirit, the belief that he was destined to found a new religion, of which he was the Messiah.

In fact, Hitler always saw Catholicism, directed to entirely different spiritual ends than his own, as his main rival, which he would in the end, having made Germany the greatest power on earth, and having eliminated the inferior races, subjugate but not finally destroy. It was his overriding ambition and intention to make it subservient to him, or, in the tactic of proselytising atheists, weaken its influence, or eliminate it altogether.

Unleashed by Reinhard Heydrich, Himmler's No. 2, *Krystallnacht* created horror and devastation on a scale hitherto unimagined. The list of activities proscribed, or places excluded for Jews, strangely enough included German forests. This provides a chilling yet extraordinary insight into the way the Nazis had aestheticised politics (similar to the way we have sexualised it today), and become what the Surrealists had called for, 'a government of artists'.

A short while after this week of atrocity the NSDAP leaders and their wives were at a dinner party with Hitler. The Nazis loved cruel, heavy-handed jokes). To Goebbels' demand for the Jews be forbidden to enter forests, Göring replied, 'We shall give the Jews a certain part of the forest and see that various animals that look much like Jews – the elk has a crooked nose like them – get here also and become acclimatised.'

Forests were sacred. The effect of forest romanticism in early German cultural history could never be underrated – for the German, as Canetti writes in *Crowds and Power*, 'army and forest transfused each other in every possible way... The parallel rigidity of the upright trees and their density and number fill the heart of the German with a deep and mysterious delight... What to others might seem the army's dreariness and barrenness kept for the German the life and glow of the forest.' Jews, be warned!

In gratitude for his invitation to the dinner the newly appointed Minister of Justice in Bavaria, Hans Frank, sent a fulsome telegram, 'My life is and remains service to your work. Heil to you my Führer.'

Pacelli's attitude to *Kristallnacht* was the same as Faulhaber in 1933: public silence and – apparently – private indifference. The Jews must look after themselves. And all during this time German women went on christening their children as Catholics and attending Mass. There were many decent family priests, while well-off Munich women much admired the august, stately presence of Faulhaber, with whom they had personal contact.

In his New Year's Eve sermon in 1938, Faulhaber congratulated Hitler's government: 'One advantage of our time: at the highest levels of the government we have the example of an austere alcohol- and nicotine-free lifestyle.'

When in 1934 a Prague newspaper had published a faked sermon, falsely attributed to him, which voiced opposition to racial hatred and persecution of the Jews he reacted furiously, and in a rage telegraphed two federal ministers as well as the Bavarian chancellery and the German embassy in Prague to 'save' his reputation – or, rather, to salvage it to save face. The telegram read, 'Faulhaber's sermon against racial hatred never delivered. Trying to withdraw false message.'

Veneration for him remained strong: as Benedict XVI, Ratzinger has never wavered in his loyalty to this dubious, at best ambiguous figure, while the road in Traunstein where his old seminary is lodged, is named after him, as is the smart Kardinal-Faulhaber-Strasse in uptown Munich.

† † †

For the time being Hitler, it seemed, once the German Catholic Church's defeat could be taken for granted, was content to take a back seat. He would not risk universal outrage by murdering the Catholic hierarchy. Fear and intimidation were enough to instil obedience. He left the dirty work of eliminating low-level protest from parishes to Bormann and Himmler, but with the luxury of the occasional intemperate outburst against

Christians, one heroic Lutheran in particular who later became a martyr:

> He had another such fit of rage at Pastor Niemöller in 1937. Niemöller had once again delivered a rebellious sermon in Dahlem; at the same time transcripts of his tapped telephone conversations were presented to Hitler. In a bellow Hitler ordered Niemöller to be put in a concentration camp and, since he had proved himself incorrigible, kept there for life.
> (Speer, 1970)

The unpalatable truth is that Hitler's successes from 1920 to 1940 'claim to rank amongst the most astounding by any individual in the history of the world', André Gide declared in his Journal. Subjugation of the Church ranked among them as one of Hitler's modt notable early successes. But he still somewhere respected the Catholic Church, and felt it was necessary to help him fulfil his mission.

While he occasionally boasted to Speer, 'Once I have settled my other problems I'll have my reckoning with the Church. I'll have it reeling on the ropes', even after late 1942, Speer reported, he maintained the Church was indispensable in political life, and that it was impossible to replace its prestige and influence by a 'party ideology'. A new party religion, he said, would only bring about a relapse into the mysticism of the Middle Ages.

6

Religious Czar and Two-Way Kardinal

No one could live under a brutal dictatorship without becoming tainted. Compromising with evil to prevent worse, a defence I was to hear many times, is always futile, but to know this after the event is as easy as, except in a very few cases, it is difficult to recognise malignancy in its infancy.

George Clare, *Berlin Days 1946–7*

While Hitler played cat and mouse with weak Great Britain and France, professing peace, and his armies and intimidating gangs, together with his fascists ally Mussolini, gobbled up neighbours and overseas territories, the Catholic Church moved further along the path of appeasement.

Four days after his election as Pope Pius XII on 2 March 1939 Pacelli proposed to his German cardinals that he would handle all dealings between the German Church and the Reich personally. He affirmed Hitler with these words, over which he dithered, unsure whether to style the Führer 'Most Illustrious' or simply plain 'Illustrious':

To the Illustrious Herr Adolf Hitler, Führer and Chancellor of the German Reich! Here at the beginning of Our Pontificate We wish to assure you that We remain devoted to the spiritual welfare of the German people entrusted to your leadership...

During the many years we spent in Germany, We did all in Our power to establish harmonious relations between Church and State. Now that the responsibilities of Our pastoral function have increased Our opportunities, how much more ardently do We pray to reach that goal. May the prosperity of the German people and their progress in every domain come, with God's help, to fruition! (Cornwell, 1999)*

Thereafter, on 20 April 1939, Archbishop Cesare Orsenigo, the Papal Nuncio in Berlin, (later disowned and dubbed by the Church 'a bent reed') splashed out on a lavish gala reception for the Führer's 50th birthday.

Pacelli instructed Cardinal Bertram of Berlin to follow this every year on the same date to send 'warmest congratulations' on his birthday, in the name of the German Church, to the Führer.

There is no mention by Ratzinger anywhere of this abject servility of his Church and his predecessor towards Hitler.

But wasn't the Catholic Church playing politics, embracing the spirit of the age, in a way it had claimed it had put behind it with the Concordat?

Ratzinger seemed later unaware of the harmful effect the Pope he admired had visited upon his people. He would adopt the official Pacelli line over his behaviour towards Hitler and the Third Reich, defending him against attacks on his 'silence' as Pius XII over the Holocaust, and becoming an ardent supporter of his future canonisation. This was in spite of the judgement pronounced on Pius by Fr Robert Leiber, SJ, his longtime German secretary: '*Grande si, santo no*' (great man yes, a saint, no).

'I am not opposed,' wrote Ratzinger, 'as a principle to a move towards stronger models of separation, where this is relevant. On the whole, the Church benefited by being forced to detach herself from the state Church systems after the First World War.' (Seewald, 1997.)

---

* With unease the present writer noted the reintroduction of the papal 'We', similar to that of Pius, in Benedict's papal utterances. John Paul abolished it in 1978. 'As we go through difficult times, we feel you should raise your thought to more joyous things of the past,' the Pope said in a letter in July 2010 to Cardinal Tarcisio Bertone congratulating him on the 50th anniversary of his ordination.

This was clearly not the case, as I have shown in the previous chapter. For, by whom was the Church forced, if not Pacelli? In wanting to make himself supreme arbiter of the Church he was playing as he thought a subtle and non-confrontational diplomatic game with Hitler (which concealed his own 'wild mood swings'), and which he thought would prevail. To some degree it might be claimed there was even a competitive element of Hitler being his mimetic double, for, he thought, he could match Hitler's evil with his own virtue and purity.

Asked by Pasqualina why he dealt with Hitler in this way he told her that he could not allow emotions or impulse to sway his decisions. But the pope is a man, whatever the gloss of 'infallibility' (something which Cardinal Newman never signed up to: see Chapter 25 for discussion of this issue) established by his predecessor Pio Nono.

Sir Robert Vansittart, a British career diplomat, admirably summed up the result to Lord Halifax, the British Foreign Secretary. 'Pacelli has effectively stitched up twenty-three million German Catholics into the evil power of the Nazi Party.'

Ratzinger's statement, therefore, appears almost shockingly naive, at best disingenuous. No one would argue that it is not beneficial for State and Church to be separate, but it was the way this happened which was so crucial, at the behest of a power-hungry cardinal and a ruthless dictator, and at the expense of a free German democracy. This was to be followed by the death of many millions of innocent Germans who had been tricked into believing as Catholics they had to support Hitler and the Nazi state.

† † †

Hitler was now fully embarked on his Nietzschean destiny. 'Ye shall love peace as a means to new war, and the short peace more than the long. You I advise not to work, but to fight. You I advise not to peace but to victory.' The immense drama approached its climax, while Hitler was well aware of the high stakes.

Earlier, in November 1936, in spite of his boast that he would have the Catholic Church on the ropes, he had, playing both sides of the street, even taken his fears and concerns to Cardinal

Faulhaber, Bavaria's spiritual leader, with whom he had been closeted in a long and close discussion at Obersalzberg.

He had emerged soberly from this heart-searching:

> Afterward Hitler sat alone with me [Albert Speer] in the bay window of the dining room, while the twilight fell. For a long time he looked out of the window in silence. Then he said pensively: 'There are two possibilities for me: To win through with all my plans, or to fail. If I win, I shall be one of the greatest men in history. If I fail, I shall be condemned, despised, and damned.' (Speer, 1970)

There are well-documented parallels of lesser political figures bent on war seeking the approval of spiritual authority. Tony Blair, for instance, flew to Rome in February 2003 to consult John Paul II, and ask for his advice and endorsement when he had already decided to take part in the invasion of Iraq. The surprise here was that Hitler's consultation with Faulhaber showed a side of his personality he normally hid: that he still had concerns or superstition about the power of the Church. It also showed Hitler thought of Faulhaber as a sympathetic ear, or he would never have consulted him.

Increasingly now, the Nazis used the harmonies of Germany's classical composers to drown the thump of truncheon and jackboot. 'Performances of the Berliner and Vienna Philharmonic, the Leipzig Gewandhaus and other good German orchestras were meant to demonstrate that National Socialism was in tune with the highest aspirations of German culture.'

† † †

The Ratzinger family had nothing to say about the invasion of Poland in September 1939, or at least nothing that has been recorded beyond a brief mention in *Milestones*. The *Diktat of Versailles* had robbed the Germans of their army. 'The activities they were denied, the exercises, the receiving and passing on of orders, had became something they had to procure at all costs. And now, unrestricted, they could enjoy these for years. The prohibition of universal military service was the *birth* of National Socialism.' (Canetti, 1952)

It had grown to full maturity. Germany was united as never before, North and South spoke with one voice. The Prussian North and the Bavarian South embraced with love and mutual regard.

The way Warsaw held out beggars description, and on 15 September, angered by the unexpected setback, the Wehrmacht High Command decided to 'pound the stubborn citadel into submission'.

In round-the-clock raids bombers knocked out flourmills, gasworks, power plants, then carpeted the residential areas with incendiaries. One witness, passing scenes of carnage, enumerated the horrors: 'Everywhere corpses, wounded humans, dead horses… and hastily-dug graves…' Food ran out finally, so that famished Poles, as one man put it, 'cut off flesh as soon as a horse fell, leaving only the skeleton'.

On 28 September, Warsaw Radio replaced the Chopin 'Polonaise' with a funeral dirge. The indiscriminate killing of Poles, including women and children (and priests) committed by front-line German troops, many of whom were Catholics, was so horrifying that even some Wehrmacht generals baulked at it, and requested transference from Poland.

But wait a minute. Didn't the German Catholic bishops believe Poles, almost universally Catholics, were their brothers in faith? None raised a voice, advising mercy and compassion.

The Nazi authorities and Hans Frank, now appointed Governor of the 'Government General' of Poland, had special orders to exploit Poland ruthlessly as a war territory and a land of booty, 'to turn it, so to speak, into a heap of ruins from the point of view of economic, social, cultural and political structure'.

On 5 October 1939 Hitler visited the subdued capital of Warsaw, stood on a podium and took the march past of Field-Marshal von Rundstedt's Eighth Army, which lasted two hours, during which security guards foiled an assassination attempt on his life by a student. He made a fleeting visit to the Belvedere Palace. He doesn't seem to have been too happy:

'The Führer's verdict on the Poles is damning,' Goebbels noted. 'More like animals than human beings, completely primitive, stupid and amorphous. And a ruling class that is the unsatisfactory result of mingling between the lower order and an Aryan master race. The Poles' dirtiness is unimaginable. Their capacity for intelligent judgment is absolutely nil...'

Direct military rule of Poland stopped in late September 1939. SS atrocities, ordered or overseen by Himmler, continued unabated. But there were still a great number of German front-line units in the country. In February 1940 General Johannes Blascowitz complained about the SS atrocities of the *Einsatzgruppen*. Frank intervened and requested personally from Hitler General Blascowitz's removal.

Von Rundstedt, the commander of the German invasion forces, also demanded an end of anti-Jewish measures and resigned his command. He was moved to plan and then execute the forthcoming invasion of France. Hitler was loath to lose one of his best military minds. Again, I cite this example, for when someone in the hierarchy spoke out, Hitler temporised.

The young aristocrat officer, Klaus von Stauffenberg, a staunch Catholic who served in Poland with his 17th Cavalry Division, remained in Poland only a short while. He is portrayed in book after book, film after film (most recently in the 2009 film *Valkyrie*), as a true military prince, who preserved the heroic tradition of an old world family, and aristocratic honour.

Yet he supported the occupation and the Nazi regime's use of Poles as slave workers and that the Polish lands partitioned by Poland in Russia and handed back at Versailles in 1919 should be colonised, in line with what the Teutonic Knights did in the Middle Ages. Even as late as May 1944, just weeks before his bomb plot to remove Hitler, he demanded a new partition.

His wife Nina said, after his death, 'He let things come to him, and then he made up his mind... one of his characteristics was that he really enjoyed playing the devil's advocate. Conservatives were convinced that he was a ferocious Nazi, and ferocious Nazis were convinced he was an unreconstructed conservative. He was neither.'

Only when Germany was losing in 1942 did von Stauffenburg finally became convinced of the need to rid Germany of the Führer and the questions his life poses suggest the answers would be far more complex than the two-dimensional, conspiratorial hero of legend. What his wife said of him seems an apposite description of this similar trait in Ratzinger of letting things come to him before making up his mind.

His staunch Roman Catholicism, like Faulhaber's, was very German, nationalistic and anti-Jewish. It believed Polish Catholics should be enslaved. He would have approved, as did the Catholic hierarchy in Germany, of racial laws and measures against the Jews. It stopped short of violence and extermination.

By the time Poland and France had been conquered and occupied, the Ratzinger family had settled well into Traunstein, where Hitler had once been billeted as a serving member of the Royal Bavarian Army.

7

Did They Resist Intimidation?

To Sonne's mind, history was eminently the area of guilt. We should know not only what happened to our fellow men in the past but also what they were capable of. We should know what we ourselves are capable of. For that much knowledge is needed; from whatever direction, at whatever distance knowledge offers itself, we should reach out for it, keep it fresh, water it and fertilize it with new knowledge.

Elias Canetti, *The Play of the Eyes*

Details as precise as a photograph pepper Ratzinger's accounts of his later childhood and youth, but they are impersonal and thin-blooded and, to be honest, not very interesting – not so much those of a writer who is interested in the world, and in himself, but more of a Church leader, a cardinal who had a position to maintain, and wanted to inspire a devotional following among those who read him.

It is as if early on, the child, who is the father of the man, is already divided into two different identities. The first is the sensitive, enquiring soul, a genius already of conceptual analysis and reactive, almost feminine empathy to concepts and ideas of Christian value.

The second is the careful, self-advancing supporter of tradition and order, who is ruthless and a survivor, and who is the driving force of the two selves, both preserved in such a careful way as to make sure in the future they are never to come into conflict with one another.

He tells us that his father had turned 60 on 6 March 1937. They had moved that year into the Traunstein house, where there was a ceiling beam with '1726' etched into it; an orchard with an apple tree, and two enormous cherry trees; a roof over the stalls and lofts was covered with wooden shingles that were held down with stones against the wind; there was a well, a weaving room; he and his brother Georg slept in a room facing south.

From the three main sources to which he wrote or contributed, the impression is that Ratzinger distanced himself from the cultural force of Nazism, its wide appeal, and especially the appalling suffering it caused on all sides. There is little apart from generalised condemnation of the 'Brown Shirts', as he calls them, the Nazi leaders he holds responsible, which conveys strong feeling or personal outrage.

He would find it difficult ever to see the Third Reich as other than a foreign import, its evil seeds sown in the decadent neighbouring Austro-Hungarian Empire; never as a purely German phenomenon, as Thomas Mann saw it, with its roots deep in German culture.

On the Nazi Party postcard, alongside Frederick the Great, Bismarck, and Hindenburg, stood the now *echt Deutsch* Hitler, with the caption: 'What the King conquered, the Prince fused, the Field Marshal defended, the Soldier saved and unified.' This was the *credo* of most Germans.

† † †

Preaching in German at Auschwitz in May 2006 as Pope Benedict, Ratzinger claimed he was there as a son of 'that people over which a ring of criminals rose to power by false promises'. Then, speaking in Italian – the switch seemed Mozartean, and why didn't he talk in Polish, for that was where he was, in Poland? – he said, 'In the end there can only be a dread silence – a silence which is itself a heartfelt cry to God: Why Lord, did you remain silent? How could you tolerate all this?' (BBC News. 25 May 2006).

Later, in Israel he was criticised for not showing more remorse. 'The pope spoke like a historian, as someone observing from the sidelines... he was part of them, with all due respect to the Holy See, we cannot ignore the baggage he carried. He never said Jews were "murdered" only "killed", never mentioned Nazis (years before, John Paul II had used the word "murdered" on his Yad Vashem visit).'

There had been from 1933 onwards, many Catholic and other witnesses who remained silent, many who refused to believe in the horror – so perhaps the responsibility lay more with men, and not with God.

One of these, not least, had been Pope Pius XII. Benedict missed out by not using this as an opportunity to recall the gullibility and silence of these men, and the complicity of those who were convinced and dedicated to those false promises, influential among which were high-ranking members of the Catholic Church. He could have said something more along the lines of, 'The Church failed by not bearing witness to her moral essence; in the face of an upsurge of monstrous barbarism it was wrong to be guided by "reasons of state" or "*raison d'église*".'

This was the truth. Yet occupying the papal throne from 2005 to 2013 he seemed at certain moments to be making the same mistake with regard to other issues, such as the clerical abuse of minors.

At Auschwitz Ratzinger made no apology on behalf of his countrymen, nor did he make a direct reference to anti-Semitism. Had he missed out the little bit of Nazi that is potentially in everyone of us; that self-awareness of which that had prompted Sir Thomas More, when seeing a murderer led to the scaffold, to say 'There, but for the grace of God, go I'?

As Hitler sought victory and believed passionately in the Thousand Year Reich, one feels that Germans such as Ratzinger and his family put up with it as an oppressed minority which got on with life as best it could, keeping what it thought to itself.

This sense of privacy, of a closed book, is strong and is deepened by the way in which in *Milestones*, as in subsequent 'frank and open' interviews, Ratzinger described those years.

When the fortunes of war changed with Hitler's rash and fatal invasion of Russia, and it began to be possible that Hitler would

lose, Cardinal Pacelli, now Pius XII, began to speak out, but only
up to a point, and in a very general way. In the famous Christmas
message of 1941, which according to some supporters, 'broke his
silence' over the Holocaust, he made his appeal for the 'victims
of war'. Later he claimed this was a protest and a denunciation of
Nazi extermination of the Jews.

But at the time he couched his speech in the most vague and
wishy-washy language, in order to placate those who urged him
to protest, and not offend the Nazi chiefs: 'Humanity owes this
vow to those hundreds of thousands who, without any fault of
their own, sometimes only by reasons of their nationality or race
are marked down for death or gradual extinction.' He never once
used the words *Jew*, *German*, *Nazi* or *non-Aryan*.

Apparently the Italian Foreign Minister Count Ciano came
upon Mussolini listening to the broadcast: 'The Vicar of God,
who is representative of earth of the Ruler of the Universe,'
sneered Il Duce, 'should never speak, he should remain in the
clouds. This is a speech of platitude which might better be made
by the parish priest of Predappio [Mussolini's backwater native
town in rural Romagna].'

Even if he had wanted to be diplomatic and ambiguous to
avoid any chance of Nazi revenge for more explicit condemnation (as John Cornwell, in presenting his case in *The Hitler Pope*
against Pius, argued), there was no excuse for his claim after the
war that he had spoken candidly and with due moral leadership. Cornwell began to question Pius's role in the Second World
War when Ralph Hochhuth's play, *The Representative* (performed
on Broadway 1964–5) depicted Pius as indifferent to the fate of
the Jews and more worried over the preservation of Vatican real
estate. Cornwell called Pius's action:

> A stunning religious and ritualistic silence... Pacelli's reticence
> was not just a diplomatic silence in response to the politi-
> cal pressures of the moment, not just a failure to be morally
> outraged in the face of an atrocity committed at the heart of
> Christendom, in the shadow of the shrine of the first apos-
> tle [which] persists to this day and implicates all Catholics.
> This silence proclaims that Pacelli had no genuine spiritual

sympathy even for the Jews of Rome, who were members of the community of his birth. (Cornwell, 1999)

He had been, said Cornwell, 'the ideal pope for Hitler's unspeakable plan. He was Hitler's Pawn.'

Perhaps this was going too far, as I believe Cornwell later admitted. To reopen the case for and against Pius with regard to his wartime 'silence' about the Holocaust is not the intention here, although the industry to exonerate him is still a huge one.

What I do underline is that Pius behaved as a 'situationist' and even a 'moral relativist' (as condemned by John Paul II and Benedict as current forms of today's evil) maintaining first and foremost as much as he could the political power of the Church and its material survival, than a wholly honest and morally integrated leader of that Church. I may well be wrong but a follower of Jesus, if his message to mankind is to be followed to the letter, would have been prepared to sacrifice Rome in following and imitating the saviour, and testing the Pilate of his day (who surely would have capitulated) but as Pius was to show, he was never prepared to do this.

† † †

The civilian population in Germany could not avoid seeing what was going on. In a circular dated November 9, 1941, and addressed by the head of the Police and the Security Services to all police officials and camp commandants, one reads: 'In particular, it must be noted that during the transfers on foot, for example from the station to the camp, a considerable number of prisoners collapse along the way, fainting or dying from exhaustion... It is impossible to keep the [civilian German] population from knowing about such happenings.' (The Black Book, 1941.)

A woman like Ratzinger's mother Maria must have seen and known 'such happenings' were going on. She must have been aware of mothers around her whose sons were part of the army or had joined the Nazi Party. Nazism had successfully created not only unlimited enthusiasm but also an atmosphere of undefined terror, and everyone must have known of the confinement of hundreds of opponents to Nazism.

The nineteenth-century Christian tradition, including both the Lutherans and Catholics, had influenced Reich women to remain wholly subservient to their husbands, and consider them their masters. The Reich repudiated the religion, but took over and continued the tradition of subservience. Vanished were the women of classical or Christian medieval character, who were more independent and even ruled their husbands by measures such as refusing them sex till they fell in with their wishes.

German women, three and half million of them, had flocked to join the *NS Frauenshaft*. Many made use of modern eugenics, abortion on demand, or, in legally prescribed circumstances according to Hitler's race laws, to curtail procreation of allegedly feeble-minded and inferior peoples.

Goebbels decreed that the 'mission of women is to be beautiful and to bring children into the world,' a mission to all intents and purposes fulfilled by most with zeal. Yet they were, in the truest sense, accomplices not victims. At every level women operated at the centre of Nazism, sustaining male moral, even if personally they felt in conflict.

When the SS man came home from heroic deeds of exterminating enemies, he entered a doll's house of *ersatz* goodness in which he could escape from his evil actions. The emotional work done by women contributed to stability. How complicit they were in their guilt later came to be largely ignored; when the war was over the Allied Control Commission failed to look into Nazi sterilisation programmes, and the part German women played in them.

We take as an example Brigitte Frank, wife of the 'Butcher of Poland', as Hans Frank, formerly Bavarian Minister of Justice, became known. She played both sides of the street. In Bavaria she was a good Catholic, where her children were christened, received Holy Communion and were confirmed by a Father R. Mayer, who, according to their anti-Nazi son Niklas, was an honest and devout priest, and an example of faith and integrity. In the Government General of Poland, she was an out-and-out ruthless collaborator with Nazism who relished every privilege she could lay her hands on – and convinced herself she was helping poor downtrodden Jews by buying at her own price (or extorting) the goods she obtained.

She kept and fed her relatives in outbuildings in the Schoberhof estate near Neuhaus am Schliersee in Bavaria. Foreign workers, imported as slaves, were free. She employed the free labour of chef, chambermaids, nurse-maids and kitchen-maids, paid from state funds, if Germans, or imported as slaves from Poland, right up to the end of the war. Two months before the Germans evacuated Poland, Frank's office manager in Krakau wrote to Brigitte, 'I have been able to ascertain that your desire to continuing employing Polish and Hungarian workers at the Schoberhof, but at the same time to having then reported as being employed in Krakow, is no longer permissible,' a blatant example of what came to be known in 2009 in Great Britain as 'flipping'.

The household held Brigitte in some contempt and defied her frustrated attempts to have them address her as 'Frau Minister'. Later one servant related how, at an elegant dinner for Nazi leaders, the chef urinated into the 'Polish Meissen porcelain' tureen, which had been filled with asparagus soup. Below stairs they fell about with laughter as it was served. Brigitte's response was 'Tell the *maître* his soup tasted delicious.'

† † †

Georg Ratzinger, born in 1924, would have been, if Hitler Youth membership since 25 March 1939 was compulsory from 14 (Seewald, 174), obliged to join in 1939. However, Ratzinger, interviewed in *The Salt of the Earth*, claims it was made compulsory in 1941, and that he was 'still too young', although he was 14, to join. In fact the real situation, which Ratzinger should have explained, was one from which he also benefited and was both more vague and more flexible as long as one did not actively oppose. Ratzinger was not altogether speaking the whole truth when he said, 'You had to join the Nazi Youth.'

In December 1936 Hitler Youth membership had been made mandatory for anyone, although apparently you could be excused if your parents did not agree. The proof for this is the fact that this loophole was closed in 1939, when parents could no longer withhold membership from their children. There was, as Hannah Cleaver, a researcher in Berlin, tells me, a distinction until 1939 between Stamm-HJ, those who had volunteered to join, and Pflicht-HJ, those who were made to join. But even then it was possible to avoid joining.

Dr Rupert Burger, a friend of Ratzinger and later Mayor of Traunstein, described how he, and it seemed Ratzinger, used his religion to avoid Hitler Youth. 'A couple of times the police came round and picked me up and took me to the meetings but I was determined not to go. I just remember the meetings, there would be a hall full of young lads and it was chaotic, really loud. We were put into groups and then I think I left. I even had a uniform... I was helping the priest perform Mass on Sundays in the military hospital in the building where I lived... I got a note saying I was needed at the Mass, signed by the commanding officer, sent it to the Hitler Youth people and never went again.' (Hannah Cleaver to author.)

The situation became even more flexible as, from 1941 onwards, massive conscription efforts to fill the spaces in a diminishing army confused the issues until boys of ten became, as *Hitler Jugend*, called up to fight.

Joseph says Georg joined the *Hitler Jugend* in 1941. Now aged 17 at least, it was more likely they conscripted him straight into the SS training camp at Konigsdorff near Bad Tolz. At first, after training, he joined, according to Seewald 'a labour service' in the Sudeten region – this, although unspoken, presumably meant as a member of the SS or Nazi labour service he *guarded* slave labourers, for it was unlikely a trained member of the SS would be on manual labour service when the Nazis had so many millions of forced labourers from occupied territories.

8

Complete Innocence and Sexual Continence

According to Joseph his family remained unimpressed by Hitler's military triumphs of 1939–41; Hitler was, according to Joseph senior, an Anti-Christ, while his wife made anti-Hitler jokes within a limited circle, and they listened to forbidden radio broadcasts. Joseph senior scolded trespassers who took a short cut across his land.

He was by all accounts deeply devout, severe, a teetotaller, and as a retired policeman saw himself with a higher sense of purpose as set apart from ordinary folk. But then we have only Joseph's word for what he said about his father. Local Traunsteinians are only prepared to talk in the most glowing terms about their favourite son who became pope.

Both Ratzinger and Karol Wojtyla were strongly influenced by their fathers, both 'Josephs', one a policeman, one a soldier who had lived a life of service and retired early. Here the resemblance between their backgrounds ends. Ratzinger grew up in emotional and material security; Wojtyla the reverse.

The family never owned anything, and early on Karol had no family. 'At twenty, I had already lost all the people I loved... I was not old enough to make my first communion when I lost my mother. My brother Edmund died from scarlet fever in a virulent epidemic at the hospital when he was starting as a doctor. After my father's death, which occurred in February 1941, I gradually became aware of my true path.' Wojtyla then was well over twenty, and was to experience four gruelling years as a labourer, then clandestine seminarian. (O'Connor, 2006.)

Probably the most remarkable thing about Wojtyla's father was that, given the anti-Semitism in Poland, endorsed by the Catholic Church leader Cardinal Hlond, he, and the Catholic hierarchy in Krakow were not anti-Semitic; as Ginka, an early Jewish girlfriend of the future pope said of his father when she had been driven out of Poland: 'Mr Wojtyla was upset about my departure, and when he asked me why, I told him. Again and again he said to me, "Not all Poles are anti-Semitic. You know I am not!"

'I spoke to him frankly and said that very few Poles were like him. He was very upset. But Lolek [Wojtyla] was even more upset than his father.'

From an early age Wojtyla had felt close to the Jewish community in his native Wadowice, and that 'relationships with Jews were a daily occurrence'. He frequently made the point that Canon Prochownik, who had buried his mother, spoke out against the economic boycott of Jews in the 1930s, and insisted that to be anti-Semitic was to be anti-Christian.

† † †

Joseph said he would never forget that 'sunny day in 1941 when we received news that Germany had launched with her allies an attack on the Soviet Union on a front reaching from the North Pole to the Black Sea'.

Yet here was their mentor, Cardinal Faulhaber, justifying and extolling the virtues of the invasion. In a pastoral letter to Bavarian bishops he wrote in December 1941 appealing to 'our believers for faithful fulfilment of their duties, to persevere boldly, for self-sacrificing work and for fighting in the service of our country in the hardest times of war'; he ended with the rousing endorsement, 'as the German Government well knows and so we observe this fight against Bolshevism with great satisfaction'.

The family needed more than its bulwark of truth and righteousness against the kingdom of atheism, it needed resistance to the equivocation of its Church.

It would seem to some degree that Joseph, while strongly asserting his family's anti-Nazi attitude, even though it militated against a deep-rooted instinct to conform to officialdom, retreated, in his description of his childhood, into a theological safe house. Most children, and young men and women, growing up in Nazi Germany were, like the Ratzinger children, intensively trained – we see at one stage Joseph receiving high marks for Nazi indoctrination – and whether they liked it or not, conditioned for life, work and death in Hitler's Third Reich.

We shouldn't disguise the fact that the vast majority loved it: most of the country, at least until late 1941, expected it to win, as it had now for its eight years of unbroken victory. The American journalist William Shirer, who had chronicled the Reich since its beginning as an eye witness, and who only left Germany in late 1940, wrote his impression of young German men:

> Though their minds were deliberately poisoned, their regular schooling interrupted, their homes largely replaced so far as their rearing went, the boys and the girls, the young men and women, seemed immensely happy, filled with a zest for the life of a Hitler Youth. […]
>
> The young in the Third Reich were growing up to have strong and healthy bodies, faith in the future of their country and in themselves and a sense of fellowship and camaraderie that shattered all class and economic and social barriers. I thought of that later, in the May days of 1940, when along the road between Aachen and Brussels one saw the contrast between the German soldiers, bronzed and clean-cut from a youth spent in the sunshine on an adequate diet, and the first British war prisoners with their hollow chests, round shoulders, pasty complexions and bad teeth – tragic examples of the youth that England had neglected so irresponsibly in the years between the war. (Shirer, 1959)

From Joseph 's own account, and from those around him, and those who wrote later of his early years, it appeared that he never once suffered or experienced the general hero-worship of German boys of his age for the heroes of the pre-war, or war, or for other boys of his age who led the youth movements, for the famous sportsmen, industrialists, film stars and so on. Could this be true? There would be nothing wrong if he had, it would be seen as quite natural and forgivable even if they were Nazis. It seems he was, from birth in this mammoth Faustian drama, cast as one of the good angels.

Not so another German writer, born in the same year, 1927, who won the Nobel Prize for Literature in 1999. He confessed (having for a long time kept quiet), how he felt a quite unreserved love for the temptations of Nazism. On his eleventh birthday, in 1938, for instance, he reports that synagogues in his birth town, Gdansk or Danzig, were set aflame and Jewish shop windows shattered, followed by rampaging SA gangs. But this did no more than elicit mild surprise in his childhood self. Other events affected him far more. The official party line:

> 'No one shall starve! No one shall freeze!' German racing drivers like Bernd Rosemeyer in his Mercedes Silver Arrow were the fastest. People gaped at the *Graf Zeppelin* and *Hindenburg* shimmering over the city or on picture postcards. The newsreels showed our Condor Legion helping to free Spain from the Red menace with the most up-to-date weapons. We re-enacted Alcázar on the playground. Only a few months earlier we had thrilled to the Olympic Games, medal by medal, and later we had a marvel of a runner in Rudolf Harbig. The Third Reich glittered in the newsreel spotlight. (Grass, 2007)

And above all the heavyweight boxer Max Schmeling was triumphant.

These feelings would seem very natural and normal excitements for a boy, and these were the reactions of Gunter Grass. His shopping list at Christmas had on it the Jungvolk's (the Hitler Youth) official uniform cap, scarf, belt and shoulder strap. For him to join the Jungvolk, he felt, 'lured him away' from the stifling, petit-bourgeois atmosphere of familial obligations.

He was only too willingly seduced, not at all coerced into obedience. While he never denounced anyone and noted the defections and disappearances in his local circle with a degree of curiosity but no particular feeling one way or the other, still he was, no bones about it, a Young Nazi. He perceived every German deed as justifiable retribution for the shame and failure of earlier years.

So here was a Joseph *doppelgänger*, same age, same passion for books, same passion for composing verse, but perhaps more compatible with the future age in which Joseph was to become Pope.

† † †

In December 1942 Georg Ratzinger is reported as having joined the Wehrmacht as a member of an Infantry Division; by now he had become a qualified radio and telephone operator, and then, as the military reverses began to pile up, he served in Holland and the South of France, finally arriving in la Spezia, Italy, as part of a unit to stem the Allied advance. Subsequent to this he took part in the fierce and bloody battles for Monte Cassino: 'We were lying in a line, a soldier every three yards, and I suddenly saw that a whole half of a man next to me was gone.'

Italy had changed sides, and on 8 September 1943 the Germans occupied Italy and Rome. Hitler asked the SS commander in Italy, Karl Wolff, to prepare a plan to evacuate the Pope and the Vatican treasures to Lichtenstein. Wolff resolved, after considering all aspects of the proposal, that to invade Vatican City and seize the Pope, or to arrest the Pope in retaliation for a papal protest, would provoke a backlash throughout Italy that would seriously threaten the Nazi campaign to repel the Allies.

Hitler took his advice, and dropped the plan, again showing that Pacelli underestimated or ignored the Catholic Church's potential strength for stopping Hitler's by now more rampant and deadly annihilation of all European Jews. In late October, when the SS entered the Rome ghetto and rounded up more than 1000 Jews, Pius refused to denounce the action.

† † †

Georg's regiment retreated through Rome, where they bivouacked at night in St Peter's Square on Vatican territory. The

retreat was shocking and shameful, although portrayed by
German at the time and after as heroic and tactically brilliant.
Georg was part of that occupational force which raped, pillaged
and applied a scorched earth policy as it defended in a series of
bloody battles fought up the spine of Italy, in which no quarter
was given by the Germans, in particular to the Italian people or
their country. Again, no mention is made of how Italians were
enslaved and forced to work for the German war effort, while
Italian Jews were added to the list of those exterminated. Rome
fell to the Allies on 4 June 1944.

Later, Georg was in action again, in Northern Italy 'next to a
lake'. A grenade exploded beside him. 'It shattered my arm, there
was blood everywhere. I tugged my arm, but it held firm. It was
a wound through the upper arm.' The doctor called it 'a marvellous million-dollar wound', presumably believing that for the
rest of the war Georg would be safe, which was not true.

In *Milestones* Joseph says his brother was only three years
older than him and does not mention the SS, stating Georg was
wounded in 1944, and then returned to fight again in Italy in the
same year.

There is a distinct contrast between the intricate attention to
academic detail and reference when it comes to the theologian's
biblical scholarship, and the vaguer and cursory admission of personal detail during this critical, formative period of his own life.

Yet nearly everyone's memories of early years, especially if
packed with action, fear and misery, as those years must have been,
remain very vivid. They form inevitably, and in any future biography, the most interesting part. Could it be that while so little is
known of Jesus of Nazareth's early life, which the future Pope is to
write up in the final volume of his *Jesus of Nazareth*, this reflects
perhaps a convenient example for omission of much of his own?

What did Ratzinger actually say about that period of the early
war, before he was called up in 1943? In *Milestones* he devotes
a few pages to writing on how the Traunstein Gymnasium had
been little affected in its teaching routines by National Socialist
political correctness. A second head was removed for ideological
reasons, but none of the classics teachers had joined the Party. He
found, thinking about it later, that a study of Latin and Greek

antiquity created a mental attitude that resisted seduction by a totalitarian ideology.

He noted how the Catholic music teacher had made them, in spite of the introduction of Nazi songs, cross out '*Juda den Tod*' ('to Judah death'), and instead write '*Wends die Not*' ('dispel our plight'). He was soon replaced, with the old system, by new, younger teachers, as Ratzinger says, 'many with excellent talents, ardent Nazis and anti-Catholic', while in 1940 religious instruction was dropped entirely.

It seems there were, in Nazi Germany, many opportunities for the talented to advance themselves, as long as they did not pursue an actively anti-Nazi line. Hence many of the intelligent and well-informed led happy and well-rewarded lives. There is only a little recollection of the immediacy of events, no presentation of the thoughts and feeling Joseph had as a child.

On the plus side, his family, given the annexation of Austria which worked in their favour, enjoyed visits to Salzburg to make the pilgrimage to Maria Plain and in particular, to the Salzburg Festival. Beethoven's Ninth Symphony (conducted by Knoppertsbusch), say, Mozart's Mass in C Minor, were among the works he recalls in particular.

'The greatest and most important and loveliest part of my childhood,' he judged at that time, 'I spent in Traunstein, where there is a great deal of influence from Salzburg. There Mozart thoroughly penetrated our souls, so to speak, and he still moves me most deeply, because his music is so luminous and yet at the same time so profound.'

Mozart himself, as his biographers including Albert Einstein recount, never much enjoyed being Mozart as a child, while he was reported as saying, on the subject of the adulation showered on him, 'But do you really love me?' Ratzinger did not add that Mozartean music, as well as the man himself, also has a markedly profane and naughty side, as well as celebrating such forbidden rites as those of Freemasonry in *Die Zauberflöte*. Many see this opera as an allegory of enlightened absolutism. *Don Giovanni*'s uninhibited zest for its hero's libertine life style, although it ends badly for him, has a strong, amoral charge. Mozart had an unashamed rakish side.

Mozart was also the idol of Ratzinger's future theological rival, Hans Küng, who wrote a spirited eulogy of his favourite composer. Küng made no secret of how Mozart fell out with the Salzburg hierarchy and its archbishop, writing to his father he 'hated the archbishop to madness', who in his turn called Mozart a 'scoundrel, rogue and fox'. Mozart also famously said, 'I want to hear nothing more about Salzburg.'

Küng quotes another admirer who claimed Mozart could intend something 'quite diabolical with his music, a jest, a nihilism behind the appearance of tender understanding, a higher form of amorality'.

Clearly, there were sides to Mozart to which Ratzinger did not respond, or did not want to be seen to respond.

† † †

Although Joseph senior did not work or earn money apart from his reduced pension, Joseph's sister, Maria, after an obligatory year in agricultural service, began work for a 'big company' in Traunstein, which 'eased the family budget', and enabled Joseph aged twelve to attend the same Traunstein seminary which Georg had joined. It may seem a little odd that Joseph, like his brother, should at such an early age, become completely sure of his priestly vocation, and not want to explore his many other talents, as had his predecessor Karol Wojtyla, who was both a gifted writer and actor.

Hitler's sharp perceptions of Bismarck's war or *Kulturkampf* with the Church had brought him to the resolution that to assault the Church directly would only make martyrs. While he turned Pacelli's self-vaunted subtle and diplomatic approach upside down and ran rings round him, he also knew that 'One doesn't attack,' as he said, 'petticoats or cassocks.'

When it suited him and he thought it politic, Hitler could be careful with the Catholic lay population too. When, for instance, in June 1941 Adolf Wagner, Gauleiter of Upper Bavaria, ordered the removal of public crosses, which produced anti-Nazi demonstrations and the signing of petitions including ones from Catholic soldiers at the front, Hitler ordered Wagner to rescind the order.

In the 1933 Concordat, a provision or concession had been made for the Church to continue to educate and train seminarians, although this training soon became indoctrinated with Nazi ideology, so that future priests would endorse, as did the Vatican treaty, the Reich's ongoing legitimacy. Even more cleverly, in a secret annex to the Concordat, Hitler agreed to grant Catholic priests exemption from any conscription imposed on German males in the event of universal military service. This provision was important, Hitler told von Papen, for it showed the world the Vatican's tacit acquiescence before they began the campaign for total rearmament. The payback for the Reich was that the German Catholic bishops and the Vatican endorsed the Nazi Party, the SS and any future acts of military aggression.

Did the Ratzinger brothers sign up under parental pressure in order to increase their chances of survival? Ultimately would they be able to make use of the legal loophole in Hitler's suppression of Roman Catholicism, which the Ratzinger family also perceived as a way to avoid too close an assimilation into the bad ethos of the Reich? It seems so. Again it should be stressed that I am not decrying what they did or didn't do, but simply the lack of openness in the future about it, and lack of self-knowledge about what effect it may have had in the wider context, especially on the personality of one who became so important for so many millions.

Were the parents playing safe, dressing their children in ornate vestments and wrapping them in a mist of Bavarian Catholic liturgy and incense? Dr Hans Küng, the fellow theologian at Tübingen University, a harsh critic of Ratzinger and his background, deplored the family's pious 'shrine to an old-fashioned God', and accused Ratzinger, when made Prefect in 1981, of still 'carrying it around with him'.

It seems both brothers did make up their minds not only very quickly but also very early to become priests, which was, as we have seen, Hitler's loophole or concession to 'petticoats and cassocks'. Perhaps in retrospect it can be seen as a shortcoming that neither they, nor their parents, wished ever to step out of their comfort zones, although both seemed equally to be blessed with gentle, conforming spirits, and of course to be seriously dedicated. But they were from the start very sheltered, and so they were to remain.

To begin with, Joseph found boarding at the Traunstein seminary a complete torture, for he was bad at sport, and although his fellow seminarians were tolerant of his physical ineptitude, and the fact he was younger than they were, he felt intense discomfort and shame. However, as the military took over more and more of German life they turned the seminary into a hospital. Georg and Joseph had to switch to being day pupils at an alternative address to which the seminary moved.

9

High Interior Exaltation

It would be uncharitable to begrudge Ratzinger his happy memories of childhood and the peace and security they brought him: he grew up in the warm and safe environment of devotion to Catholic values with which Joseph senior and Maria surrounded and embraced their family. But given the world's perception of his Nazi-influenced background and his unfortunate sobriquets given him when he became known, perhaps he could, as well as keeping his happy memories, have seized the initiative to give a wider and broader acknowledgement of what life was really like in the Germany in which he grew up.

In spite of the darkening social and medical catastrophe that spread inevitably from total war with the Soviets, Joseph's next year, 1941–2, was one of 'high interior exaltation, full of great hope for the great things that were gradually opening up to me in the realm of the spirit'. So here we gain a strong impression of withdrawal, of not wanting to face reality but remain in the realm of the spirit.

Once more he showed his youth passing in a sharp contrast to the youth of Wojtyla, who experienced at similar ages a dark foreboding, a Job-like sense of oppression, and later wrote plays about destiny and Poland's doom. Wojtyla had to weather the trials of hunger, loneliness, and hard physical labour, which he interiorised in a poem:

Listen to the steady pounding of the hammers
Such a familiar sound. It makes us look within
To reflect on the power of the blows.
Listen now as an electric current
Cuts through the river of stone.
Inside a thought grows
Slowly by the day, that the greatness of
Work can be found in man.

(Wojtyla, quoted in O'Connor, 2006)

While every day in Germany the newspapers told of some soldier's death and almost every day a requiem Mass had to be held
for a young man, the Ratzinger family still seemed to be able to
feel itself largely untouched or favoured by providence.

Before they moved to Traunstein Joseph had found a desire
to teach had awoken inside him – more than this, it excited him
greatly. So too did writing, and even in elementary school he
wrote poems, Christian poems and nature poems, for he found
great delight in 'expressing myself and passing it on as well. So
whenever I learned something, I also wanted to pass it on.'

By now Joseph was experiencing at first hand 'the German
Christians' makeover of Christ as an Aryan. 'As a Galilean, they
said, he was no Jew.' (*The Salt of the Earth,* p. 249.) No one in
Germany could really avoid knowledge of what was happening
to the Jews, who were being deported east never to return.

But the German Catholic Church, as well as the larger centralised Catholic Church under Pius XII, was no longer able to
practise what later Ratzinger would define as an essential of the
Church, in an important phrase: he states, as well as enunciating
the truth that 'there is a judgment over me' as an orientation
for the Church's preaching and pastoral ministry, that 'She must
also be able to threaten the powerful.' This is of course arguable,
although Ratzinger believed it, and continued to do so when he
became Pope. This it had singularly failed to do with Hitler, nor
did Ratzinger ever make mention of the fact.

I can find no admission by Ratzinger either before or after he
became Pope that the Church was weak in the 1930s, although

he analysed its theological changes and currents of thought in detail. As that decade came to an end the Nazi Party was well on the way to severing all its ties with organised Christianity.

At grass-roots level there was much heroic opposition from priests and Catholic lay people to the run-down of denominational schools, but the leaders were terrorised or intimidated, and by the summer of 1939 all such schools had been turned into community schools, while all private schools run by the churches were closed down or nationalised, their staffs of clerics dismissed. The Vatican remained obstinately unresponsive to the complaints of some German bishops.

Pius XII refused to condemn the German invasion of Poland. As General Franco came to power in Spain he watched this with great joy, hoping this precious land 'will return to the old Catholic traditions that made it so great'. But Franco's long-term influence on an '*ancien régime*' church was, as seen in the present decline of the faith in Spain, disastrous.

Pius remained in his ivory tower, as described by Carlo Falconi in his *Popes in the Twentieth Century*, 'a man interested in systems and abstract ideas... Pius XII was paralysed by his fear of contact with other men, their cleverness, or shrewdness disarmed him, their vanity and passions bewildered him. He became an object lesson in what all popes ought not to be, following in the footsteps of Pius IX, who was 'psychopathetically fixated on his own infallibility', according to Falconi.

When by the time it became difficult to deny the reports of the mass murder of Jews, he advised the German bishops to be cautious and exercise restraint. Archbishop Clemens Graf von Galen refused to believe these 'unconfirmed' reports, which were dismissed as BBC anti-German propaganda. When von Galen did courageously speak out by condemning in 1941 the suppression of religious houses, and the killing of the mentally ill, Pius wrote to Bishop von Preysing in Berlin (who was anti-Hitler) that von Galen's sermons brought him more consolation and satisfaction than he had felt for a long time.

Significantly, when local Nazis asked Hitler to arrest von Galen, Goebbels told Hitler that if this happened there would be open revolt in Westphalia. Hitler also cancelled the T.4 euthanasia programme, as he wanted no further provocation of the churches for the rest of the war.

The following episode is of significance, too, in considering the behaviour of Pope Pius XII. In February 1942 Archbishop Prince Sapieha, leader of the Polish Catholics, sent news to the Vatican about the concentration camps newly set up me near Krakow, whose inmates were 'deprived of all human rights, handed over to the cruelty of men who have no feelings of humanity. We live in terror, continually in danger of losing everything if we attempt to escape, thrown into camps from which few emerge alive.' (Williams, 1982.)

Sapieha insisted this letter be committed to memory and destroyed by Father Risso Scavizzi, its priest-courier to Rome, and he warned Pius' diplomatic secretary of state, Giovanni Montini (the future Pope Paul VI) that the publication of such information (about Oswiecim – Auschwitz) could provoke further persecution.

In May 1942 Pius and Montini heard for the first time of the mass extermination of Jews in Poland, Germany and the Ukraine from Father Scavizzi and other Knights of Malta chaplains who travelled back and forth from those countries to Rome.

Scavizzi reported that when he told Pius, 'I saw him weep like a child.' Later Sapieha said, of the Jews in Krakow,

> … the worst thing of all is that those unfortunates are left without help, cut off from the whole world. We cannot, we must not say so for fear of shortening their lives. We are living through the tragedy of those unfortunate people and none of this is in a position to help them any more… There is no difference between Jews and Poles… (Falconi, 1970)

All Pius could comment to Von Preysing and others was that to speak out was important (as long as it was not he who was doing this), 'since the very difficult and general political situations of conflict require the head of the whole Church [i.e. himself] to exercise restraint in his public statements.'

That is, silence.

10

A Contrast of Two Adolescents

The year 1943 saw the lives of Joseph and his exact contemporary Gunter Grass converging, as all those boys born in 1926 or 1927 were called up as 'Luftwaffe auxiliaries'. Contrary to a widely held view which seemed to delight and repeat in labelling him as a 'Hitler Youth', Joseph, while having to register, managed to avoid taking part in Hitler Youth activities. Brother Georg did join, but soon after was drafted into the army as we have seen.

Returning at weekends to Danzig, Grass comments, as an ordinary 17-year-old who felt the push to leave home:

What the Luftwaffe auxiliary who wore a uniform by day heard in his pyjamas, when his father fell upon his mother during his weekends on leave, was unbearable.

Yet it is far from certain that the two of them went at it when the son lay awake on the couch within hearing range; in fact, it is more likely they took his presence into account and left each other alone. But the mere expectation of those noises in their more or less unchanging sequence was enough to keep me awake. In the dark I had a clear picture of all the variations on marital coupling, and in my cinematic version of the act the mother is always the victim: she yielded, she gave the go-ahead, she held out to the point of exhaustion.

The hatred of a mother's boy for his father, the subliminal battleground that determined the course of Greek tragedies

and has been so eloquently and sensitively updated by Dr Freud
and his disciples, was thus, if not the primary cause, then at least
one of the factors in my push to leave home. (Grass, 2007)

Nowhere can I find any similar or parallel sense of sexual awakening in Joseph, who here again presents a strong contrast to
the young Karol Wojtyla in Krakow, a subject of Frank's corrupt
regime, who was 20 years old by now.

Grass sought a way out of the restrictive family by volunteer-
ing: he tried to join the German navy as a submarine recruit. No
luck came to him in his urge to be independent, his will to grow
up, 'to be a man among men'. They made him give up his chic
Luftwaffe uniform, which irked him, for the annoying Labour
Service garb – 'shit brown, it made us look shitty'.

The 'betrayal' of the Italians (according to the Germans),
and the struggle over Monte Cassino which he referred to, was
another point of contact with Joseph's family. Humiliated, Grass
traipsed about wearing the headgear – 'a felt hat that looked like
a big lump with a crease down the middle … we dubbed it "arse
with a handle".'

Georg suffered, according to his brother, the indignities
of Labour Service before joining his regiment. Joseph had a
clearer run in his chic Luftwaffe gear, at least until later in 1944.
As a Traunstein seminarian, continuing part-time studies at the
Chiemgau Grammar School in Traunstein, he was next obliged
to join a Flak battery in Ludwigsfiel, whose task with its 18 heavy
anti-aircraft guns was to defend the BMW war factory at Allach,
which made fighter engines.

Joseph's job was that of range-finder, to spot approaching
bombers and supply readings to calibrate the guns to hit their tar-
gets. He says no one who was there could remember ever having
hit one of the approaching aircraft with 'incendiaries and other
bombs' (he wrote thus, although he may have been mistranslated
– anti-aircraft guns did not fire incendiaries and bombs).

Again, here, Ratzinger was perhaps being a little disingenuous, not wanting to be identified with the death of allied airmen,
although he must have been a willingly and complicit member
of the team, using advanced (and brilliant) German technology

of the day, and worked during the heavy air-raids under extreme pressure when laying down a lethal barrage. Not to hit an allied bomber would have been a surprisingly poor record for 18 heavy ack-ack guns, and given the time he was there and the intensity of the air-raids – over a year – as part of the crew, quite unlikely.

It would seem he had no inclination to report or remember what had been shot down or missed, and thus show his participation in the fighting, or to report the deaths of allied airmen, which from bombing sorties was numerically very high. It is a further pointer to the future when war, thanks to technology, would become even more impersonal and inhuman. A range-finder, calibrating time, velocity and distance, was just as much responsible for killing the enemy as an infantryman with a bayonet.

His barracks at Ludwigsfiel had an electric fence separating Joseph from a prison camp where inmates from nearby Dachau, taken to work by heavily armed SS men, worked as slaves.

Apparently, when Joseph senior ran down the regime, his mother used to say, 'Not so loud or you'll end up at Dachau.'

About this the later Ratzinger reported, 'Even if they [the Dachau inmates] were being handled better than their companions in suffering in the actual concentration camps, the dark side of Hitler's system could not be missed.' Again, this is surely a bit understated and euphemistic in relation to such monstrosity, while Joseph himself during this relatively long period manning the guns now escaped to bomb-devastated Munich three times a week to continue his classes at the elite Maximilian Grinner Gymnasium.

Somewhat ambiguously, a report card marked 'Air Force Assistant report', under the seal of the swastika, and stamped with other Nazi emblems, registered his industry and exceptional skill in such subjects as biology and history, which were taught with a specifically racial bias.

In February 1944, serving still in the Luftwaffe (and he must have been efficient at his job to have kept it so long) in Unterföhrling and Innsbruch, like Georg now, he was in the communications branch.

His final Luftwaffe posting was in Gilching, to defend the Dornier factories at Oberfaffenhofen against US bombers. Here, 'from where the first jets soared into the air', his battery received a direct hit which killed one man and wounded many, although Joseph escaped unhurt. Again, in reports of this, the impression we gain is of a very detached young man – the 'non-coms' horror, the non-socialiser who can't march, and who instead of carousing or card playing writes satirical hexameters in Greek on his superior officers.

He looked on the Western allies' invasion of Germany which came very soon, in July 1944, as 'a sign of hope… there was a great trust in the Western powers and their sense of justice'. This was a reflection with hindsight in *Milestones* and one wonders how German Catholics really felt.

Even that most independent of German archbishops, the towering, six-foot-seven-inch Clemens Graf von Galen of Münster, who had practised 'selective resistance' to Hitler, still stalwartly thought of himself as first and foremost a German. When on 31 March 1945 American troops entered Münster, he spoke of 'this day of shame, when the enemy enters our city'. Germans were, and above all remain, patriots.

† † †

Meantime, by mid 1944, superior officers had handed 17-year-old Gunter in his demeaning Labour uniform a 98 carbine, taking 'literally', as he said, in their arms drill, the expression, 'A soldier's gun is a soldier's bride.'

There was one exception, an out-and-out rebel who refused to do any drill. He was, Gunter noted, removed and taken off to 'quarantine'. By now the Allies had landed at Normandy, while only weeks later followed the von Stauffenberg attempt on Hitler's life. The Nazis wasted no time: along came to Grass's unit a Reich Labour Service leader with a tightly knit retinue, who reeled off 'clipped pronouncements about shame and craven betrayal, that is, about the base and insidious plot on the part of a coterie of well-born officers – unsuccessful, thank heaven – to assassinate our dearly beloved Führer, and about merciless revenge, the "extermination of this vile clique". And on and on about the Führer, who – "It was truly a miracle!" – had survived.'

Although there were whispers of defeats Gunter feels his faith in his Führer instantly recharged, for

...faith in the Führer was not hard to maintain – it was child's play, in fact: he had remained safe and sound and was what he claimed to be, his gaze steady, ready to meet the eye, his field-grey uniform free of flashy medals. He was everywhere portrayed with only his Iron Cross from the Great War, majestic in his simplicity. The voice seemed to come from on high. He was impervious to attack. Did he not have the protection of something beyond understanding, of Providence?

(Grass, 2007)

It was still religion (*religio* in Latin means a binding back) which bound the German people to Hitler.

When his Labour Service unit was disbanded Gunter found himself back in schoolboy shorts. His response? He volunteered to join, as Georg Ratzinger had done, as an SS recruit, and train as a Panzer gunner in the Bohemian woods, with the aim to 'plug breaches in the Nazi defence'. He was now, he says, among crack infantry mercenaries like 'a father of the *Landsknechts* – Someone who stood for freedom, liberation'.

He found the Waffen SS had a European aura about it, for it included separate volunteer divisions of French and Walloon, Dutch and Flemish, and many Norwegian and Danish soldiers.

'There were even neutral Swedes on the eastern front in the defensive battle, as the rhetoric went, to save the West from the Bolshevik flood.' And he did not find, he said, 'the double rune on the uniform collar repellent'.

† † †

Joseph, in complete contrast to Gunter, evades or avoids virtually all personal, graphic memories of his war service, just commenting that this time 'brought many an unpleasantness, particularly for so non-military a person as myself'. Particularly? What about the millions killed, maimed, uprooted, dispossessed?

Gunter confesses 'as long as I was a believing Catholic, the transition to non-belief was smooth – my penis paid off as a ready perennial subjection for confession. I ascribed the most outrageous sins to it.'

The young Grass, describing his Nazi youth and strange coin-
cidences and similarities which underline this doppelgänger role
with the young Ratzinger, reflected in a way a suggestion that
there would always be, and would remain, a barrier, or an immediate sublimation, in Ratzinger.

As the devoted Seewald pointed out, there had never been any
girlfriends, and, by implication any sexual stirrings or sexual life
for Joseph. So what do we make of Grass's observation in his
autobiography: 'Lie or her younger sister, Deception, often hands
over only the most acceptable part of a memory, the part that
sounds plausible on paper, and vaunts details to be as precise as
a photograph.'

Did the latter part about the acceptable part of memory apply
to Ratzinger, and if so, would it be likely to become a grave
handicap to him as Pope?

Grass's account, in his delayed confusion decades later, planted
the questions which still need to be asked, if they can never
finally be answered:

> Because so many kept silence, the temptation is great to dis-
> count one's own silence, or to speak about oneself all but
> abstractly... the ignorance I claim could not blind me to
> the fact that I had been incorporated into a system that had
> planned, organised and carried out the extermination of
> millions of people. Even if I could not be accused of active
> complicity, there remains to this day a residue that is all too
> commonly called joint responsibility. (Grass, 2007)

He was exactly the same age as Ratzinger.

Joseph's Luftwaffe service ended in the autumn of 1944. Then,
the reverse of Grass's experience, he was pressed into Labour
Service, supplied with the uniform Grass had worn with such
disgust (no pictures of Ratzinger in this remain), and sent to
Burgenland on the Austro-Hungarian border.

Here his duty was to guard a huge conflux of Reich slaves
forced into building a southeast defence wall with anti-
tank ditches and minefields to halt the Soviet armies. As with
Grass the Nazi non-coms issued Ratzinger with a gun, but he

disclaimed any knowledge of how to use it, ot any training: 'We had in any case never learned to shoot.'

This appears disingenuous. All his early life until his father retired there had been guns around in his house, while the policeman had been out frequently on all-night duty. For one period they lived in a police station. Joseph Senior must have possessed at least one revolver and other weapons, probably a carbine. It seems hard to believe that as a state policeman in those violent times he hadn't had cause on more than one occasion to use a firearm. Moreover, Joseph had by now since the age of 16 been in military service: to claim complete ignorance of the workings of lethal weapons was surely far-fetched.

His task at the Burgenland was not clear: if he was guarding massed foreign deportees he would not be using a spade, but carrying a carbine. A newly conscripted soldier in most armies carries a rifle at all times, and during training live rounds or blanks are issued and fired. Yet, Ratzinger says, his 'weapons were not loaded'. And then the guards like himself were pushed around mercilessly by long-term Austrian Nazis, 'fanatical ideologues who tyrannised us sharply'. NCOs are like that in every army, not only Hitler's.

He tells how an intricate military drill taught them how to lay down the spade solemnly, how to pick it up, and swing it over the shoulder. 'The cleaning of the spade, on which there should not be a single speck of dust, was an essential part of this pseudo-liturgy.'

This whole scene was horribly punctuated by a rare graphic image Ratzinger gives of what he and his fellow 'spade-guards' saw on the outskirts. This was 'the way of the Cross of the Hungarian Jews, who passed by us in long columns'.

The account doesn't quite add up. He couldn't have been part of the slave labour gang if he was a guard. He felt brutalised by his officers, yet at the same time he guarded and presumably had to exhort and drill slaves to work. While he could have carried a carbine, and wielded a spade at the same time, we are sometimes not sure if he was a guard or a badly treated worker.

Like Grass he was approached to join an SS unit, and take up active as opposed to camp or garrison duties. He must at least have looked potentially the right material. Fanatical SS recruiting officers woke up his squad at night and quizzed one soldier at a time, taking advantage of their exhaustion to bludgeon them into agreeing to 'volunteer'. Each had to step forward to face the recruiters on his own.

Joseph had the good fortune to say he intended to become a priest, and this spared him, for under the terms of the Concordat he was granted a valid excuse. He found the insults and abuse he thus incurred tasted 'wonderful' because they freed him from threat. How come? The next two months he stayed where he was.

In 20 November they abandoned the defence wall. The military command sent Joseph by train through Vienna and Salzburg, both now reduced to rubble, to Traunstein, to await his call-up papers at home to join the Wehrmacht. His new unit was the Traunstein Artillery 179th Grenadier and Training Battalion. The summons duly arrived. When it did he had a new uniform to put on, his third.

11

Example to the German Bishops

Hitler said it was the German misfortune to have the wrong religion. Hitler's views on Christianity, expressed many times in one form or another, were (like those of his atheistic counterparts in the UK today) generally sarcastic and contemptuous. But as we have noted before, they could also be quite ambiguous and contradictory. It is intriguing that he sometimes aligned the German superman dream and world domination with Mohammedanism:

> Distinguished Arabs told him that when the Mohammedans tried to penetrate beyond France into central Europe, in the 8th Century, they were driven back at the Battle of Tours. Had they won this battle the Western World would be Mohammedan today. For they believed in spreading the faith by the sword, and subjugating all nations to that faith. The Germanic peoples would have become heirs to that religion. Such a creed was perfectly suited to the Germanic temperament. Hitler said that the conquering Arabs, because of their racial inferiority, would in the long run have been unable to contend with the harsher climate and conditions of the country. They could not have kept down the more vigorous natives, so that ultimately not Arabs but Islamised Germans could have stood at the head of this Mohammedan Empire.
> (Speer, 1970)

Hitler usually concluded this historical speculation by remark-
ing: 'You see, it's been our misfortune to have the wrong
religion. Why didn't we have the religion of the Japanese, who
regard sacrifice for the Fatherland as the highest good? The
Mohammedan religion too would have been much more
compatible to us than Christianity. Why did it have to be
Christianity with its meekness and flabbiness?'
(Speer, 1970)

His devoted disciple Hans Frank in Poland had the triple misfortune to be surrounded, as head of the 1 per cent of Germans
who ruled the 99 per cent of Catholic Poles, by a population
who hardly at all conformed to the Führer's idea of Catholicism
as weak and feeble. It had of course been so in his native Bavaria,
with the German bishops led meekly into self-destruction by the
appeasement and silence of Cardinal Pacelli, later Pius XII. Hitler
ordered Frank upon assuming office in Poland to make use of
the Church to keep the Poles, 'quiet, stupid and backward'.

Frank, himself a lapsed 'Old Catholic' with a wife who, in spite of
her venality, loudly protested on every occasion her devout attachment and moral rectitude, as well as her admiration of Cardinal
Faulhaber, saw at once more accurately than Hitler the nature of
the beast he had to subdue and keep at heel. Of course being also
who he was, with a need to intellectualise and rationalise everything in his fine mind, he could be quite eloquent about it:

The Church is maintaining a remarkable aloofness. But this
is only a method which has recurred constantly in Polish history. The Church, as long as there were still other centres of
operation available, has always kept itself in reserve as the final
nucleus of Polish nationalism. To Polish minds the Church
is the central rallying-point, silently shedding a constant ray
of light and in this way acting as a sort of inextinguishable
beacon. Whenever all was darkness in Poland, there was still
Our Lady of Czestochowa and the Church. You must never
forget this. For this reason the Church in Poland has no need
to be active. Catholicism in this country is not just a religion; it
is a necessity of life. (Hans Frank diaries)

In spite of this measured statement and the almost euphemistic directives to colleagues and security police to pay attention to the activities of the clergy and 'intervene' in cases of the use of the Church for political ends, the religious community was systematically and without mercy brutalised. Mainly the Gestapo and SS did this, with Frank turning a blind eye to the murder and torture. And of course the repression, different from the effect it had in Catholic Bavaria except in certain exceptional cases of very brave, defiant priests, only served to strengthen and harden faith, causing Frank to bluster and threaten even more, and proclaim even harsher restrictions.

> I observe in increasing measure that the Church is beginning to become unpleasant. While until now this mighty ideological bloc in Poland has, strangely enough – so to speak – been loyal, the Church is beginning here and there – apparently as a result of the stiffening of certain political situations on this continent – to become an embarrassment. I would like to stress straightaway that I shall not stop at anything here and even have bishops arrested immediately if the slightest thing occurs. I request you in this connection to take the severest steps to ensure that officials in uniform are strictly forbidden to visit Polish churches during a service.
> (Hans Frank diaries)

But he did recognise ultimately he did not have the resources or the will to break the power of faith over the hearts and minds of the Polish people. It was this unwavering faith, a few thousand quislings and collaborations apart – and even in the case of left-wing believers – that unified the nation and underpinned the prevalence of instinctive, spontaneous and social support for the Resistance.

What a contrast it made with the compliant German people and Catholics especially in the Catholic heartland, Bavaria. Why? Because the Church here had lacked leadership in the 1930s, and the Polish Church kept its autonomy (especially in its distrust of Montini before and after he became Pope). In Poland there was an underlying unspoken trust and share of service value which stopped the Gestapo from infiltrating and crushing the Polish Resistance. 'Resisters were able to serve without ever learning about the links to the unseen chain that bound them to their superiors.'

The Polish Resistance was therefore imitating the hierarchy and courage of the Catholic Church at its best and most ideal, which it had fallen lamentably short of in Nazi Germany. The German cultural 'New Order', just as the 'New Soviet Man' later, was doomed from the start in Governor Frank's 'Gestapoland'.

To illustrate this resistance, an anti-Nazi activist recalls how he arrived in Warsaw from London one day after narrowly escaping discovery and arrest when crossing Germany. Leaving a secret meeting in the centre of town he was stopped by a Gestapo agent. He said he had just been to visit his dentist. Pressed by the agent he gave the telephone number of the dentist, a woman, who when phoned, without hesitation told the Nazi he had just been with her.

Deeply frustrated in his work, Frank tried out the tactic he employed with the German legal profession in the 1930s – playing both sides of the street.

His children had been christened in Faulhaber's Munich diocese by the good priest Father Mayer. He would even encourage his employees to attend Mass and say prayers for him and his family. He knew how the faith kept people in social order, and encouraged obedience and acceptance of authority, or in hard times, adverse fate and hard striving. He published a book in 1944 called *The Cabin Boy and Columbus*, which implied or claimed he had kept a residual belief in the faith, although this may well be a further example of his religious hypocrisy. It seemed, or so it would emerge, he still went on praying privately while he had his own German Catholic curate, Father Burger, whom he would appear to have seen often, and may even have said Mass privately in Wawel Castle.

In public utterances and his endless Government General decrees he waged an increasingly hostile battle: this was the Nazi official line and he took a savage and theatrical delight in denouncing the Church: 'If, as is claimed, Catholicism is really a dishonour for a nation, then all the more Catholicism must I wish for the Polish race... If Catholicism is a poison, then one can only wish this poison on the Poles. The same applies to other things as well.'

As the security situation worsened in 1943 Frank sounded almost weary when he spoke in the same vein to Luftwaffe officers on 14 December 1943:

> The Polish clergy and the Polish schools are my chief enemies precisely because I have to put up with them for reasons of general policy. I am aware that the Polish priests and teachers are systematically keeping this country in a state of unrest.

On 11 February 1944, he spoke along the same lines to Party officials: 'We cannot carry out any Church or school policy. I am intelligent enough to realise that these curates are our mortal enemies.'

In the dock at Nuremberg in 1946 on trial as a war criminal he converted back to Catholicism, and, before he was hanged, prayed to Jesus for mercy. How sincere his prayer was, and whether it could or should have been heard, is a subject outside the scope of this book.

Ratzinger in *Milestones* wrote that 'Despite many failings, the Church was the alternative to the destructive ideology of the brown rulers; in the inferno that had swallowed up the powerful, she had stood firm with a force coming to her from eternity. It had been demonstrated: The gates of hell will not overpower her.'

Had this been true? Surely it was the Polish Catholic Church, rather than that in his native Germany, which gave the example of standing firm. His own had most definitely not.

12

More Dissolving Battalions

While Joseph marched in Bavarian Grenadier uniform through the streets of Traunstein swinging his arms, reluctantly singing military songs, and with a rifle digging into his shoulder, Gunter Grass suffered hair-raising escapes on the Eastern front in East Prussia, near Peterlein. The Soviets overran his unit. Grass escaped from his Panzer tank with minor wounds and fled from the advancing Soviets, ripping off his SS insignia as he went, for this would have meant instant reprisal, and donning an ordinary Wehrmacht uniform, which was tantamount to desertion.

Like Ratzinger, Grass retained his *amour-propre* with the compensatory reflection he had not fired, directly, on the enemy. What had kept him from aiming and pulling the trigger as the Soviets bore down on them 'was more like reason, or the absence of necessity. That is why the claim I have so often made – namely, that during the week in which the war had me firmly in its grasp I never looked through a sight, never felt for a trigger, and thus never fired a shot – is at best a way of alleviating in retrospect the shame that remains. Yet something else remains: the fact that we did not shoot. What is less certain is when I exchanged my uniform jacket for one less onerous. Did I so of my own accord?'

Grass had shed his collar ornaments for an ordinary Wehrmacht jacket, and moved west as fast and as far as he could in order to surrender to US troops rather than the Russians. Very many Germans on the run at this time suddenly remembered they had 'a distant relative or acquaintance in Bavaria in order to be released into that region, because the American sector appeared to be the most secure and promising'.

Meanwhile Georg had been awarded an Iron Cross, Second Class, for repairing damage to telephone connections. Again, the non-combatant activities of the Ratzinger brothers is brought to the fore and underlined, but I am not sure of the exonerating effect of this, except of course that it meant they never directly killed anyone.

Then neither did most Nazi leaders, as they were later at pains to establish at Nuremburg before the judges, and with the US psychologist Dr Gilbert whose job it was to observe them – they were just carrying out orders. Of course no one is suggesting the two Ratzinger brothers were remotely guilty of war crimes, but they were Reich soldiers, and there was only a difference in degree between accurately calibrating the range with *Deutsches Technic* to shoot down a US Super Fortress, and the mass machine-gunning of advancing assault troops on an invasion beachhead. War today in 2013, as Karl Marlantes points out in *What It Is Like to Go to War*, is more like the war Joseph Ratzinger fought than the mass slaughter his brother was involved in at Monte Cassino.

Georg lasted in combat until 2 April 1945, the day President Roosevelt suddenly died, giving rise to Hitler's hysterical belief the tide had suddenly turned, and he would win the war after all. Georg recalls that it was on 14 April, 'a marvellous day weather-wise', when they had been holed up in a bunker where they were ordered to repair wiring connections. The Americans dropped incendiaries, and the whole hill was on fire.

'Our own artillery was shooting short, onto us. There was a heavy barrage, day and night, and someone next to me cried out, "I've been hit, my arm's gone, my foot's gone."' The American Army captured Georg alive. Suddenly, his war was over.

Joseph was by no means yet out of danger. In February 1945 he had gone down with a blood-poisoned thumb: a doctor pre-scribed amputation, but he avoided this when a medical orderly sent him home and his mother looked after him. He was back at Traunstein barracks on 16 April. Several weeks later, when Hitler's 'heroic death while defending Berlin' had leaked out, he decided to quit barracks and go home.

SS men roamed the area, it seemed, hanging deserters from trees; Joseph, technically a deserter, felt threatened, but as fortune would have it, he came across fairly benign men who still wore uniform but who took no action against him. Two members of the SS on the run insisted on requisitioning their house for quarters, and sleeping there. Berated by his father 'voicing to new faces all his ire against Hitler', says Ratzinger, the SS men also let them be. Next day they disappeared.

'A special angel seemed to be guarding us,' says Ratzinger, in the kind of unguarded statement someone like him surely should never make. For, one might ask, was it the same Bavarian angel that guarded Hitler so many times, and that he felt must have saved him from so many assassination attempts?

It seems most unlikely, in such trigger-happy, fragile-tempered times, Joseph senior should suddenly have become so outspoken and have attacked Hitler (who had just committed suicide after saying 'Suicide is only for cowards') – and without a thought for the safety of himself or his family; especially now that safety was at hand. Before the United States Army took over, the rich, idyllic Bavarian farmlands had become a happy hunting ground for savage reprisal of all kinds, and of all political or military complexions, a throwback to the lawless Munich of 1919, or the Reich's later bestial birth. Jewish prisoners of war, who had escaped in a horrific last spasm of Nazi ideology, were rounded up by the score by roaming SS, and shot or hanged.

Traunstein survivors from that epoch recall nearly seventy skeletal figures marched through the town centre street, where some of the locals offered food, but others leered and laughed. Surely the Ratzinger family were there too and saw them. Twenty kilometres further south, the SS shot them. Murder and fear stalked the idyllic summer countryside.

13

Strange Meeting If True

Both Gunter and Joseph wore their tattered and faded Wehrmacht uniforms until after the end of fighting. They were lucky it was the warm time of year. Gunterhad been placed as a prisoner in a harsh open air camp at Ulm near the Czech border, policed by the American Third Army −'the GI's might have come from outer space,' he thought.

Joseph was picked up by US troops who took over the Ratzingers' modest abode as their headquarters (surely, therefore, not that modest). Wearing civilian clothes, but now identified as a German soldier, Joseph had to put back on his Traunstein Regiment uniform; his mother and father lamented seeing him depart yet again. He 'slipped a big empty notebook and a pencil' into his pocket, which seemed 'a most impractical choice, but this notebook became a wonderful companion to me, because day by day I could enter into it thoughts and reflections of all kinds. I even tried my hand at Greek hexameters.'

The Allies incarcerated Joseph first at the military airport of Bad Aibling, in the Bad Kreuznach prisoner-of-war collection camp. Here he and thousands of German POW's camped under guard and slept outdoors. And here the US Military held many 14- or 15-year-olds from Hitler Youth battalions which were more or less wiped out in the defence of Nuremberg. Hundreds of thousands of new Hitler Youth had been trained since September 1944, and sacrificed in battle where they displayed 'marvellous courage': 'it is a pity about this young and valuable blood,' commented Werner Haupt, 'when it has to be shed in such fighting'.

In this first place of imprisonment, Ulm, Gunter had found, working as a skivvy in the camp kitchen – he spoke English – three ivory dice and a leather dice cup, as well as some mementoes of the Siegfried Line from the First World War. Now, transferred to Bad Aibling, he struck up a temporary friendship with a fellow prisoner:

> I used them to play dice with a boy my age, the friend I had so longed to have in the dark pine wood, who now actually had a name, Joseph, and spoke a bookish, Bavarian-tinted German. It rained a lot. We dug a hole and would huddle under his tarpaulin for shelter. We talked about God and the world, about our experiences as altar boys – his permanent, mine very much auxiliary. He believed I thought nothing was holy. We both got deloused. It didn't bother us in the slightest. Like me he wrote poems, but we had very different plans for the future, which later, and then only gradually, became history. For the time being the Siegfried Line pins were more important.
> (Grass, 2007)

Joseph did not recall meeting Grass. Did it happen, or did the fictional master of *The Tin Drum* make it up, as often autobiographers tend to do? Grass ventured into relating the encounter with more detail: he tells his devoutly Catholic sister how as a 17-year-old POW he had sought refuge from the rain under a tent with a boy his age and how they chewed caraway seeds to stave off their hunger.

'My sister doesn't believe my stories on principle, and she tilted her head distrustfully when I said his name was Joseph, he had a marked Bavarian accent, and was a dyed-in-the-wool Catholic.'

'So what,' she said. 'There's a lot of them about.'

Grass insisted that no one could be as fanatical, and at the same time tender and loving when referring to the Only True Church 'as my pal Joseph. He came, if I'm not mistaken, from somewhere near Altötting.'

His sister became even more suspicious.

'Are you sure? Sounds a bit far-fetched to me. Just like one of your stories.'

'Well, if my camp experiences under Bavarian skies are of no interest to you...' Grass answered.

To which she replied, 'Oh, go ahead.'

He conceded a certain lack of confidence to make himself more believable – 'We were just two among thousands' – but refused to rule out the possibility that his pal Joseph, who was as lice-ridden as him, whom continuous hunger had driven to chewing caraway seeds from a bag, and 'whose faith was as securely bunkered as the Atlantic Wall once was, might well have had the surname Ratzinger and so be the man who today as Pope claims infallibility, if only in that familiar shy way of his, speaking softly, the better to enhance its effect'.

Grass sounded credible enough with the 'securely bunkered' faith. But not to his sister, who laughed, he says, as only off-duty midwives could: 'It's just another one of those yarns you told to pull the wool over Mama's eyes.'

'Who knows,' Grass self-deprecated once more. 'I can't swear that the spindly kid I sat with in early June '45 in the Bad Aibling camp, looking out over the Bavarian Alps when the sun was out and huddled in a tent when it rained, actually had the name of Ratzinger, but that he wanted to become a priest, was not interested in girls, and was planning to study all that damned dogmatic claptrap the moment he was released from captivity – of that I'm sure.'

Grass remained convinced it had been Joseph with him at Bad Aibling:

> ... gazing up at the less than communicative sky, behind which Joseph saw the heavenly abode while I saw a gaping void, we both responded by writing ostentatious verse, which, however, proved insufficient. That is why we let the dice make the final decision as to who would become what. To needle my pal, I claimed that, as church history demonstrated, even an atheist could become pope.

... Joseph threw three points more. Call it bad luck or good.
So I became a mere writer, whereas he... But if I had thrown
two sixes and a five, then today I and not he would be...

Si non e vero e ben trovato. Joseph was certainly at that camp –
that much is true. They then, in a somewhat curious, reverse way,
transferred him to the one near Ulm, 'an area of enormous farmlands where fifty thousand prisoners had been brought', the one
from which earlier Gunter had departed. This 'was not always
fun, existing in tents (if lucky) and a ladleful of soup and a little
bread each day. Here the Christian roots of European civilisation,
tubers which had long been frozen in the long winter of Nazism,
began to put forth shoots again.'

On the horizon Ulm Cathedral's spire and tower reminded
him 'of the indestructible humaneness of faith. Some few priests
who were there began to celebrate Mass. Not exactly a huge
crowd (of the 50,000 prisoners) came. Theology students in their
final semesters and academics – journalists, art historians, philos-
ophers met formally and a wide-ranging program of conferences
developed that brought the structure to our empty days.'

The private, mystical distance from war now became Joseph's
reality. Even as a prisoner of war he found a comfort zone which
was not far from being a first academic cloister. In the comfort
zone, even though it was a prisoner of war camp, the German
inborn gift for organisation became manifest; groups and sub-
groups, each with its field to hoe. 'Everything ran according to a
timetable, everything was thorough and punctual.'

How virtuous we were, he was saying. We kept our beat. He did
not mention how SS uniforms suddenly vanished from his fellow
prisoners, or had been swapped for German Medical Corps.

Frisch Weht Der Wind
Der Heimat Zu
(Fresh blows the wind back to the homeland)
J.W. von Goethe

Joseph's constructive intellectuals and fellow faithful in sight of Ulm Cathedral might well have behaved as characters in his favourite Hermann Hesse novel, *The Glass Bead Game,* 'where passion dominates that does not signify the presence of greater desire and ambition, but rather the misdirection of those qualities towards an isolated and false goal, with a consequent tension and sultriness in the atmosphere. Those who direct the maximum force of their desires toward the centre, toward true being, toward perfection, seem quieter than the passionate souls... In argument, for example, they will not shout or wave their arms. But I assume they are nevertheless bursting with subdued fires.'

Intended seminarians apart, the vast majority of Germans had no qualms, and often little restraint about their reversal from conquerors into victims. As Grass noted, 'the crimes coming to light with peace, the flip side of war, were making victims out of perpetrators.'

Most began to orientate themselves, covering up as best what they did or failed to do, towards the new leaders, and what could be saved or papered over, and what hierarchical structures that remained, chief of which was Cardinal Faulhaber's diocese of Munich, and those of his fellow bishops, some of whom had shown themselves far from resistant to Nazism.

US forces arrested Governor Frank in his Bavarian home, to which he had fled with the Leonardo masterpiece, *The Lady with Ermine*, a Rembrandt self-portrait, and 43 volumes of his diaries. While the Frank family hit penny-pinching and hungry hard times, he continued from prison to appeal to Faulhaber to obtain papal clemency. Niklas Frank, his son, believed that their fortunes began to change when, even though they had moved out of the Schoberhof into less grand dwellings, Faulhaber sent his twelve-cylinder ecclesiastical buggy (the same one which had stimulated Ratzinger's imagination to take the cloth) to Neuhaus with vittels, which dwarfed the American care packages. Niklas reported in his book *Die Mutter*, his account of Brigitte's life, that Faulhaber's final judgment on her husband was, 'A genius and a Catholic'.

They were invited to the Archbishop's Palace in Munich, and people, recorded Niklas, started to treat them once more as being in the league of big shots. Faulhaber, who had welcomed the German invasion of Russia in 1941, 'with great satisfaction' – only Berlin's Bishop Konrad von Preysing had refused to go along with this – played an equivocal and somewhat defiant role. He protested, on 20 June 1945, on behalf of imprisoned NSDAP members and German military prisoners, claiming, in a joint letter with the Lutheran Bishop of Bavaria, Hans Meiser, to the US command in Munich that imprisonment and atrocities and unclarified sudden death in POW camps would make it difficult to rehabilitate the German people. Niemöller took a very different line, similar to that of Grass.

It would seem that once Governor Frank's trial began in November, Brigitte felt Faulhaber's patronage and support rather rapidly ground to a halt – so much so, that when the Governor saw his conversion would not impress the Vatican and make it intercede with the Nuremberg judges, he threatened to reveal secret agreements made between the Vatican and the Nazis, which he soon realised would not exactly fit in with the general drift of his whitewash and his image as the penitent convert.

The number of Nazis who received help from the Vatican to disguise themselves, to filter through military checkpoints, or work escape routes through the Vatican itself, through Switzerland or Sweden, or devise other means of flight, has been estimated at over 30,000.

The main organiser of this, known as the Vatican Ratline, was the notorious Austrian anti-Semite cleric, Bishop Alois Hudal, Rector of the Pontificate Santa Maria dell-Anima, where he looked after the interest of German-speaking Catholics in Italy. A close friend of Hudal was Montini. Through his office Hudal arranged papers, passports, exit visas and work permits for escaping Nazis, among them many well-known criminals such as Klaus Barbie, Adolf Eichmann, Heinrich Müller, Gustav Wagner and Franz Stangl.

Hudal, it was alleged, convinced Montini that leniency was needed, and as the war ended he converted from pro-fascist to anti-communist, then was appointed by Pius XII as the official Spiritual Director of the German People in postwar Germany.

Frank had tried to pull his own Catholic strings through Brigitte and Cardinal Faulhaber and through Bishop Hudal, whom he believed had offered to arrange his escape. Meantime, with the competition cut down to nil, and with his mistress now grown deaf to Hans's repeated appeals to write to him, attend the trial or visit him in the cells, Brigitte could again now have Hans all to herself. She did all she could to create sympathy for Frank, defend her children, excuse, whitewash his record; and later publish his prison confession *Facing the Gallows*.

The question remains: Were there secret documents? Joseph Ratzinger's refusal as Pope to authorise scrutiny of Vatican documents relating to Pacelli's pre-war diplomacy in Germany and the Second World War until 2014, which has been criticised by some Jewish leaders, suggested there was something to cover up, even if there wasn't.

Not surprisingly there was considerable medical and scientific as well as worldwide public curiosity about this clutch of 'the greatest group of criminals the human race has ever known'. Even so, sartorially speaking, the Americans treated them with great consideration – stripped at first of their suits they donned under order cotton gabardine fatigues, dyed black. Then the Americans allowed them to choose for cleaning from their clothes the ones they wanted to wear. 'Every detail,' said Albert Speer, 'was discussed with the commandant down to the matter of sleeve buttons.'

Every night their suits were pressed for the next day's session. Psychologists made them constant objects of observation, and gave them Rorschach and IQ tests for evaluation of their mental processes and personality traits. Surprisingly most defendants, who saw themselves as members of the *Herrenfrasse*, were only keen to show to their vanquishers their intellectual prowess, and all scored very highly.

Both the American psychiatrists, Dr Douglas Kelley and Dr Gilbert, gave Frank and the others the inkblot tests. The cigar-puffing Kelley declared, 'In my life I've run across some strange birds, but I've never met twenty-one people who considered themselves so pure and lily white.'

The inkblot tests established most of the Nazis were essentially normal, suggesting to Kelley that the potential to act like Nazis may exist in many of us. He added, importantly, 'the almost utter destruction of the whole world will have gone for nought if we do not devise some conclusion concerning the forces that produce such chaos'. He extrapolated from observation that the leaders were not spectacular types, and that there was 'little in America today [1947] which could prevent the establishment of a Nazi-like state'. His observations flew in the face of the general prevailing demonisation of the Nazi leaders as one-off monsters of evil (a convenient theory to which Ratzinger also subscribed). However he did believe that Hitler was the exception – 'abnormal and mentally ill.' He never met Himmler, Goebbels, or Bormann.

He seemed to confirm Thomas Mann's thesis that Nazism was an underlying cultural phenomenon of the German people.

† † †

Ratzinger could be challenged on his statement, repeated by his brother Georg, that resistance to Nazi ideology 'was impossible', therefore implying that the German people were not culpable for going along with it. Pastor Niemöller's poem, quoted above, makes the opposite observation. Resistance had been possible, but it did not happen on a large enough scale. Many did resist, so maybe some of those who risked their lives would, and did, find Ratzinger's claim insulting.

At a parish level many brave priests spoke out against the Nazis and did what they could to minimise the suffering of victims, or hide them. Fr Johannes Prassek of Hamburg, together with Edward Müller and Hermann Lange, known as the Lübeck Martyrs, was one such outspoken critic of the Nazi regime who dedicated his pastoral work to Polish slave labourers. Arrested by the Gestapo he was killed in 1943.

Many of these were executed or imprisoned. The hierarchy was left alone. Even Grass, who at 17 embraced the ideology, was aware of, and mentioned those who resisted. He believes Germany's guilt remains a constant factor in the life of the nation. During his trial Hans Frank at Nuremburg said Germany's guilt would last a thousand years – but then retracted the statement, and said the Allies who defeated Germany were just as culpable.

Behind the Ratzinger coverage of those early years is the assumption that he was just an ordinary person. One can well believe that had he been an average person he would not have had the courage to do more. But by no means was he ever an average person. He became the Pope, the successor to St Peter, who was crucified upside down for his faith, and the disciple of Jesus, who said he was the son of God, who was spat on, tortured, then crucified.

When Pius, as already reported in his famous Christmas message of 1941, which according to some supporters, broke his 'silence' over the Holocaust, had spoken out for the victims of war, he couched his appeal, in what he later claimed was a protest and a denunciation of Nazi extermination of the Jews, in the most vague and wishy-washy language, in order to placate those who urged him to protest, and not offend the Nazi chiefs.

Speaking in 1946 to the Palestinian Supreme Council of Arab People, just before the allied judges passed final judgment on the Nuremberg criminals, Pius pronounced:

'It is superfluous for me to tell you that we disapprove of all recourse to force and violence, from where-so-ever it comes, just as we condemned on various occasions in the past the persecutions that a fanatical anti-Semitism inflicted on the Hebrew people.'

He had never before spoken out even once against a 'fanatical anti-Semitism'.

Moreover, even more extraordinary, in its Pecksniffian self-righteousness, or moral relatavism, was that when he created three new German cardinals in February 1946, he reminded the world of 'another Germany'.

This, he claimed despite the crimes committed in her name by criminals who had declared war on their country's historic Christian values, still deserved an honourable place in the company of nations. Yes, by all means true, yet it still had to earn it.

In so doing he rejected the notion of collective guilt for which he, and Catholics generally, had over the centuries believed the Jews to be responsible. His view, it seemed, rather late in the day when one considered both his anti-Semitic statements and feelings, and his stance aligning the Jews with Bolshevism in Nazi Germany, was that the Catholic Church rejected the notion of collective guilt.

Guilt was always personal in Catholic teaching, he maintained. Later this was set out plainly in the Second Vatican Council declaration that 'neither all Jews indiscriminately at that time [of Jesus's death], nor Jews today can be charged with crimes committed during [Christ's] passion (*Nostra Aetate* 4)'. But it was too little too late.

We need to be clear that the way Pacelli affected the Catholic Church in Germany when he served as Papal Legate and controller of the Vatican's foreign policy, and later the Vatican itself during the war, had a devastatingly and lasting effect on the Church. There is little doubt that Pacelli, although he later made gestures and said words of self-exculpation was – if not the Hitler pope, or not *exactly* the anti-Semitic pope – far from being the 'sign of contradiction' that was expected from Catholic leaders. He was 'married' to his age, which is why there has since been such a divorce.

The statement made by Abe Foxman is applicable: 'It cannot be denied that a certain insufficient resistance to this atrocity on the part of Christians can be explained by an inherited anti-Judaism present in the hearts of not a few Christians.'

This, as will be seen later in the Bishop Williamson affair, reached into and had a strong effect on the public perception of Benedict XVI's papacy.

First of all it alienated all those who somewhere, even if they could not put it into words, felt the Catholic Church had let down the world before and during the war, and needed this explaining by the hierarchy how and why. This was especially true of French Catholics in the postwar period, who saw how prominently the Church had been used to bolster the collaborationist Vichy regime of Pétain. Like Pacelli, whose canonisation Benedict whole-heartedly supported, Benedict had been naïf, or blinkered, in his understanding of the Nazi leaders, and how Hitler, in particular, a genius, was both everyone and no one, who made rings round the clerics, and mocked and scoffed, as did Mussolini, over the Church's conduct and pronouncements.

In G.K. Chesterton's Father Brown stories, Father Brown roots out the criminal in any crime scene because he has identified within himself the criminal instinct which we all possess, and which used to be called by most believing Christians, and in particular by the Catholic Church, 'Original Sin'.

'No one,' says Father Brown, 'is really any good until he knows how bad he is, or might be…till he's squeezed out of his soul the last drop of the oil of the Pharisees; till his only hope is somehow or other to have captured one criminal and kept him safe and sane under his own hat.'

One doesn't receive much sense that Pacelli, since that early time as papal legate when he adopted the opulence and trappings of a temporal prince, travelling with his railroad car full of his dietary needs, and at later times with monkey gland injections, had ever squeezed out of his soul the last drop of Pharisee oil.

With his extraordinary aloof and autocratic manner, which extended even to making sure the paths were cleared of gardeners whom he did not want to see as he strolled in the Vatican gardens, and his carefully studied and staged (and highly impressive and convincing) air of humble piety, he would sometimes seem near to qualifying more for the chamber of papal rogues. By contrast, Benedict consciously and carefully in outward behaviour adopted a humble, listening pose. But was this a pose, and did he emulate Pius's aloofness in spirit? Those who have witnessed it close to, say it could not possibly be.

The Berlin Philharmonic, conducted by Furtwängler, played Brunhilde's last aria and the finale from *Götterdämmerung* in the capital's unheated concert hall only days before Hitler committed suicide.

'I have the most intimate familiarity with Wagner's mental processes,' the Führer had said. 'At every stage of my life I come back to him. Only a new nobility can introduce the new civilisation for us. If we strip *Parsifal* of every poetic element, we learn from it that selection and renewal are possible only amid the continuous tensions of a lasting struggle.'

In present-day global culture and politics, cloned aspects of Hitler's character and mentality live on. If mankind is again faced with moral challenge of the enormity presented by Hitler's regime, we must hope that it will have better moral guidance than that of Pacelli, Pope Pius XII, and the German bishops.

15

A Conflicting Message

On release from Ulm's POW camp on 19 July 1945, Joseph returned home to his joyous family, and could begin to get on with the rest of his life. 'There was no longer any doubt about my calling. I knew where I belonged.'

Printed by now on the heart of Joseph in his 19th year, the age when so many Germans first experienced the words of Hitler and his presence, were those six years in which the Reich had risen to its satiety of gluttony and destruction, and then fallen to its nadir of defeat and desolation.

He had, by the end, withdrawn into an inner mystic state similar to that of Karol Wojtyla at a similar moment in Krakow, in the wilderness Hitler had made of Europe. For both their 'hidden self' had endured in patience and silence until the 'hidden God' made his appearance. Both Karol and Joseph hungered for the isolation in union with God. But they came from different polarities.

Having experienced the darkest hell of Nazism, Karol had come to the judgment that liberty was not the liberty that Mephistopheles promised Faust in Goethe, 'the freedom to fulfil one's deepest desires'. The Germans had been there and done that – but that liberty was and is, in the deepest measure, the extent to which man is capable of love. Karol's life was to become dedicated to the growth and expansion of that birth of love. This was the result of his direct experience of Nazism.

Germany had descended to ground zero, to a condition of almost universal death. For a deeply religious person death was the place of greatest concentration, and the true artist, opposite to the charlatan and mountebank artists of the Third Reich, and their enthusiastic German *claque*, didn't look the other way.

War, as not only Joseph perceived at first hand, but even at the end Hans Frank acknowledged, perpetuated the most evil and dangerous of human traditions. The Catholic Church in the 1930s and during the Second World War, like the Western powers before they partially came to their senses under Churchill's leadership, had reduced itself to impotence. In particular the Catholic Church in Germany, aided by the German Papal Nuncio Pacelli, revealed ignorance or poor perception of the true enemy, identifying it here with Bolshevism and the Jews, and as such displayed a quite terrifying short-sightedness in the name of political expediency. In Pacelli's case this fulfilled his ambition for power, which he believed he knew how best to use. This pusillanimity gave Hitler the green light to see how far he could go. The politics of Hitler's adversaries in those years just staggered from one makeshift solution to the next.

In one young man, at least, the direct experience of being absorbed into Nazi culture, its corrosiveness and dislocation, had led to a withdrawal into solitude, into the desert of biblical times, which this young man would, from then on, view as contemporary with his own times.

His gift from this time, his turning around of the darkness of Nazi Germany, was to see all time as eternally present, and in particular to see Jesus Christ as alive in his own times. As such, and in time as a theological witness to Christ, he was to become uniquely empowered to expound and represent his religion. His German background and experience played no small part in this, in so far as they shaped him into what he was:

> For the desert is the place of silence, of solitude. It is the absence of the exchanges of daily life, its noise and its superficiality. The desert is the place of the absolute, the place of freedom which sets man before the ultimate demands. Not by chance is the desert the place where monotheism began. In

that sense it is a place of grace. In putting aside all preoccupations man encounters his Creator.

Great things have their beginnings in the desert, in silence, in poverty. It is not possible to share in the mission of Jesus, in the mission of the Gospel, without sharing in the desert experience, its poverty, its hunger. That beautiful hunger for justice of which the Lord speaks in the Sermon on the Mount cannot be born in the fullness of satiety... And let us not forget that for Jesus the desert did not end with these forty days. His final, extreme desert was to be that of Psalm 22: 'My God, my God, why hast Thou forsaken Me? And from that desert sprang up the waters of the life of the world.

Pope Benedict XVI, *Journey to Easter*

PART TWO

THE COVERED-UP CHURCH

The Church has been corrupted by power at least
since it became the pet religion of the Roman Empire.
Quentin de la Bédoyère

How Stonewall, the gay rights campaign group, chose to portray Pope Benedict
XVI in September 2012, showing the young Ratzinger in 1941 as a member of
Hitler Youth. 'With France's plans to legalize same-sex marriage, ex-Hitler Youth and
current Pope Benedict XVI told a group of French bishops visiting Castel Gandolfo
that the introduction of gay marriage will threaten the family in France... The Pope
is directly calling upon the French Catholic lobby to interfere in the affairs of a
government. Swinehund!' [*sic*]

16

Theology First, Life Second?

At first, joyfully reunited with his family, Joseph helped, in the ground zero that Germany had become, to set up his former religious school in Traunstein, which had been a hospital, into a seminary again. At the start of 1946 both Joseph and Georg began their life dedication to 'understand faith' in Freising seminary with the specific aim of helping Germany rebuild its soul.

Nearly two years later Joseph parted from Georg, who didn't aspire to become more than a priest and a musician. Joseph meanwhile furthered his studies, adding philosophy to theology to obtain his doctorate and set about tackling some of the fundamental issues that remained part of his lifelong search as a teacher for the truth of revelation, one of which was the relation of dogma to history:

> The Christian reality had been conceived as the Absolute, the self-manifestation of immutable divine truth. But now it has to let itself be interpreted in terms of the categories of history and of historicity.
> (Ratzinger, *Sprich e dogma* (Milan, 1970)

He identified strongly with St Augustine, whom he called a second self: 'the passionate, suffering and questioning man'. In the straitened conditions of post-war Germany, surviving on minimum food and comfort, the growth of a genuine encounter 'between God and myself – especially through the richness of the Roman liturgy' cemented his decision to enter the Church. He knew, then, he was without a direct desire to start a family.

Cardinal Faulhaber ordained him priest, together with Georg, in Reising Cathedral on 29 June 1951.

'The grand and venerable figure of Cardinal Faulhaber impressed me greatly,' wrote Ratzinger later. 'You could practically touch the burden of sufferings he had to bear during the Nazi period, which now enveloped him with an aura of dignity. In him we were not looking for "an accessible bishop"; rather what moved me deeply about him was the awe-inspiring grandeur of his mission, with which he had become fully identified.'

Everyone knew where his heart lay, but maintaining throughout the war years a certain luxury and grandeur, Faulhaber had not suffered that much. In view of this, Ratzinger's tribute does not quite strike the right note. This was a prince of the Church who had ordered his clergy in 1933 to obey the new chancellor, in stark contrast with Cardinal Konrad von Preysing of Berlin who said that their country was 'in the hands of criminals and fools'.

'The Jews can help themselves,' Faulhaber had said when persecution was rife; 'the Nazi handshake with the papacy is a feat of immeasurable blessing.' And, much later, 'Without doubt the chancellor [i.e. Hitler] lives in faith in God.' As we have shown, Faulhaber, a hero in Ratzinger's eyes, had presented a certain ambiguity in dealing with the Nazis, on occasions praising Hitler rapturously, and had wholeheartedly supporting the German invasion of Russia. No doubt like Pius, who subsequently, it is claimed, suffered terrible nightmares about his role in the war, by the end he silently abhorred Hitler. But a cardinal's red robe signifies the readiness to sacrifice blood for your faith, perhaps not always literally, but at least a sacrifice of some of your luxury and trappings of office.

The culture went on, for in 1948 Hans Meisser, the Lutheran Bishop of Bavaria, proclaimed in a sermon that 'the eternal Jew doesn't die. We cannot free him from his curse.' The clergy were in a double bind. They could not admit they were complicit with the Nazis by entertaining anti-Jewish feeling, at the same time, as they did, claiming they were pillars of resistance against Hitler.

Joseph Ratzinger photographed in August 1943. (Press Association Images)

Dated 1952, the photograph shows Priest Joseph Ratzinger holding Mass in Ruhpolding, Germany. (Press Association Images)

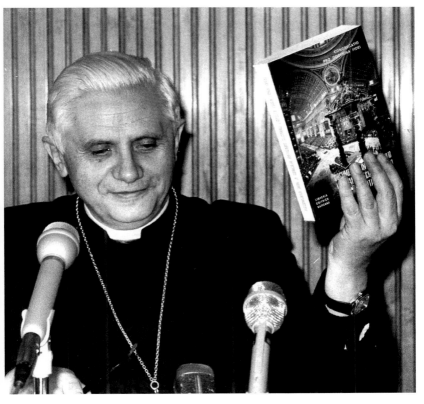

December 12, 1985; the theologian. Joseph Ratzinger presents a book with the documents issued by the Congregation for the Doctrine of the Faith during a press conference at the Vatican, when he was Head of the Congregation. (Press Association Images/Bruno Mosconi)

September 11, 2002; Cardinal Joseph Ratzinger with Pope John Paul II during mass in St. Peter's Basilica. The closest of confidants, Cardinal Ratzinger watched as Pope John Paul II, once a strapping athlete, steadily deteriorated in his later years. Burdened by Parkinson's disease and crippling hip ailments, Pope John Paul could no longer walk or talk at the time of his death in 2005 at 84. A disturbing vision of papal frailty that surely affected the future Pope Benedict XVI. (Press Association Images/Pier Paolo Cito)

The Vatican May 1, 2011; Pope Benedict XVI celebrates the ceremony of Beatification of Pope John Paul II in St. Peter's Square. (Press Association Images/ Stefano Costantino)

April 19, 2005; Pope Benedict XVI greeting the crowd from the central balcony of St. Peter's Basilica moments after being elected. (Press Association Images/Domenico Stinellis)

Pope Benedict XVI greets pilgrims at the end of his general audience in St. Peter's Square at the Vatican, Wednesday, February 27, 2013. At his final general audience he recalled moments of 'joy and light' during his papacy but also times of great difficulty. He also thanked the people for respecting his decision to retire. (Press Association Images/Luca Bruno)

January 2008: a student wears a mock mask of Pope Benedict XVI under a mitre reading 'Stop Homophobia' as he protests at La Sapienza University in Rome. Students and professors were mobilising against the Pope's visit later that week to Rome University, in a protest the Vatican described as smacking of censorship. Pope Benedict was scheduled to deliver a speech during a ceremony to inaugurate the academic year. (Press Association Images/Gregorio Borgia)

Argentina's Cardinal Jorge Mario Bergoglio is elected as the Catholic Church's new Pope Francis I, the first Latin American in the role, on March 13, 2013 at the Vatican. Cardinal Bergoglio was elected in a swift five votes of a conclave of 115 cardinals, and immediately appeared to say the Lord's Prayer to crowds on the Vatican plaza. (Press Association Images/Eric Vandeville/ABACAPRESS.COM)

But Joseph was completely unaware of all this. Just at the moment, 'when the elderly archbishop laid his hands on me a little bird – perhaps a lark – flew up from the high altar in the cathedral and trilled a little song of joy, and to me it was like encouragement on high.'

The following four weeks were an unending feast for the happy brothers: 'Everywhere we were received even by total strangers with a warmth and affection I had never thought possible to that day. In this way I learned first-hand how earnestly people want a priest, how they long for a blessing which flows from the power of the sacrament. The point was not my own or my brother's person.' (Joseph Ratzinger's 'Happiness Day', Zenit)

† † †

Joseph served as an associate pastor in the Most Precious Blood parish of Munich, at one period standing in for the priest at Moosah, ministering to a very large community of 10,000 people. But he soon moved on, summoned to the seminary at Freising where he completed his doctorate in 1953, saying he suffered from the loss of human contacts and experiences afforded in the pastoral role. He was now, at the age of 26, a doctor of theology, and applied for his *habilitation*, entailing the production of a scholarly work which proposed and defended a thesis. This took him four years, and interestingly, in view of his future three-volume *Jesus of Nazareth* (2007–12) the theoretical part of his thesis was rejected, so he had to cut it and present to the academic committee just the 'historical' part of the original work.

By now, as he said later of himself in other situations, books were his advisers, and this constant formation of his mind and soul meant that for the rest of his life he was primarily a theologian and teacher, fascinated by the different concepts of Christian revelation, and the conflicts between modernism and tradition: 'Revelation is always something other than what is written down,' he said (quoted by Aidan Nichols in *The Thoughts of Benedict XVI*).

As such he was very much apart from the internecine religious fighting that went on in Bavaria in this period, the sometimes

bitter disputes between Catholics and Protestants over who was
responsible for the guilt and misery that had brought Germany
so low, and especially whether the Church had been part of it.
He went first to Bonn as professor of fundamental theology,
then in 1963 he was appointed dean of the Theology Faculty at
Münster University.

† † †

Hans Küng, identified as 'gadfly' in Peter Hebblethwaite's illuminating biography of Pope Paul VI (by the same token Ratzinger
is 'arch-theologian'), picked out Joseph as a brilliant young
theologian, and brought him from Münster into the Tübingen
Theology Faculty in 1966.

Küng had known of Ratzinger since 1957, and described him
at their first meeting during the Second Vatican Council as 'very
friendly, though perhaps not completely open... For me he is
more a "*timido*" with an invisible spiritual anointing.'

Any potential disagreement or divergence of religious or political thought between the pair did not bother him: on the issue of
whether or not they might be at odds he said, 'One can deal and
work with the best people; it is the bad ones who create problems.'

Unashamedly open in his views, the Swiss-born Catholic
priest Küng was handsome, dynamic, and made no bones about
using publicity to advance these views and his written works to
'intervene' between the Magisterium (the office and exercise of
formulating doctrine in the Catholic Church) and wider, freer
theological debate. This later led to his being criticised for reducing 'authenticity in dialogue' by those who preferred Church
debate, like Joseph, to remain protected and in private.

Outspoken as he was from the start with his progressive views,
Küng supported 'collegiality' (that is the bishops' participation in
policy-making) in the Church, as opposed to papal primacy, and
saw Ratzinger as a like-minded theologian who would remain
committed to reforms.

Silver-haired before he was forty, when Ratzinger moved to
Tübingen he was still known as the *enfant terrible*, a 'dangerous'
liberal reformer who even liked 'evangelical theologians of the

Protestant faculty'. When Joseph spoke in his lectures of Jesus or Holy Writ his words approached the intensity of prayer. There was a dynamic rhythm in his combative statements: look how he repeats the word 'scandal' here:

> It is a secondary, self-caused and thus culpable scandal if under the pretext of defending the rights of God, only one particular situation and the positions of power are being defended. It is a secondary, self-caused and thus culpable scandal if on the pretext of protecting the unchanging nature of faith only one's own past is defended. It is a secondary, self-caused and thus culpable scandal if on the pretext of safeguarding the whole of the truth the opinions of school are perpetuated which... have long needed the revision and reinvestigation demanded by the authentic originals...

There had been little or nothing in his previous academic record to contradict this. When the genial John XXIII, at the age of 78, was elected pope in 1958, he was seen as a transitional pope. He called the Second Council, known as Vatican II, a daring and unexpected move to proclaim and reform the Catholic faith in a new way for his day, while still protective of its traditions – '*aggiornamento*' was the term he employed.

The Council began on 11 October 1962. From the start the Auxiliary Bishop of Krakow, Karol Wojtyla, 'a young Pole with an immensely strong face', had a place, mainly as an observer. The much younger Professor Ratzinger had already been noticed by Cardinal Joseph Frings of Cologne and included in the policy-forming body because of his original and progressive lectures.

Frings had listened to Ratzinger advocating a liberalising of the Church, which was held on too tight a rein with too many laws, many of which 'helped to leave the century of belief in the lurch, instead of helping it towards redemption'. Frings asked him to prepare a paper on 'The Council and the Modern Intellectual World', which he proposed to deliver in Genoa, and then adopted Ratzinger's material almost word for word, provoking a sensational response leading to a summons to a papal audience.

This, Frings feared, would lead to his own dismissal. But John loved the lecture and Ratzinger's views, claiming they said everything 'he was trying to say but could not'. On the strength of this Ratzinger became a *peritus*, a theological adviser and Frings' close aide, evaluating and proposing progressive measures, in which capacity he continued after John XXIII died in 1963, and Paul VI was elected pope.

Up to this time Pius XII's encyclical *Mystici Corporis* (1943), had emphasised, in dealing with the nature of the Church, what John's vision of his Council sought to address: namely the identification of the mystical Body of Christ with the Roman Catholic Church. Pius's encyclical denied, in its exalted view, the reality that Catholics and Protestants met and died together under SS rule, and therefore might be, with God's grace, on an equal footing.

No distinction surely could be made between Dietrich Bonhoeffer, the Lutheran pastor, and Fr Alfred Delp, S.J. both of whom were hanged expressly by Hitler's order on meat hooks. Would one go to hell, the other to heaven? Pope John saw, in his ecumenical aspiration, other religions not only equal but compatible with Roman Catholicism.

Another young German, the Jesuit Karl Rahner, a colleague of Ratzinger, also objected to *Mystici Corporis*, wondering how with this literal identification of Christ with the Church how sin could possibly worm its way in, which it clearly did. He used the phrase 'the sinful church' but also talked of 'the church of sinners' – for which he was condemned by the 'Holy Office'. Rahner's description might be considered only too appropriate for 2010.

On 8 November 1963 Cardinal Frings addressed the Council with a speech Ratzinger ghosted, censoring the methods and behaviour of the Holy Office (the CDF or Congregation for the Doctrine of the Faith, aka the Inquisition) as a cause for scandal. Frings (and Ratzinger), like Küng, favoured greater collegiality among the bishops, liturgical reform, more ecumenicalism and interreligious exchange, and greater Vatican transparency.

By now Hans Küng with others was growing more defiant towards papal authority, expressing later the view in his book *Infallible?* that 'if the canon lawyers of the "progressives" had voiced the theology of "collegiality" with the same skill that the Roman canonists used to defend papal primacy this would have changed the whole course of church history'. Ratzinger too joined in the enthusiastic approval for *ad experimenticus*, when every aspect of Church life was scrutinised and explored for change.

John's death in 1963 left many questions unresolved, while the increasing supremacy of the progressives over the traditionalists troubled the new pope Paul VI, the former Cardinal Montini, who as mentioned above was reckoned a close associate of Bishop Hudal. He began seriously to vacillate between reform and holding fast, commenting 'as a result of human frailty, charisms may at times be confused with one's own disordered ideas and inclinations'.

Was it conviction or ambition which was to show Ratzinger which path to follow next?

Küng's description of how he was sidelined by Paul, and Ratzinger preferred to him, throws light on how, if Küng is to be believed, Ratzinger shifted his allegiance and even his integrity to further his ambition in the Church hierarchy. In December 1965 Küng had a one-to-one audience with the new Pope in which the latter told him that he would have preferred he had written nothing. He could do much good, 'if you were to put your great gifts at the service of the church.'

Küng answered that he was already at the service of the Church. But of course he soon realised the Pope meant conform, with trust in him, to *his* idea of the Church. Küng went on to raise the disputed question of contraception, offering a small memorandum, and 'finally on the basis of the papal reservations about the pill [how this] unexpectedly ended up with the question of infallibility'. Neither of these pleased the Pope, in contrast to the different route of Ratzinger, who, Küng commented, 'evidently has subsequently taken the way open to him directly or indirectly in some form by the pope'.

What Küng lamented was that the new spirit and breadth of universality, of sensitivity to the world, opened up by John XXIII, was, with hesitancy and trepidation, being closed down by Paul VI.

† † †

After the end of Paul's Council, which had implemented many 'reforms' and set up commissions to continue procedural change and revision (among them the use of the vernacular in the Mass, Offices for Christian unity, Non-Christian Religions and Non-Believers) Ratzinger, advanced by Küng who found him and his sister a place to live, quickly established himself in the theological promised land of Tübingen as a popular lecturer and tutor.

He and Küng were in many ways opposites. Küng behaved with panache and dressed with fashionable elegance, drove a white Alfa Romeo, and was popular with journalists, with whom he engaged in combative polemics. He criss-crossed barriers.

Joseph, far from being outspoken or impetuous, was still mild-mannered, and walked to work or took a bus (later he had a Citroën 2CV). Every day he said Mass in a girls' school chapel; he was unworldly, and one of his assistants told how once, in a restaurant, he ordered sausages for himself and all his students, unaware they might want something more and different, and would have liked to make their own choices. When this was pointed out he revised his habit and let everyone choose what they wanted.

In one public debate, in which both professors took part, Küng stated how much he had liked John XXIII as pope, upon whose death the London *Times* commented that few pontificates had so captured the imagination of the world. His papacy, said Küng, had been pastoral rather than jurisdictional. Joseph would not comment, so students started to chant, not altogether with sympathy, 'Rat-zin-ger! Rat-zin-ger!...'

He then, very studiedly, stood up and spoke. He said he had taken into account all aspects of the arguments. Very carefully he did not take sides. From then on his and Küng's relationship started to break up, 'through a slow and silent process of internal detachment... a progressive estrangement without confrontations', as Ratzinger came more and more to change his standpoint.

Ratzinger has denied this, claiming he had followed a straight line since Tübingen. But Küng says, 'even in Tübingen my colleague, who for all his friendliness always seems somewhat distanced and cool, had kept something like an unenlightened "devotional corner" in his Bavarian heart and shown himself to be all too stamped by Augustine's pessimistic view of the world and Bonaventura's Platonising neglect of the visible and empirical (in contrast to Thomas Aquinas).' (Courrier de Rome, 1998.)

There was one dramatic episode which stood out, and weighed more heavily with him than anything else, and finally fractured the Küng–Ratzinger bond.

In the late 1960s, like everywhere else in the world, student unrest erupted in Germany and spread from Bonn and Berlin to Tübingen. In Paris, under red and black flags, the students of the Sorbonne proclaimed 'It is forbidden to forbid', and 'The past is bourgeois propaganda', or 'Don't come back, God.' The French authorities on the whole, in spite of the general paralysis, with Gallic nonchalance let the insurrection run its course and wear itself out: hadn't André Malraux, the Minister of Culture said, 'Christ, an anarchist who succeeded. That's all.'

In Berlin several deaths occurred, and in Bonn the Red Brigade bared its fangs. In more reserved Tübingen, students occupied the university parish church of St John and made speeches demanding a voice. They shouted for the democratic election of chaplains. Less charitably, they chanted '*Unter der Taleren der Muff von tausend Jahren!*' ('under the cassocks the filth of a thousand years').

Although Tübingen erupted with less violence than more combustible centres, the theological faculty and lecture halls could no longer serve as a Ratzinger safe house. Arriving at work he found himself having to step over students who prostrated themselves on the faculty steps in his path. He tried to reason with his students, but his soft voice was shouted down.

Max Sechler, a former assistant of his, commented, 'he was lost when opposition became violent. He does not know how to scream [*sic*], he is unable to make himself heard above voices raised in anger.'

He seemed at first to sympathise, to take it seriously. One student he tried to tackle, Karen, 'a beautiful blonde [however] disturbed... a girl who later died unexpectedly.' (This is all we know about her.) Then he recoiled at the students who 'complicated his life'. He even called it a 'psycho terror inflicted on him by students'. This was now 1968 and student riots had erupted in numerous university towns of Europe.

Another priest who knew him at the time, and later retired from a Münster parish, said, 'He could no longer stand reading manifestos which described Jesus and St Paul as sexually frustrated beings, or called the cross a symbol of sado-masochism. It made him sick.' To his assistant Peter Kuhn he commented, 'We have opened the door to drive out a devil from the home; let us hope that in doing so, we have not let seven others enter.'

During the événements Kuhn recalls dropping Ratzinger off late for a lecture, braking the tiny car so fast the number plate with its Tübingen registration fell off amid derisive laughter from students. At another time a Canadian doctoral student brought him in a satiric cartoon of Paul VI in a Catholic magazine: 'When I showed it him with a wink he gave me a severe look.'

What perhaps is more surprising is that he made no comparison in his mind with the infinitely more bloody left-wing coup in Munich fifty years earlier, when Communists were on the rampage, and briefly took over, and priests joined the insurgency – and then especially how the crackdown, the imposition of the reactionary animus, gave a fillip to Hitler and the Nazis.

He commented, rather pompously, and was criticised by Küng for his 'timid' response, that revolutionary winds, 'based on Biblical hope, enough to preserve its religious fervour, it eliminates God and replaces him by political actions by man'... So, said his assistant, 'his shock was tremendous when protests became sacrilegious, parodies, bourgeois rebelliousness, a devastating corruption of the things that he most treasured'.

Somewhat stealthily, it appears, he made plans to move, or took the opportunity of an offer (who knows if he organised it, or not?). He left Tübingen in a hurry. 'Things were not going well,' Kuhn told a friend.

'I have seen the face of this atheistic religiosity unveiled, the psychological terror, the lack of restraint with which they could abandon every moral consideration as a bourgeois remnant where the ideological goal was concerned', Ratzinger further complained. 'Anyone who wanted to remain a progressive in this context had to give up his integrity.' He needed 'a less agitated context and did not want to be involved in continuous polemics. He was not one who relished or enjoyed a fight.'

Yet in the same summer and winter upheavals Ludwig Raiser, a Christian university teacher who was a Protestant, gave an example which contrasted strongly with Ratzinger's reaction. He endured sieges, abusive insult, sit-ins and public debates without summoning the police. He listened to the students. He felt the responsibility of scholars and teachers compelled them to join in the thinking, and that however distorted the student interpretation of what was happening, 'We should seek to understand that in the world-wide unrest of young people an age is announcing itself for which the traditional forms of life and behaviour will no longer be adequate.'

Only, Raiser thought, a struggle for the truth, carried on in intellectual freedom and mutual respect, would win over the young generation. Crucially the task, by tackling the ideologically fixated minorities, was to help the great majority, 'which is critically doubtful but not fixated, to form a well-founded judgement'.

So did Ratzinger, in his pessimistic crisis of anxiety, traumatised like his predecessor, simply give in and leave? When you row a boat under a long dark bridge, the echoes of your voice, like those of your past, last longer and sound deeper.

Like that threatening invasion of the nunciature in Munich fifty years before, to which it was in some ways similar, and which left its indelible mark on Pacelli, the student revolt apparently triggered, as far as one can say about this iceberg of a man, nine-tenths of which remained invisible below the surface, a deep and long-lasting emotional response.

Küng, hearing of his erstwhile friend and colleague's departure for Regensburg, exploded with shock and fury. He felt he had been let down. Ratzinger had, he said later, 'sold his soul for power in the church'. He failed to 'fulfil any of the hopes of reform-orientated Catholics', while he was 'always stressing the nice sides of faith and the church and leaving the harsh church rules that still exist unmentioned'.

Küng continued to maintain that the extreme conservative wing, by which he meant men like Archbishop Michel Lefebvre, of the Church was small, and that Christian unity did not blur the differences but transcend them. You could, he told the English Catholic writer Piers Paul Read, affirm the importance and pastoral primacy of the see of Rome, but also want to limit it to 'the norm of the Gospel and not see it act in a worldly spirit'.

As for clerical celibacy, he declared that while he never denied that celibacy was a good thing for the priesthood, 'to be married is a natural way to be and it was not a special obligation' – such as clerical celibacy was – but 'a human right'.

Küng did not waver from his mission, now to be seen much less as 'gadfly' than important in the context of Ratzinger's future life and in the Church itself, especially in his belief that there should be more account taken of dissent in the Church, and that the Pope should be a common pastor for all Christians. Küng was especially concerned that the 'Holy Office' or 'Sacred Congregation', responsible for disciplining the Church, should be abolished: people were right, he told Read, to continue referring to it as the Inquisition, 'which makes you think of burning heretics. There is no institution in the Catholic world which has done so much harm to orthodoxy as this terrible organisation which like the secret police in Russia changes its name all the time and its methods slightly, but...' Küng would find agreement here from Read's godfather, Graham Greene, who in 1989 said he blamed the fact that so many priests were abandoning their ministries on those who were now in authority in the Church.

'Don't you find?' Greene told his *Sunday Times* interviewer, 'that the Roman Curia reminds you a little bit of the Politburo,' adding, 'But even the Politburo is changing.'

† † †

Secrecy, in all its forms, was an 'essential condition of the holy office, in which there existed an 'abhorrent system of secret denunciation.... the centre and culmination of all the rest'. But here again was an ambiguity, a mystery. Did Joseph really want power in the Church, while disclaiming his interest in it all the time?

Whatever his doubts and self-questioning he had learned along the way not to be become involved in the *agone*, the desperate struggle that so many people feel with their faith, with their doubts, their conflicts, which was especially true of the intensity Paul VI brought to his vocation.

'We live at this high temperature,' Paul had said, '...because we have renounced so much... we have foregone many, so many legitimate and sacred things in order to be in the *agone,* in the contest, to be athletes of the spirit'. Paul had become increasingly depressed and racked with doubt, to which Wojtyla, then a bishop, was particularly sympathetic. Paul saw his Council ending in disaster, clouds and storms, more seeking and uncertainty, as having created more problems than it solved.

'If Nietsche were to be acknowledged,' he said, 'as the prophet of the modern world, what would remain of the Gospels, and where would the modern world end?'

But what had Ratzinger renounced? Very little, it seemed, except his academic studies, and even these he could pursue to a degree. He always managed to arrange everything he wanted. By his own admission he had never been much of an athlete of any kind, and he was not cast in the mould of an athlete of the spirit like Paul.

He would not entertain doubt. He was determined he did not live at a high temperature, but a calm, equable one. Much later, in 1984 he insisted there had been no shock and no trouble with his students.

'I did not change,' he told Vittorio Messori, 'it is they who changed.' Surely this disclaimer was naive. Students had been rioting ever since there have been students, while they figured endlessly in Church history. And what about their behaviour earlier in the Bavarian heartland?

Even later he told Seewald, 'Personally I had no problem with the students. But I saw how tyranny came to be exercised, in many ways that were brutal, even.' This suggested too he saw the whole of his wartime life through rose-tinted glasses.

† † †

Back at Regensburg in Bavaria, once the Roman military camp Castra Regina, now the site of three hundred churches, he could be at peace. The hills nearby were pronounced and rolling, the forests lush and impenetrable, known as 'the roof of Europe', and the tranquil Danube ran through the old imperial city untouched by bombing. Here, in Goethe's words,

Über alle Gipfeln
Ist Ruh,
In allen Wipfeln
Spürest Du
Kaum einen Hauch.

(Over all the mountain tops there is peace; over all the tree-tops you can hardly feel a breath of air.)

Reunited with brother and sister he could nestle down in his perfect theological habitat.

He built for himself, his brother and sister, a two-storeyed house in the leafy suburb of Pentling, bought from royalties from his *Introduction to Christianity*, and all three moved in. Since 1964 Georg, after the death of their mother in 1963 (Joseph senior had died earlier), was *Kapelmeister* of the Cathedral, and director of the Domspatzen, its renowned youth choir.

Now, in the Chair of Theology and Dogma at Regensburg University, Joseph could settle above the fray in his frenzy-free island, tended by his faithful sister in 'my little paradise' where they kept three beehives; later the honey would be sent to Rome. All was harmony of the spirit. The brothers kept up the practice, and the musical imagery which binds them together: customs and realities follow the rules of music, into which, it seemed, not only had Schopenhauer's or Thomas Mann's perception of music not entered, but also the twelve-tone systems of Berg and Schönberg, and other modern atonal composers were forgotten.

In 1974 they exhumed the bodies of their mother and father in Traunstein, and moved them to their local cemetery in Pentling, only a few hundred yards from their house. They ate ready-made food for none of them knew how to cook. The holy family was once again reunited in the holy harmony of early days in an atmosphere of piety and prayer, what Küng had called the family's pious shrine to an old-fashioned God. And so in their little idyllic fortress they thrived. His sister was always with him when Joseph went to Mass. 'Here come Joseph and Mary,' parishioners joked.

After uninterrupted years of teaching and the production of theological titles, among them his best-known 1968 *Introduction to Christianity* and his *Eschatology: Death and Eternal Life* (1977) which he deemed 'my most thorough work. and the one I laboured over most strenuously', which 'detaches eschatology from politics', Ratzinger seemed to have developed a slightly valetudinarian attitude to life and looked forward to approaching fifty and 'savouring the final stage of academic wanderings'.

This was now a well-defined component of his character, what Thomas Aquinas called the *anima pusilla* or petty soul. Yet he would not be long now in finding, the opposite, the *anima magna*, or grand soul, which would counterbalance his quieter qualities and open up for him a hitherto undreamed of path in life.

† † †

Discussion of Ratzinger's theology and ethical thinking has been kept in these pages to a minimum. All I can say about them, not being a specialist but a general reader, is that, always clear and lucid, they have something of the quality of Mozart, his favourite composer.

Again, to emphasise the attachment to musical values in his character, Salzburg is only twenty miles away from Traunstein. There were other Mozartean parallels, too. He said in 1996, 'His music is by no means just entertainment; it contains the whole tragedy of human existence.' As already mentioned, Hesse, a writer concerned with equilibrium and harmony, was another favourite: *Siddhartha*, Hesse's novel of oriental mysticism, was one, he claimed, of his three favourite books, together with the Bible and St Augustine's *Confessions*. The English academic Nicholas Boyle commented that Ratzinger saw his own story not as that of Siddhartha, who goes his own way to Nirvana through worldly and sensual experience, but Govinda, his counterpart, the institutional and ascetic Buddhist.

It is worth mentioning his self-confessed anti-Thomism, which long before had set him apart from the life and teaching of St Thomas Aquinas, one of the founding fathers of Catholicism. His dislike of the views of Aquinas had never been disguised, although his dismissal was open to question when he said, 'I had difficulties in penetrating the thought of Thomas Aquinas, whose crystal-clear logic seemed to me too closed in on itself, too impersonal and ready-made.'

Yet Aquinas was generally thought to be outward-looking, believing truth could be grasped through a disciplined reflection on the world. Karol Wojtyla said Aquinas 'explains how, with the gifts of the Holy Spirit, a person's whole spiritual being becomes responsive to God's light, not only the light of knowledge, but the inspiration of love'.

It seemed to Ratzinger that Thomists, like Wojtyla, whose optimism was profound, were altogether too optimistic about human nature. His pessimism about the corruption of the human condition at times looked so Lutheran 'that he has to assert his differences with Luther a trifle self-consciously,' wrote Adrian Hastings (*Tablet*, 3 February 2001).

† † †

By now the Ratzinger side of his character, as opposed to the earlier more gentle Joseph, was clearly fired up for advancement, and had been leading behind the scenes since the end of Vatican II, a traditional fight-back against the progressives, the subversive Dutch and Belgian clerics who still advocated radical change. So then quite suddenly we hear (and in a fairyland, Bavarian twist), Paul VI made this small, delicate gentleman, always smaller than ever imagined, Archbishop of Munich, and then almost straight away a cardinal.

In elevating him in one swift leap, and in spite of his minimal pastoral track record, Paul was acknowledging that here was a sound, traditional churchman, a strong culmination of outstanding theological aptitude and simple Bavarian piety. Above all he supported Paul in such crucial issues as contraception and papal infallibility, which Paul, the '*timido*', feared questioning or reforming.

'It was quite clear,' observed Graham Greene, 'that the majority of bishops under Paul VI were in favour of contraception, but he ignored it and went his own way, even though he made it clear it was his own way and could be changed.'

17

Rapid Advancement

In this dramatic switch from an academic career, from theological adviser, and university posts, to the exalted appointment of Archbishop of Munich and Freising, Pope Paul VI had made Ratzinger in 1977 the first diocesan priest for 80 years to be promoted to the responsibility of direct Church governance, in charge of 750 parishes and the spiritual welfare of two million Catholics. At first he responded with enthusiasm to this new role, energetically visiting parishes, giving direct simple addresses which went down well. Seewald described the impact he could make:

Already as a professor he was used to speaking in packed lecture halls in front of up to a thousand students. As Bishop of Munich he commanded the Marianne Platz with tens of thousands of listeners. And I myself have experienced how in the country he can hurry towards crowds with his little steps, as if he were meeting old acquaintances he had not seen for years. Then he is able, with a really delicate method of his own, almost imperceptibly to cast his spell over a crowd, rather as one guide to the kite with small movements. And as soon as he starts a sermon, his listeners feel almost hypnotised, as though he is casting a spell over them, as if some sweet scented dew were streaming out of his words and sinking into their hearts, beguiling them. (Seewald, 1997)

But he was less impressive to his brother clergy who thought he lived too much inside his head, while he was not an effective administrator. Wolfgang Beinert, a future Regensberg professor, told of the valedictory dinner for Razinger leaving the university when he stood up and said to the company, '"Until now I have sat with you on one side of the table. Now I am moving to the other side." This took us aback.'

Some critics discerned a patchwork quality in his character as he changed university posts four times in eight years. There was a querulous streak, as well as the high, squeaking voice, which in arguments could antagonise colleagues; his encounters at the faculty in Bonn had been 'tension filled' – and so on. Sometimes he was called a poor judge of character, despite his correctness and politeness. A common complaint was that he lacked *Menschenkenntnis*, a knowledge of human nature.

How would he fare in what was now a very exposed position of great responsibility at a time when such a post, unlike that of his revered predecessor Faulhaber, was subject for the first time in history to severe public scrutiny?

† † †

At his Episcopal ordination he took the motto: 'Co-operators of the truth'. He explained the motto by seeing it, on the one hand, as 'the relationship between my previous task as professor, and my new mission', going on to say, that 'in spite of different approaches, what was involved…was following the truth and being at its service.'

On the other hand, he said, he chose this motto because 'in today's world the theme of truth is omitted almost entirely, as something too great for man, and yet everything collapses if truth is missing'.

At once it was clear that by 'truth' he meant something very different from that pursued by the world at large. Something very specifically defined by theological reasoning.

His active role as archbishop was brief, and he remained untried in episcopal responsibility. Paul VI died in 1977, his life work and aim unfinished. After the briefest of reigns as John Paul

I, the newly elected Albino Luciano, Archbishop of Venice died, and in October 1977 Wojtyla was elected pope in a highly unexpected result of a second conclave. In this, Ratzinger played an important part, having become more orientated towards Rome, towards which his ambitions were now clearly apparent.

One of the new Pope John Paul II's first foreign trips was to Munich, which Ratzinger organised, and then as the two men became closer, the result of this was that he would never to have to prove himself in what a theologian, primarily a teacher and inspiration for priests, makes of governing his episcopate as a bishop.

John Paul appointed him (by now he was known for his severely traditional views on birth control and sexual morality) as chairman of the Synod of Bishops on the Family. This too would be a short-lived post. He was firmly moving in a different direction from that of the closeted academic.

'But there can certainly also be spiritual power without much worldly satisfaction,' commented Küng, from whose two monumental memoirs of 1983 and 2007 it is almost possible to extract a life of the future pope. 'He complains that he had to give up an *oeuvre*, an overall theological work, for the sake of his career. "*Tu l'as voulu, Georges Dandin, tu l'as voulu.*"'

This quote from Molière was apposite, for Ratzinger has always maintained perhaps disingenuously, and sometimes even naively, that what happened to him in his 'rise' was not of his own volition or initiative, and that although he had played no small part in it, it had been directed and willed from elsewhere, i.e. 'above' or 'on high'. Having fallen out as friends and colleagues, he and Küng were now cast as protagonist and antagonist in this ongoing Church drama, which was to last well into their eighties.

Several events of his tenure of the Munich episcopate, two known at the time, another discovered only later, did not augur well for the future. This was, as Ratzinger's first biographer after his election points out, his only direct major experience as a pastor prior to becoming pope in 2005. 'How those years look,' says John Allen, 'depends to a great extent upon whom you ask.'

First, he played a part in John Paul's decision to revoke Küng's professorial licence to teach at Tübingen, which suggests he was low on human scruples and even basic friendliness when it came to Church governance, and could 'put the boot in'. Here at once we see that, in the exercise of power, core Christian values (e.g. 'Love thy neighbour as thyself') are compromised in relation to Church rules. 'Despite his politeness in many situations,' commented one German journalist, 'there's a kind of paranoia there too. Hotheads have on occasion made unfounded accusations against good men, and Ratzinger has not the sense to discount such complaints.'

Secondly, exercising a right he enjoyed from the Bavarian concordat established by Pacelli in 1924, he removed, another former friend and colleague, the much admired Rahner, who called it 'an injustice and misuse of power'. Here he was perhaps revealing for the first time the play of forces still unresolved from his early life. As small episodes and incidents lead to larger ones, this was a crucial event, a landmark in his life. Some priests likewise in his diocese found him aloof, and said he failed to communicate well with them.

The other event concerned a Father Peter Hullermann…

† † †

Germans love their mountains. Vacations in the mountains, climbing and rambling, breathing in the pure air, admiring the spectacular views, is a pleasure countless millions have savoured and enjoyed.

In 1979 Wilfred T, an eleven-year-old Westphalian boy from the industrial town of Essen, was excited by the thought of taking a holiday in the mountains with his loving and trusted priest, Father Peter Hullermann, 31 years of age.

'Hully', as he was affectionately known by his boys, had been serving in his Essen parish since his ordination. He was noted for his accessibility, his humour, and his ability to connect: 'touchy-feely' was how his parishioners might have thought of him, in literal translation, they said, 'a priest to touch'.

He possessed the charisma to create a young church, and pass on his love of liturgy in enduring fashion to a young generation. In fact, he had the qualities of an ideal confessor in the post-Vatican II years of the 1960s and 1970s, dedicated to the Christian community spirit and love, and opening out the Church to the modern world.

One night of their mountain sojourn, after Hully had encouraged and cajoled his young charge to join him in a few drinks, he took Wilfred to his bedroom, locked the door, stripped him and then – his own father confessor – forced him to perform oral sex.

The abuse came to light. The Church authorities, responding to accusations of molestation by Hullermann of Wilfred and the children of two other families, mollified the parents or otherwise gained their silence, and suspended Hullermann. They sent him 500 kms away – so far that no one should hear about it – to Munich in Bavaria, where he came under the jurisdiction of Joseph Ratzinger, Archbishop of Munich and Freising.

Here he was placed under the care of a psychoanalyst, Werner Huth, who demanded as a condition of his treatment that he should stop drinking alcohol, have a friend to keep an eye on him, and never again be put in a situation to interact with children. As Hullermann refused to believe there was anything wrong with him, Huth placed him in group therapy. The psychoanalyst believed he could not be cured, but could learn to redirect his sexual desires.

Shortly afterwards, 'within days', on assurances he would no longer have children in his care, Hullermann was returned on the order of Ratzinger's deputy, Vicar General Gerhard Gruber, to clerical duties. From February 1980 to the end of August 1982 he practised unrestricted pastoral care in a Munich parish.

Gruber took full responsibility for this, saying Archbishop Ratzinger did not know, However the *New York Times* (23/3/2010) reported having proof that Ratzinger was copied into a memo stating 'Hullermann would be returned to pastoral work "within days"'. This contradicts later denials, and the Pope's dismissal that this, and media outrage over other such cases, was 'silly gossip'.

In late 1982 Hullermann was moved on to the parish of Grafing, and from 1984 began teaching high school children six hours a week, even though there was some vague mention of the 'previous proceedings'. Less than two years later a court convicted him of sexually abusing minors (this time it was not specified how), giving him an 18-month suspended sentence, five years of probation, and fining him 4,000 marks. The court ordered psychotherapy , which he resumed with Werner Huth.

This was not the end. From Grafing he moved to Garching an der Alz where he served for 21 years as curate, chaplain, and administrator in various institutions. Then he made a sudden, unaccountable departure, marked by public celebration with brass band and the firing of salutes, which suggested the Church's insistence he had not offended since 1986 was far from the truth, but also that he was so popular he could get away with it. He moved and took up another post in the parish of the Bavarian spa Bad Tolz.

Father Hullermann's history would never have been revealed but for a bizarre incident.

On Sunday, 15 March 2010, he was celebrating Mass in Bad Tolz, where in 1945 Joseph, as a captured 18-year-old German prisoner-of-war, had been detained in a POW holding camp. Hully was again engaged in parish duties as once more a popular and much-fêted pastor.

In his homily he made reference in general and vague terms to the abuse scandals both of a physical and sexual kind, now dominating German and world headlines. A young parishioner whose marriage he was shortly due to celebrate stood up in his pew and began to shout about the priest's past secret. He stepped down, left, and went into hiding.

Father Rupert Frania, in charge of the Bad Tolz parish, reported that he knew nothing of Hullermann's previous history of sexual abuse: 'They should have told me before,' he said.

18

The Panzer Kardinal

When Ratzinger arrived to settle in Rome in 1981, called there by John Paul II to run the Holy Office, the Congregation for the Doctrine of the Faith, aka Inquisition, nothing was known of the Hullermann case. His image was magnified in the public domain as an unattractive figure who lacked charisma. One biographer of popes called him a rigorous conservative: 'small, compact, handsome with silken, silver hair (and as an eminent British theologian has noted, 'a cruel mouth and bedroom eyes'. He had a poor speaking voice (squeaky, querulous) and to some extent didn't at that time exactly contradict the harsh sobriquet 'God's Rottweiler' and 'iron-clad cardinal', the '*Panzer Kardinal*'.

On the other hand he was, to his supporters and admirers, an 'earthy Bavarian of friendly visage', an 'aggressive German of lordly air', 'an ascetic who carried his cross like a sword'. For the next 24 years he was to exist largely as John Paul II's shadow, or 'the papal enforcer' – a modern equivalent of Chief Inquisitor.

He quickly gained the reputation of using harsh methods for the survival and unity of worldwide Catholicism. He was, after all, the son of a lifelong Bavarian state policeman, and to enforce law and order must have been to some extent an inherited trait. He saw it as his duty to keep order – to make sure the rules were obeyed. In pursuing this as he did he was accused of bad and discourteous behaviour, lack of charity, and of being a bully in his relentless pursuit of orthodoxy.

Even milder critics, such as Fr Henry Warnsbrough, an English scholar who worked with him on the Pontifical Bible Commission, said, 'I don't know how someone so polite, so perceptive, so open, so intelligent, could have put his hand to so many severe pronouncements.' To sum up from a distance, one might say the overriding impression he gave, in spite of his actions, was one of ambiguity. Here again a trenchant if harsh observation of a US lawyer at Nuremburg trials on the Germans on trial might be considered – 'To tell you the truth, they think whatever you want them to think.' But equally the iron fist in that velvet glove image applied to the man.

For, fulfilling the anxious need of a church losing support in Europe, he cultivated the very successful manner and demeanour of a humble, shy, retiring churchman, which, with his exalted rank, commanded respect and affection. The Roman Curia was intent on reinforcing its centralised power and influence, not devolving authority to bishops all round the world. When appointed archbishop by Paul he knew he had read the 'sign of the times' correctly, by which he meant the signpost to his own advancement, and had understood the Pope's unhappy state of mind over the direction of the Church, but also his reluctance to turn to the more palpably reactionary and splenetic cardinals who resisted change for support for they would give the Church a bad image.

The problem was the Church itself, which with its ruling body the Curia, lacked confidence and therefore swung between compliance in courting a popular, feel-good image, and restrictive, sometimes bellicose assertions of authority, along the lines that Catholicism's task was to fight the modern world, expose its lies and folly.

It was, in some respects, similar to the new and awkward position the male of the species found himself in much of the advanced world, where traditional male/female values had broken down.

† † †

To John Paul and to the Roman Church elders Joseph was new, young blood. Always open and ready to listen to others, an academic ostensibly open to fresh ideas, 'listening to the other in the otherness of their thinking', he was now ultimately and deeply attached to those values which to some extent he hid from himself as from others, changed from reforming the Church to retrenching it in the safety of autocratic tradition. It was not in his temperament to maintain the style of princes of the Church of similar belief, like Pacelli and Faulhaber, so he wisely discarded this, although maybe in heart and disposition he was inclined to want to follow them.

He emphasised, from his modest background, that he was never at home in august circumstances, never proprietorial, and he discarded pomp and ceremony, misplacing his crosier, for example, and was at first mindless of ill-fitting vestments. Having moved to Rome, he lived in a flat opposite the Vatican. At first he walked to his office, but as he became more high profile he was stopped so frequently for blessings that he started to use a car to take him the short distance.

He would look and remain ordinary, a simple soul, retain his colourful Bavarian accent, all these gave the right signals to the faithful. But he was far from being an ordinary, simple personality. For one thing he had an extraordinary, even photographic memory, which is hardly an everyday attribute.

He also, it seemed, copied from and retained in his orbit, so to speak, his old friend and now antagonist, Hans Küng, who kept biting and goading, true to his mission to reform the Church. There were so many shades and shadows from his Bavarian background, which still had, and were to retain, a presence in his personality and actions. He was far from the earlier progressive who proposed liberal reforms, and who had once signed up to a scheme that bishops should serve only eight years in office, and then retire.

† † †

One of John Paul's greatest gifts was that he knew how to deal with the Germans, the traditional enemy of Poland. He had lived as their slave and vassal in Krakow, been threatened on a daily basis with extermination, and for four-and-a-half of the most formative years of his life worked as labourer first in a quarry, then in a chemical fertiliser plant making material for explosives. He understood the German mentality both from inside, their motives, and their way of thinking and acting.

One of Wojtyla's most overlooked initiatives as a bishop before he became pope was the move he made towards that reconciliation of the Polish Catholic Church with its German counterpart, which had been so superior and arrogant towards it during the Second World War. A deep and genuine spirit of reconciliation towards the German people motivated him strongly, and he set about achieving this in a very unconventional way: he planned with the Polish bishops that they would begin by apologising for the wrongs the Poles committed towards the Germans.

From his own direct experience, and from the start, he knew man's dual nature. 'Each of us carries two people within the human person. One is who I am, the other is who I should be. This is a very deep tenet of the human person and its inner life. It is not a deception, it is a reflection of reality. He who denies it either lies or... is very deficient. This applies particularly to the young... Human life is not conventional – it is turbulent, uneven. Man tipped the original balance and continues to live in it restlessly. And it is difficult for him to restore the tipped balance. It will not happen without struggle, one has to be prepared for it, one has to love it from the start.'

He understood, even if he had not read Carl Jung, the need of men and women to work through their shadow side, the need also of any person to actualise and become aware of all sides of the self before achieving integrity and maturity. He could mix easily with friend and foe, with Catholic bishops who had clicked their heels when they said '*Heil Hitler!*', and later with Palestinian leaders, like Yasser Arafat, who brought their revolvers along to an audience with him in the Vatican. He could dandle on his knee Leo, the infant son of the specious Blair, make the gesture of offering him communion when the rules forbade it, and cock a snook at the priapic Clinton.

In November 1965 he and the Polish bishops had sent a letter expressing understanding of the suffering experienced by the Germans, ending with the words, 'We forgive you and ask for your forgiveness.' When the Communists in Poland heard of this they reacted with a furious campaign against the bishops with the war cry, 'We will not forget and we will not forgive!'

Workers at the Solvay Plant where Wojtyla had worked in the war, wrote to him saying 'There is nothing the Germans have to forgive us for, since the direct guilt for the outbreak of the Second World War and its bestial course fall exclusively on German imperialism and fascism, and its successor, the German Federal Republic.'

Wojtyla persisted, explaining that he had once been a Solvay worker, and that their request of forgiveness would maintain its proportions, in accordance with the Gospel. 'Never has it been so, in the relations between people. Especially over such a long period of time, that people would not have something to forgive for which to ask mutual forgiveness.'

Although the workers remained adamant, Wojtyla achieved his aim of reconciliation in the end, just prior to his election as pope, when on a German visit he delivered discourses and meetings to heal the rift and reinforce the two churches in 'truth and in love ... to heal the wounds of the past'.

The enrolment by a Pole of his traditional enemy was John Paul's most conspicuous appointment, equivalent perhaps of Ratzinger, on becoming pope, appointing as Secretary of State a Brazilian or a Nigerian, or a secular or gay man as his close adviser (had he really embraced the spirit of contradiction he advocated), and thereby breaking out of his safe German zone.

Their differences made them good partners. John Paul was an extraordinary communicator, often with an uncompromising message (over the Western 'culture of death', or the way capitalism was aggressively spreading totalitarianism of a different kind from that of Hitler or Stalin). By his passionate performance and stirring example – and especially with that example of resistance to suffering in final days – John Paul brought the Church to the forefront of world attention. He lived his love story with God in the glare of universal publicity. But for all the force of his logic, and the power of his words, what he said to the millions of '*à la carte*' Catholics in the West tended to be absorbed and applauded in the moment of his presence, but then largely ignored.

Perhaps Ratzinger, observing him, saw that sometimes a more nuanced and gentle approach could penetrate in a different more pervasive way. We could now detect sometimes a humorous self-awareness in this complex personality. Condemning a Catholic dissident to a period of penitential silence (i.e. not being allowed to teach) he said this measure might be inappropriate or redundant, but added that 'objectively considered, it wasn't bad to invite someone to reflect longer on a difficult question. Perhaps it would do us all some were someone to tell us, "You should stop talking about that for a while, you shouldn't keep publishing frenetically, but give things a chance to mature."'

But there was substance in the charge that he lived too much inside his head, that he lacked *Menschenkenntnis* – the skill of summing up people, and that, as a Jesuit voiced it, he was 'too tense and anxious to make a good Parish priest'.

One drawback was that he did not consult with those beneath him in rank. From an intellectual point of view no one could challenge him. It didn't augur well when he said in his first homily, 'I am not alone. All the saints of God are there to protect me, to sustain me and to carry me.' He made no mention of his fellow workers in the vineyard – the bishops.

He stuck, too, to well-trodden paths. The earliest journalist to be allowed into Ratzinger's space on his appointment was the same one who had interviewed John Paul II successfully.

Vittorio Messori, collaborator with John Paul on *Crossing the Threshold of Hope*, met the cardinal in the South Tyrol, where Ratzinger's cultivated counter-image of modesty and simplicity worked its spell. At times, commented Messori, 'I could see he looked disturbed, but he could also laugh heartily when relating an anecdote, or commenting on a barbed reply.'

He seemed to Messori isolated. He stayed on his holiday alone, mixing with other priests on vacation, or visiting 'acquaintances' from Bavaria. He gave Messori a response that became standard in the future when confronted with the horrors of Auschwitz, on a visit to Poland, or meeting the victims of sexual abuse. Worded with slight variation this became his stock reaction to horror: 'More than ever before, the Lord today has made us conscious of the fact that he alone can save his Church. The Church belongs to Christ and she depends on him to care for her.' It called for 'patience, that daily form of love'.

The main result and effect of *The Ratzinger Report*, intentionally on the part of its subject, was the disarming of the harsh image into something more urbane, careful, and listening. And it worked, for the wider discerning public was amazed at how different he was in reality from the media image. But the exorcising of Ratzinger's trauma or emotional reversal over liberalism still continued to be exercised or taken out on those who spoke for freedom of criticism. He disciplined many, among them Father Charles Curran, who defended the right to public dissent from Church teaching, Archbishop Raymond Hunthausen, another American, who tolerated homosexuals as priests, the Brazilian Bishop Dom Pedro Casaldaliga, and a Sri Lankan who proposed blending Eastern thought with Christianity.

In 1981 John Paul appointed him specifically to take charge of dealing with clerical sex abuse cases. Here, for all the defence offered later when these cases came to light in March 2010, of his treatment of these as Prefect in their exposure, it seemed his first concern was defence of the Church not of the victims, and keeping the cases hidden from public attention. On the other hand, emphasising the ambiguity of the man, there were those who said he did everything he could to change the Church legislation, making it easier for priests to be quickly laicised if found guilty of abuse, instead of the previous way of sending the offenders to another parish where, after either denial or confessions of their crime, they were free to commit the same offence. The perpetrators, or most of them, had no doubt either convinced their bishop of their innocence, or confessed in the confidentiality of the confessional and been absolved, done their penance and signed off with a 'go and sin no more'. This was surely the faith delusion, in defiance of common sense, when they, confessors and penitents alike, were sure before God they wouldn't do it again. But with sex crimes it would never be enough. It came from the closed order, and closed ranks, nature of the Church.

'Cases of this kind,' to sum up the Prefect Ratzinger's attitude, 'are subject to the pontifical secret.' In other words they should

be kept away from public attention and scrutiny, and dealt with
by the Church itself. It didn't stem the trend.

In 1984, three years after revoking Küng's professorial licence,
Ratzinger invites him to lunch in Bavaria. Now a world-famous
theologian, the hierarchy's disapproval of Küng has helped his
career (encouraged in the general spirit of repressive tolerance
towards dissidents) to flourish even more than before. Clad in a
simple black gown, Ratzinger comes down the broad steps of a
large convent to greet him smiling:

'You're doing very well, Herr Küng.' It is perhaps significant he
gives him a lay title.

In what follows Küng raises the question of the large number
of religious women in Quebec who have left their order. They
should have been given more freedom in dress and lifestyle, proposes Küng.

This doesn't go down well, for the Prefect then accuses Küng
of contributing to the loosening of discipline. They don't even
manage to get on to the subject of papal infallibility, which Küng
opposes. They differ over every issue 'as much as a Ptolemaean
and a Copernican differed over the heavens in the transition
from the Middle Ages to modern times' is Küng's comment,
while Ratzinger remains silent.

† † †

The 1980s saw Ratzinger's influence in the Vatican at its height.
He spearheaded the crackdown on liberation theology in
South America (echoing here Pius's enthusiasm for Franco and
Salazar). It is a surprise in some ways that John Paul stood behind
him on this (although he did waver in passing strictures on the
conduct of Archbishop Oscar Romero, the only archbishop
since Thomas a Becket to be killed saying Mass). He must have
remembered his own popular Church leaders in Poland who
supported the anti-Nazi resistance with guns and dynamite, as
well as with prayers.

Ratzinger reigned in 'collegiality' where he saw it. In a 1986 document, a letter to the Bishops of the Catholic Church on the Pastoral Care of Homosexual Persons, now considered infamous, he denounced homosexuality as 'a more or less strong tendency [again that ambiguous Bavarian phraseology which could be, for example, substituted by 'a more or less weak tendency'] towards an intrinsic moral evil'.

He went on: special concern should be directed towards those who have this condition, with 'the assistance of the psychological, sociological and medical sciences'. Clearly he did not count any homosexuals among his friends – or at least not open homosexuals – nor did he appear to appreciate their gifts and personalities as no different from other human beings, and in every case just as unique and worthy of value. It was an extraordinarily naive and inflammatory statement, which led to witch hunts of Catholic organisations and gay Catholic priests. Later he would rule that anti-gay discrimination was not unjust and in certain circumstances may even be 'obligatory'.

Yet he distinctly and quickly told another journalist in 1996, when asked how many ways there were to God: 'As many ways as there are people.'

† † †

Ratzinger must surely be one main intellectual cleric over the last thirty years responsible for the lamentable lack of historical perspective the Vatican brought to its past. The nineteenth-century role of the pope, as established by Giovanni Mastai-Feretti, Pius IX, called the first pope of modern times, was utterly inappropriate to the present world. This inappropriateness had little to do with the much fought over hang-ups of religious controversy (abortions, contraception, celibacy, homosexuality, genetic engineering, stem cell research, etc.) which engage so many minds today.

It had to do instead with the earlier Pius IX, like Pius XII, in following the political situation in the mid nineteenth century, reacting to the diminution of papal political power. He sought to compensate for this by guile and the use of his authority to increase the spiritual entitlement and power of the Church in a way no previous pope had ever dreamed of.

What Pius did was to lay down, on the secular or even ideological principle of tyrants, sacred or spiritual laws to compensate for the loss of papal territory and actual political control in the new state of Italy.

'Nature abhors a vacuum', said Goethe, and being without statehood was that vacuum that the papacy of Pius, under the winning aegis of its brilliant leader, filled by creating new definitions for the Church, thus gaining an enhanced spiritual authority. No one would deny there were not positive beneficial effects at that time for society and for the individual of his consolidation of spiritual weapons in the Vatican's armoury as it was forced to disband its military identity, but the long-term effects of this on the Church have, it can be claimed, been deleterious, as they have tended to set churchmen apart from the rest of mankind.

Three of these steps taken by Pio Nono, as he was known, are still of greater importance than the many innovations and achievements of his 32-year-long reign. The Immaculate Conception of the BVM or Blessed Virgin Mary, the first, was a definition he created on 8 December 1854. It may be claimed, even by those who may find it hard to believe literally, to be of neutral and lasting aspiration value as a feature of faith.

The second was of more debatable value: the publication, on 8 December 1864, of his encyclical *Quanta Cura*, the Syllabus of Errors, which 'denounced the principal errors of our times', among which were the ones the pope cannot or should never reconcile himself to, or agree with: progress, liberalism, and modern civilisation. Here he would find a follower in Ratzinger, who came as pope later to expend much effort denouncing the 'evils' of the age, the secularism, materialism and so on – with an effect that in the European heartland of Catholicism was largely negative and counterproductive.

John Paul II did not attack the secular world as such. He did attack the proselytising imperialist or neo-fascist ideology of capitalism, as it adopted and adapted many of the methods of the Third Reich, which was very different. Ratzinger saw, from the moment of his change of heart over reform, his Church and secularism locked in opposition to one another. He placed his authority squarely behind that nineteenth-century centralisation of Vatican authority begun as regressive consolidation by Pius IX, and fatally pursued by Pacelli.

In the age of Pio Nono such attacks on secularism, which were to become the hallmark of Benedict's papacy, were of particular power and influence because the benefits of secularisation and materialism were not within reach – indeed far beyond the reach – of the vast majority of the European or world population. They appealed by promising rewards in the hereafter to the masses, who then could be manipulated by the increased number of priests, to whom ordination with its material benefits of property, good education, and social standing brought freedom from poor backgrounds. The attacks and promised rewards gave priests power and entitlement. The rule of celibacy, too, helped ensure lasting Church ownership of its property.

By 1999 even Cardinal König, Emeritus Archbishop of Vienna, and a key figure in John Paul's earlier election, felt compelled to cry out at Razinger's policies and repressive measures as Prefect: 'I cannot keep silent, for my heart bleeds when I see such obvious harm being done to the common good of God's Church.' The doctrinal congregation must be able to 'find better ways of doing things'.

The third action of power-hungry Pius had been perhaps the most important – and in the long run possibly the most destructive. Pius was, it must be remembered, also at one time like Ratzinger an ardent liberal and nationalist, and had been elected as a moderate progressive.

Then from his defiance of Italian nationalist military force he fled Rome in disguise, and he turned into the entrenched reactionary, again perhaps in similar negative reaction followed by Pacelli and Ratzinger, and surely dissimilar to the reaction of Jesus of Nazareth – as reported in the synoptic gospels.

His third action was the crowning psychological victory of one who had been stripped of prestige and humiliated. This was the 'vengeance is mine' summons to Rome of the First Vatican Council (1869-70) to affirm the centralisation of authority and governance in the Holy See. His achievement here was the

Council's declaration and carrying of the notion of papal infallibility (18 July 1870, *Pastor aeternus*) in faith and morals, which was surely a notion wedded to its age, one when paternalistic control held full sway, suffrage was far from universal, and when women were still considered the second sex.

Again, linguistically, this had incorporated or deeply embedded in it an ambiguity, for did 'papal infallibility' mean the Pope himself was 'infallible' – as popularly believed, was this what it meant, or (even worse a notion) that the institution was 'infallible'?

We are talking here not of precise, theological definition, argument over which can be, and has been, endless, but of the meaning it conveys to the ordinary believer or non-believer.

As John Paul wisely pointed out in 1979, 'The theologian's contribution will be enriching for the Church only if it takes into account the proper functions of the Bishops and the *rights* of the faithful... It is the right of the faithful not to be troubled by theories and hypotheses that they are not expert in judging, or that are easily simplified or manipulated by public opinion for ends which are alien to the truth.'

Whatever 'papal infallibility' actually meant in theological or non-theological terms it has sadly shown its shortcomings and its dark side (and absurdity in view of papal history), not only over the recent abuse cases, and the shrill absurd Vatican pronouncements upon the response to these, but previously in mid-to-late twentieth century history.

As Prefect, Ratzinger reinforced the idea of infallibility, while John Paul, with his experience of a besieged church in Poland, adhered to it fully, although more in the spirit of maintaining unity and papal authority than in the sense (in English at least) of being not liable to be deceived or mistaken, or incapable of erring. He saw it as useful for the strong presence of the Church in the world, and as a means of curbing seething discussion on social issues or theological disputes. Perhaps he was wrong in this. But he did apologise for the Church's errors or '*mea culpas*' when popes were clearly not infallible, of which Ratzinger did not wholly approve.

As Paul VI said in his 1971 *Octogesima Adveniens,* 'in view of the varied situations in the world, it is difficult to give one teaching to cover them all or to offer a solution which has universal value'. Today papal infallibility looks like an outdated concept with inept associations, like President Bush calling for a 'crusade' against Iraq, or 'Holy Inquisition' retained as the title for Ratzinger's office. Better wording could be found to convey the idea that the pope is the ultimate and final doctrinal judge.

Cardinal Newman, whom Benedict beatified in September 2010 on his trip to the United Kingdom, put his own conscience before obedience to 'infallible' papal pronouncements. He said, 'No Pope has any power over those eternal moral principles which God has imprinted in our hearts and consciences.'

Ratzinger, when a *peritus* at Vatican II, formulated the same principle:

> Over the Pope as expression of the binding claim of ecclesiastical authority there stands one's own conscience, which must be obeyed before all else, even if necessary against the requirements of ecclesiastical authority. This emphasis on the individual, whose conscience confronts him with a supreme and ultimate tribunal, and over in the last resort is beyond the claims of external social groups, even the official Church, also establishes a principle in opposition to increasing totalitarianism.

John Paul, with Ratzinger backing him up, maintained an effective showmanship of authority which depended on his populism and palpable openness – the capacity to inspire love of God through his example – and the severity of his pronouncements, which everyone respected even if they did not concur. He bucked the overriding trend which had begun, as Peter Hebblethwaite showed in 1969, when the highly respected Belgian Cardinal Léon-Joseph Suenens, in a widely reported interview, broke the taboo on senior clerics publicly criticising the pope, which hitherto was only done between consenting adults and in private. Suenens attacked John Paul on the very issue that Ratzinger alongside John Paul upheld, namely frustrating collegiality, and for his exaggerated concept of the papal office.

The old-fashioned idea which later one saw in Ratzinger as Benedict XVI still trying to maintain, was that dignity and the power of the office were upheld by silence; like the British Royal Family, a pope did not reply to charges against him (John Paul tended to disregard this, but Benedict would reinstate it). De Gaulle maintained a lofty, Olympian silence very effective in its time. Churchill thundered, 'Never apologise! Never, never, never!' This increasingly became, as Peter Hebblethwaite writing about Paul VI pointed out, 'a handicap masquerading as an advantage'.

The best indication of this irresistible trend was pointed out to John Paul on his triumphant visit to the USA in 1989 when Archbishop John May, who was President of the US Conference of Bishops, told the Pope, 'Authoritarianism is suspect in any area of learning or culture...Therefore to assert that there is a Church teaching with authority binding and loosing [*sic*] for eternity is truly a sign of contradiction to many American who consider the divine right of bishops as outmoded as the divine right of kings.'

This, the Archbishop went on, was the reality for bishops living and working in the United States.

Ratzinger's habitual response suggested otherwise. While he agreed that what he termed this 'difficulty' was common to all 'modern societies', it was shaped by a 'defective notion of freedom as personal wilfulness'. What was needed instead of authoritarianism was 'authoritative doctrine'.

To put his reply in a nutshell, he was against modern society: 'It is the hallmark of the truth to be worth suffering for,' he told the Archbishop, 'in the deepest sense of the word, the evangelist must also be a martyr. If he is unwilling to be so, he should not lay his hand to the plough.'

This was unrealistic. Was he suggesting, in the 'deepest sense', that bishops should become martyrs? His support of such figures as Pacelli and Faulhaber suggested he thought that for the good of the Church senior Church figures should not at all be prepared to risk their own skins, to martyr themselves, but to preserve themselves and survive.

For most people 'freedom', in the new materially prosperous world, was not personal wilfulness, but a freedom to fulfil personal desires and ambitions (including those of culture and education) on a hitherto inconceivable scale. Once again he was producing the kind of hypothetical argument that would convince no one except a theologically sympathetic Catholic intellectual, more often than not middle or old-aged, who would interpret 'freedom' and 'truth' in academic accordance with his or her (mainly his) own thinking and traditional Catholic teaching.

Ratzinger campaigned vigorously against religious pluralism in the 1990s, claiming in his 2001 document *Dominus Jesus* that non-Christians inhabit 'a gravely deficient situation' compared to Catholic Christians. Here was confirmation that deep inside Ratzinger (and if you consider it alongside his anti-Thomist position as well) there was apparently the Jansenist conviction of God 'pre-selecting' those to be saved. Cynics might well argue that this is not that far removed from the *Führer Prinzip* in which only those who joined the NSDAP could enjoy the promised land.

It is very disconcerting to read of Hitler and Ratzinger being 'chosen' by God to follow a certain path in life (and, equally Bush and Blair), even if the path 'chosen by God' was utterly different for Ratzinger than for Hitler. It suggests both were projecting onto God, fate, providence, whatever term they like to use, deep subjective urges which they had then to obey, and therefore could not resist.

John Paul's explanation in his writings, and his use of words, about his life choices and what happened to him (like his escapes from death) showed a very different approach, completely in accordance with the idea of free will. He took personal responsibility for his choice, while not denying the workings of God or providence in the subsequent outcome of an action or event. 'Man proposes, God disposes' is the French proverb to which John Paul signed up constantly.

'God proposes, Man obeys,' is possibly how Ratzinger saw it. And of course it is only through the man in the frame that God's proposal is known.

There was a very definite Wojtyla–Ratzinger connection, although it was hard to know what was John Paul's goal, and what the effect of Ratzinger's reactionary conviction or its opposite, his restraining hand. They were playing, according to some, 'good cop/bad cop' with the faith, although who was which at any particular time no one could say. 'If Ratzinger didn't exist the pope would find someone just like him,' an insider said. Ratzinger shied away from answering anything to do with this topic.

What is for sure is that John Paul would never have called Buddhism an 'auto-erotic spirituality', as did Ratzinger; when for instance some of the extreme practices of Ignatius Loyola for the highest spiritual aims might be said to come from suppressed sexuality (and have been defended as such by some Catholics such as Piers Paul Read); nor was he at all critical of Islam in the way Ratzinger could claim: 'Islam was at the head of the slave traffic, and by no means displayed any great regard for the blacks. And above all Islam does not make any sort of concession to inculturisation' – and even: 'One has to have a clear understanding that it is not simply a denomination that can be included in the free realm of a pluralistic society.'

Notice here, when it suited him, that Ratzinger could employ 'free' in a very different meaning from his usual use, in a secular sense— and with approval. One is reminded of Pius's racial prejudice against black GIs 'freeing Rome' in the liberating, occupation force of post-conflict Italy in 1945.

On 16 April 2002 four hundred Bavarian mountain guards from the Tegernsee fired a salute to celebrate Ratzinger's 75th birthday. This old-fashioned, somewhat militaristic gesture passed unnoticed, yet had its resonance.

Seventy-five is the age limit for cardinals laid down by the Council, but Ratzinger was retained on the grounds of indispensability. Uta Ranke-Heinemann, a contemporary doctorate student of Ratzinger's at Munich, made this assessment of Ratzinger's twenty-plus years as Prefect:

To me Ratzinger is an enigma, because on the one hand he is so intelligent, and on the other, well, I can't believe the assertions of Christianity that are such enemies to reason... Only arrogant Christians are able to count God 1, 2, 3, and to make this God in their image and likeness as father and son...

When I was in Italy to promote my book *Eunuchs for the Kingdom of Heaven* there was an article in a small Italian newspaper about how Ratzinger and I had been students together. The article misquoted me, 'Ratzinger had the aura of a Cardinal and the highest intelligence, with a total absence of *humanitas*...'

She had been misquoted, she said, for what she actually wrote was 'with the total absence of the erotic' [she means this in the sense of connected with 'eros'].

Another striking example of what Ranke-Heinemann objected to in Ratzinger came in her telling observation, 'Jesus did not police sexual intercourse'.

Sad proof of this 'policing' is in a letter of 15 July 2004, still as prefect, in the year before he became pope, written on his behalf by his close aide Monsignor Dr Georg Gänswein:

Most honoured Dr Lindemann,

Thank you for your friendly letter of 15 July that Cardinal Joseph Ratzinger considered most carefully. In response to your question I can tell you the following: because contraception as such is not acceptable ('*intrinsice dishonestum*' *Humanae Vitae* Nr 14) Catholic physicians may not prescribe the so-called 'Anti Baby Pill'. This does not mean, however, that therapeutic measures for treatment for illnesses are prohibited, even if these result in temporary infertility; in that case, one is not dealing with contraception but with medicinal therapy (*Humanae Vitae* Nr 15). By analogy, the theologian's argument is well founded of taking and prescribing a 'pill' (but not an abortifacient) but in case of serious danger of rape of mentally ill women is permissible as an '*ultima ratio*'.

Cardinal Ratzinger thanks you for your faithfulness to the teachings of the Church and wishes you God's blessings from his heart.

With friendly greetings
Msgr Dr. Georg Gänswein.

19

Election as Pope: The First Year as Benedict XVI

Ratzinger, surprisingly in view of low public expectations, rose to the sombre and moving occasion of John Paul's death on 2 April 2005. On March 30, from his apartment window above St Peter's Square, the Pope had blessed the city and the world, but was unable to speak. Next day he was stricken by a violent shaking chill as he was being taken to Mass. His last words murmured in Polish were, 'Let me go to the house of the Father.' Ratzinger led the funeral ceremony in a frail but piercing voice, recalling that last public appearance high above St Peter's Square:

'None can forget how in that last Easter Day of his life, the Holy Father, marked by suffering, came once more to the window of the Apostolic Place… We can be sure our beloved Pope is standing today at the window of the Father's house. That he sees and blesses us.'

The end of his tenure of the Holy Office had left its Prefect tired and dispirited. There was no doubt through it he had felt keenly his constant unpopularity. He had said earlier, in 1992, that he had never wanted the post. Later he tried to hand in his resignation, but without success.

The sensitive Bavarian, who had as 'Cardinal Sisyphus' been opposing the assault of enemy troops, had apparently lost his zest for life, his light-heartedness. The most senior guardian of the Catholic faith admitted 'quite unguardedly that he did not want any more. "I'm already old, at the limit, and I feel less and less able, physically, to do that, and I also feel quite exhausted."

"Are you a happy man?" Seewald had enquired.

"I have come to terms with my life.'"

Shortly before the conclave which elected him pope, he had outlined the current situation of the Catholic Church as he saw it:

How many doctrinal winds have we seen in these last two decades? [he stated in a homily] How many ideological currents and changes in intellectual fashion! From Marxism to liberalism and libertinism; from collectivism to radical individualism; from atheism to a vague religious mysticism... Whilst relativism – this is to say, allowing oneself to be carried here and there by any doctrinal wind – seems to be the only belief that is accepted today. We are creating a dictatorship of relativism that recognises nothing as definitive and whose only ultimate value is the individual and his wishes.

How he should see this as being any different from any past period in history was not clear. The only time within public memory when a majority in free societies did not or could not uphold the ultimate value of the individual person (which was important in Catholic thinking, and always stressed by John Paul II) was during the Nazi rule in Germany, and then in those countries which had to unify and resist to bring about its downfall.

Yet here also, if one makes a rather outrageous claim, in his empirical approach and his insistence on reason, he was being markedly Protestant and English. The parallels with Cardinal Newman were strong. In contrast to Wojtyla's tendency towards didacticism, Benedict apparently showed an Anglo-Saxon or even scientific and secular way of reasoning. It is a paradox that Benedict's way of reasoning was much closer than it appeared to be to that of humanists, secularists and scientific rationalists, in other words those who saw him as the enemy. Often, his shortcomings were their shortcomings, and they were mirror images of each other.

Satan, noted the American biblical scholar Elaine Pagels in her book *The Origins of Satan* defines negatively what we think of as human. The historic drawback of Protestantism in England, which it had tried to shake off but never lost, was that it was never very popular, and as established by the Tudors was a religion imposed from the top down. The quality of the Catholic Church was that it offered, in the words of Canetti in *Crowds and Power*, the very opposite: 'deliberation, calm, and spaciousness. Its very name contains its chief claim, which is that it has room for everyone. Its expectation is that everyone will turn to it.' In other words it spreads from the bottom up: its apostles and disciples were ordinary men, its leader chosen by God a carpenter's son.

John Allen, the experienced Vatican watcher of the *National Catholic Reporter*, expressed the view that there was no way Ratzinger did not plan, or prepare very carefully, that the conclave's vote should go to anyone else but him. He explained the election process as little more than banal: 'You can say the Holy Spirit dictated the outcome,' or as Ratzinger disingenuously claimed, God chose him, but Allen lists very good reasons why Ratzinger 'got the most votes'.

First, arranging the funeral and delivering the moving oration put him straight away in a prime position to be chosen. 'His performance during the interregnum was perfectly calibrated to remind his conservative base of support of what they admired about him,' but also to reassure the rest he was not a man of his public image, 'not a brooding and dictatorial figure'.

Secondly, his age. The cardinals did not want a long-serving pope. (If only they had adopted the younger Ratzinger's proposal for a fixed term of years, they could have chosen someone much younger.)

Most of all, 'Ratzinger ran the best campaign...' And frankly there was little else in the College of Cardinals, appointed largely by John Paul II and himself, but a conservative base, while the liberal progressive elements were disunited.

After two days and three ballots at 5.50 pm on 19 April 2005, by 100 cardinals out of a total of 115, Ratzinger was elected as Benedict XVI as the 265th pope. It was a foregone conclusion: he was of advanced years, and a pair of safe hands. A fat pope follows a thin one, a short reign follows a long. With this instant,

almost overall approval from the cardinals in one of the short-
est conclaves in the history of the Church, faces fell all over the
world. It was assumed Ratzinger would turn back the clock
even more than John Paul II had in his declining years. 'A rigid
conservative out of step with the times' (Archbishop Tutu); 'a
catastrophe'; 'a hard man with no compassion' – these comments
grew into a worldwide chorus. Would there now be a change in
Joseph Ratzinger? Or had he been someone who had not yet
fully realised himself?

When first elected pope he chatted to a German pilgrim. 'I got
quite dizzy, I had thought I had done my life's work and could
now hope for a peaceful end to my days.'

He told God, he said, 'Don't do this to me! You have younger
and better men who can do this work with different verve and
strength...' He compared his election to a death sentence.

'This time [the Lord] didn't listen to me.'

† † †

Now here he was, thirteen years later, accepting God's will and
choice for him.

His fellow German and Chancellor, Angela Merkel, registered
great pride, but his opening appearance as Pope betrayed a lack
of confidence, utterly without any sign of the self-importance
of one 'who's made it to the top'. Some saw it as this, but others
noticed the satisfaction, even little signs of triumph.

A Vatican press campaign seized the initiative, disarming critics in the media. Cardinal Kaspar of Vienna came to his defence
against critics: 'Clearly he's not a clone of John Paul II... he's a
pastoral man, a man who can explain faith. It's not only important to have the truth, but to communicate truth. And he is very
able to do this... and have a good impact in a very religiously
indifferent world.'

His most harsh critic as ever, Hans Küng, noticed the strong
change which had come over him almost at once. He declared,
'The papacy is such a challenge, it can change anyone.' Küng did
not add, either for better or for worse, but he was prepared to
give him a chance.

Benedict invited him to Rome and the pair met and talked for four hours over dinner. Kung's hopes rose that here was 'the opportunity to make the spirit of the Second Vatican Council the compass for the whole Catholic Church, including the Vatican itself, and thus to promote the needed reforms in the Church' (*Irish Times*, 16 April 2010). They discussed an initiative in the dialogue of religion, but excluded any reference to a demand for reform.

Was the inner man ready to fill the role of pontiff of the world's estimated 1.2 billion Catholics?

Reason was one thing: but would it establish Ratzinger as a good leader of the Church?

In so far as Ratzinger as pope had any overall strategy, it soon became apparent that what he would do was oppose the post-modern and secular loss of faith primarily by opening theology to universal scrutiny with an appeal to reason. Optimism in some quarters ran high.

† † †

The new approach was at its most evident on a human level in his first encyclical, *God's Love*. Here he took up the charge of Nietzsche that Christianity had poisoned Eros, i.e. physical love, and refuted the charge with reservations, even making an academic joke about it. 'The epicure Gassemi used to offer Descartes the humorous greetings "Oh Soul!" And Descartes would reply "Oh Flesh!"'

Elsewhere he argued, 'True Eros is part of a unity in duality, a reality in which spirit and matter "compenetrate", and in which each is brought to a new nobility... [It] tends to rise "in ecstasy" towards the Divine, to lead us beyond ourselves; yet for this very reason it calls for a path of ascent, renunciation, purification and healing.'

The laconic response of the UK's respectable religious weekly *The Tablet* was, 'Sex please, we're Catholics!'

It seemed he would do what he could do best: argue rationally.

† † †

In Benedict's first year no theologians were publicly censored, there was no condemnation of sexual sin, no sweeping dismissal of Vatican personnel. The image of personal fastidiousness supplanted the wooden clogs and sackcloth aura of John Paul, who never carried money, and never owned a house. Benedict had acquired the one he shared with his brother and sister on the outskirts of Regensburg.

Pope watchers glimpsed below the papal robes (too short until they were changed) dainty feet in white plimsolls; he was compared even to Hercule Poirot in his pernickety choice of apparel: Nike hat; quilted white jacket for skiing in Val d'Aosta; Serengeti sunglasses and a Cartier watch.

Apart from the hobby he enjoyed of playing the piano – he was much-lauded as a pianist, but there was doubt as to whether he was very competent – he held a pilot's licence and 'flew' the papal helicopter to the summer residence of Castel Gandolfo. Did he take off and land by himself?

Probably not – here is another President Bush-like image. His favourite foods include the somewhat *ersatz* Bavarian potato ravioli and pancake strips – and Bavarian sausage. With his love of cats as well as Prada shoes, and his gatekeeper Monsignor Georg Gänswein, a former ski instructor, nicknamed by the press for his good looks 'Gorgeous George' or 'The Black Forest Adonis', he sometimes seemed pandered to, as well as pampered.

The ambiguities remained.

† † †

Benedict's first encyclical demands closer scrutiny. When John Paul became pope in 1978 media saturation had not reached its hollow instantaneity and overkill of what was meant by 'love'. In contrast Ratzinger had from the start as pope the mien and behaviour of a quiet, contemplative theologian; a clear and gentle voice, quite high-pitched. He received applause coyly, and if admirers shouted he would put a finger to his lips to silence them – in other words he didn't raise or seek adulation, but rather, instead, prayer.

The publication of *Deus caritas est* was an event awaited with excitement by Catholics. We know from what he said Ratzinger had never had girlfriends or for that matter boyfriends. No romantic friendships or amorous episodes, little history of other jobs or ambitions prior to his becoming ordained as a priest, and now pope, had ever been reported. When *Milestones* (1997), his autobiographical sketch, was launched, he was asked why he didn't mention any girlfriends: 'I had to keep the manuscript to a hundred pages!' he joked. He had never pursued any romantic or sexual contact with any other person. We tend to assume he was just not interested, although this may not be true. He did say he thought about marriage, but without much conviction, and that it was not for him. He didn't give the impression he found the idea attractive. Neither he, his brother, nor his sister, married, nor, it would seem, ever dated a member of the opposite or same sex. It would seem, too, that his father, who advertised when over forty for a wife, had little natural inclination towards the first of the forms of *amor* his son defines: *eros, philia,* and *agape.*

He said that the avoidance or omission of *eros*, together with the emphasis on *agape*, pointed to a new vision of love which Christianity brought to the world. Christ certainly preached it, and made it central, but it was not exactly new.

Greek, Roman and other civilisations had just as viable and valid notions of love. History shows it was the fortunate conjunction of Roman Law and administration (which was secular) and Christian compassion which created the dynamic of European civilisation and the development of democracy. It was only in part due to the new Christian vision of love.

'Eros,' wrote Benedict, 'is... supremely ennobled, yet at the same time it is so purified as to become one with agape.' This was high-sounding and wishful, just as was the claim that the sensually beautiful 'Song of Songs' was not about erotic love in a very direct way. David stole Bathsheba and murdered her husband in order to gratify his desire. *Agape* is not a sole prerogative of married people, but often the reverse, and can exist in any human relationship, just as pure or gross selfishness or self-gratification can raise its ugly head in the most disinterested guise in Catholic married love. Here Ratzinger's romanticising super-ego had again taken over.

In these three pages about *eros* Pope Benedict entered once more his Bavarian fairyland. 'Marriage based on exclusive and definitive love becomes the icon of the relationship between God and his people and vice versa' was not only vague, but forgot whole areas of the relationship between God and man, the Fall, Original Sin, for instance, and failed to address the marked sexual differentiation between man and woman, and the tangle of loyalties and commitments in family relationships.

Especially questionable was Benedict's final sentence claiming the Bible's superiority over other literature. He wrote: 'This close connection between *eros* and marriage in the Bible has no equivalent in extra-biblical literature.'

I cannot vouch for German literature except that I have read (in English) Goethe's *Faust*, most of Thomas Mann's great novels, Gunter Grass, Brecht, and Hesse, and all cover the *eros* connection with marriage. With regard to Russian literature (*War and Peace*, *Anna Karenina*, *The Brothers Karamazov*, to cite three titles among many), this claim was equally absurd. As for English literature of love and marriage Shakespeare, Chaucer, Milton, George Eliot, Blake, D.H. Lawrence – do we need to say more?

For further exploration of this ambiguity of the inner man we go back to the 'frank' interview scenario. Seewald, the interviewer, was quoting back at Ratzinger his own words to the effect that 'intellectual problems... unveiled to me the drama of my life and above all the mystery of truth'.

Ratzinger explained how in the Freising seminary young Germans back from six years in the war were filled with a real intellectual and spiritual hunger. Well, not the only hunger, surely – one should qualify this. The cardinal was then asked if he was allowed to talk about sex.

'Yes, of course,' answered Ratzinger. 'After all one has to talk about everything human... the insistent questions of the Christian people impel us to talk about everything human, compel us to deal constantly with this area of human existence.'

He was hardly very keen. Questioned as to whether he had a negative attitude towards sexuality—he once called sex a sort of floating mine and a 'ubiquitous power'— his reply didn't serve to deny or contradict. He said, 'Sexuality forms man's entire bodiliness, whether male or female... it moulds the person most deeply.'

What did he mean by that? He went on to condemn present-day sex: 'far from the totality of the person and the co-existence of man and woman [sex is now offered in]... a neutralised form as merchandise.'

When was it ever otherwise? Compared to slavery-dominated epochs of history, and the poverty that bound women to men, the early decades of 2000, relatively, are humane and concerned as never before with the person's sexual identity, and sensitive and nuanced to gender in a way that the Church could never envisage. And yet the present-day merchandising of sex was due to what Ratzinger called a 'specific threat which did not exist in earlier times'.

When we look into the past, at those upsurges of hidden power, of secret hubris, of privately indulged vice everywhere, it was surely healthier, both spiritually and bodily, for all the tackiness and embarrassment, that sex should be all around us and out in the open. 'One need not be a chamber to be haunted,' wrote Emily Dickinson, 'One need not be a house...'

Moreover the sexual revolution everyone had experienced over thirty years ago or more, which they say began in the 1960s, wasn't driven only by hedonism and rebellion, but also just as much by an authentic search for identity and authenticity (which are far from being a neutralised form of merchandise). This revolution also sought and still seeks, which the Church had caught on to with John Paul II, to restore or find the balance between the flesh and the spirit, which both a repressive morality and a material, industrial conformity had dislocated.

One shouldn't have underestimated the extent to which people were searching for moral codes to guide their sexuality for themselves and for their children, and here, what the Church urged on people, with its denigration of sexuality, its horror at the dionysic spirit, its rigid gender roles, and refusal to take part in discussion, was woefully inadequate.

Seewald pointed out to the Pope that in the Middle Ages public brothels existed, which in part the Church ran. The reply to this again evaded anything personal in his response. St Augustine, he said, believed it was better for prostitution to exist in an 'ordered form' – presumably he meant legalised. He then slipped out of identifying himself with that notion by more ambiguous, euphemistic statements that typified so much of his thinking on urgent human issues. 'One could definitely appeal to the reflections of the great Father of the Church, who was realistic enough to see that man was always tempted and threatened in that area, that whole religions have slid in that area.'

Rather than expose his thoughts he changed the subject sharply, he escaped quickly to safer ground, that of condemning the lapse in medical ethics. You could almost feel that embarrassment, so unlike his predecessor, his retreat, contaminating the open question–answer nature of the encounter.

In this first encyclical the Pope seemed unprepared fully to confront, as did St Augustine in the opening words of his *Confessions*, the tortured and powerfully motivating experiences that a person's experience of sexuality provided – in contrast to Karol Wojtyla in his book *Love and Responsibility*.

Love, *eros*, takes many forms and colours many aspects of life. 'We crave depth of soul but crave too the pleasure of sensuality,' writes Ronald Rollheiser in one of his weekly columns that are syndicated around the world. Benedict shied away from exploring and confronting the issues this subject presented.

20

12 September 2006

Benedict's first foreign trip was to his native Germany, the first of two, from 15 to 21 August 2005. The high points were two appearances on the Marienfeld, an ex-coalfield near Cologne. At the twentieth World Youth Day he called on some 700,000 young people who had gathered from around the world to show kindness and compassion. A crowd of one million gathered the following day for the open-air Mass he celebrated, in which he urged everyone to be guided in their lives by the Christian faith.

The second trip, in late May 2006, was to Poland, the first ever made by a German pope, and in Warsaw he was cheered by tens of thousands of people. In Krakow he urged about a million gathered in a park for Mass to devote themselves more fully to justice and solidarity. He visited Auschwitz (see Chapter 7), calling for reconciliation and forgiveness. As he settled more into his papal role it began to become clear that Benedict's idea was of a restored or 'reconstructed' Catholic Church – more compact and coherent in unity than before – in the style of Chancellor Adenauer's postwar Germany reconstructed from the ashes of war – from a reduced but more sound base.

Here the image of Germany, of a dead and failed nation, from 'ground zero', revived and restored to life and power... would seem to have become lasting for him – an example that he now would copy in the methods he applied to the Church.

As pope he would seem to have discovered his greatest skill – the Adenauer 'touch'. Up till his election this had been a buried gift, and now there was much approval, even surprise that he was now taking the Church in a different direction, even into a different dimension. Not visceral, not a showman, not working the crowd in his public exhortations, not in any way rhetorical.

Gone was that searching stare that looked into the heart of everyone, the evangelical stance, the firm grip of the artisan's fist. Benedict in a different way deliberately distanced himself from the shallow world of political leaders in a less striking manner.

He was most unlikely to comment on them in the forthright way that John Paul did – as he had on President Clinton – or have his private words widely reported, yet he could show his feelings in quite a subtle way sometimes, as he did over one visit to the Vatican of Cherie Blair, when in a cursory audience he granted her she flouted protocol and wore the white that only Catholic royalty was supposed to wear. She invited him to Britain in May 2007, years after John Paul's visit in 1982, but he wouldn't come.

On a two-day visit to Spain in July 2006 – his visits abroad were always very brief – he stressed the indissolubility of marriage and criticised what the exaggerated notions of freedom had led to in Western culture – unremarkable and quite expected by now, but warmly welcomed. His reputation as a quiet, humble, inoffensive pope grew and grew. No one wondered if this was the true man, or that something deeper, and even darker, had yet to make an appearance. Yet unhappily and paradoxically it then suddenly did. Benedict's most visible moment to the world suddenly arrived in September 2006.

He was in Bavaria, where he drew crowds of hundreds of thousands in Munich and Regensburg on the 12th September. In an academic lecture, given at his home Regensburg University, he quoted a Byzantine emperor who had referred to Muhammad, prefacing the emperor's words with 'He addressed his interlocutor in an astonishingly hard – to us surprisingly harsh – way:

"Show me just what Muhammad brought that was new and there you will find things only evil and inhuman, such as his command to spread by the sword the faith that he preached."'

The main theme of his lecture was the tendency or way God had been excluded from reason. The lecture was called, 'Faith, Reason and the University'. He made a finely nuanced distinction between the Islamic teaching – 'There is no compulsion in religion' – and the practice of forcing a faith on people through violence.

In the course of his citing examples and drawing distinctions, this quotation, 'things only evil and inhuman' was snatched out of context, not qualified by how he had introduced it, and blazed across the world media as if he had uttered the words himself, which he had not, and they were his personal opinion. This was the case for the defence.

But according to Küng the address 'disseminated errors about Islam, about the Reformation and about the Enlightenment as the de-Hellenisation of his own (Hellenistic-Roman) Christianity', and, added the eminent theologian, 'unfortunately it wasn't just a slip.'

It was the effect of his referring to the Prophet as 'evil and inhuman', as it became simplified, that triggered worldwide hostile reaction from Muslims, demonstrations and threats, effigies of the pope being burned, and the related murder of a nun, the beheading of priests, and the persecution of Christians in Iraq and elsewhere. Fanned by the press, fury and counter-indignation and contempt erupted everywhere, prompting one senior Vatican official to call it a 'multi-media phenomenon bordering on the absurd which unleashed the crowd's vindictiveness'.

Benedict did his best to limit the damage, and regretted the effect his words had had, but never apologised in the full and unconditional way his detractors hoped he would, which suggested it was not just a slip. Those who defended him argued he had a perfect right to quote a fourteenth-century Byzantine emperor in a legitimate desire to create constructive debate in a world in which religious violence happened every day. Those who did not want to see that he might have regretted what he said, called it a 'piss-apology', and claimed he should never have said sorry at all. At any rate it seemed he managed to antagonise both sides. Worse of all, he had given the world press a handle on him, a sound-bite, which would, like his 'once been a Hitler

Youth' label, even if not quite true, be forever trotted out by the media until the end of time.

The more sinister interpretation put forward by some was that he was being a 'dog whistler for Islamophobia', that he wanted to polarise world opinion by means of coded inflammatory references embedded in careful language for deniability. Here the arguments run that the 'labyrinthine nature of Vatican statements lends itself to such layers of meaning'.

Once again the earlier Ratzinger would seem to be contradicting himself, or at least being ambiguous: 'Islam is organised in a way that is opposed to our modern ideas about society... not simply a denomination that can be included in the free realm of a pluralistic society.' The fact, if it is true, that Islam was organised in a way that is opposed to our modern ideas about society, surely should make it closer to Ratzinger's own view. If you want to get on with Islam, you stress what Islam and Christianity have in common, which is what John Paul II did.

In September 2005, when now as Pope he had met with Jewish students, he was quoted as saying, 'Islam can adapt to democracy only if the Koran is radically reinterpreted,' a statement that the Vatican denied that he ever made. Anti-Islamic sentiments voiced by other senior clerics, such as Cardinal Pell of Sidney, considered a 'stalking horse' for Benedict in this respect, were surely a waste of time and counterproductive, for they alienated rather than convinced or shored up support, although they may have reassured the conservatives.

† † †

Subsequently, toward the end of 2006, Benedict made a visit to Turkey, a Muslim but secular country (with only 32,000 Catholics), in the face of death threats. Islamic fundamentalists protested, while Tayyip Erdogan, the prime minister, showed indifference towards the Pope, saying 'I don't plan my diary around the Pope's diary.' Many said he should not risk going, especially in view of the fact that his predecessor had been threatened in the pages of *Millyet* by Ali Agça, a Muslim who announced 'I will kill the commander of the crusade who arrives

in the guise of a religious leader', and two years later in St Peter's
Square almost succeeded. He went, bravely refusing to wear a
bulletproof vest.

As well as wanting to pay homage to the early roots of
Christianity to be found in Turkey, here, probably again deliberately, he brought the focus onto a dialogue with Islam, and
gave out a much more unequivocal message when he prayed
with the grand Mufti of Istanbul in the city's Blue Mosque. He
weathered with humble and diplomatic acceptance the prime
minister's snub, which won the latter round, so was it atonement
that accepted the Regensburg address was a blunder, or was it
simply a shrewd, diplomatic move?

He met other Turkish leaders, including President Ahmet
Necdet, and Athenagoras I, the Patriarch of the world's 250 million Orthodox Christians (although there were only 2,500 in
Turkey). In spite of previously voiced opposition when he was
a cardinal to Turkey joining the European Union, he was made
welcome, visited more mosques, and called for more Muslim–
Christian dialogue. He urged again all religious leaders to 'utterly
refuse' to support any form of violence in the name of faith: 'to
kill in the name of God is an offence against Him'.

If he had been aware and calculating in what he had said at
Regensburg, which was more than likely, then he made a serious
mistake. Priests, fellow Catholics had died as a result of it. He
should have known that remarks were always taken out of context and distorted. It was not the healing hand and spirit of the
visit that the world was to remember, but the provocation.

† † †

Prime Minister Tony Blair's conversion in 2007, just opportunely
after leaving office – having voiced in 2005 his conviction that
God had endorsed and sanctioned his decision to invade Iraq in
2003 (he had found Pope John Paul II in no such mind) – acted
out his conversion in public. He set up a Faith Foundation. He
and Cherie had made a point of visiting Benedict XVI, drawing him into their seductive, photographic Charybdis, although
he looked shy and abashed. So it was on this other hand that

Benedict deferred to let the Blairs make use of his office, for by this he would seem to be endorsing the Blairs' religious belief, while they were also admirers of Küng. Perhaps he should have taken a leaf out of another religious leader' books, such as Poland's Archbishop's Sapieha, who during the occupation pointedly refused to pose with Germans.

Seewald, who saw Ratzinger before and after he became pope, explored the deference and the elaborate humility. He wrote of the earlier time, 'His behaviour really did seem very humble, though not as humble as in later years, and occasionally there was a flash of something like boasting. Which was doing very nicely, against the background of a father who had kept geese. When I asked what the actual reasons for which the committee members had elected him to the Académie Française, he did not say, "Well, no, listen…" but remarked drily that "when distinguished people decide something, there is no need for any reason to be given".'

This was a rare moment in the accounts when modesty departed and the mask slipped. Seewald commented, 'Which means, "This reporter may be quite likeable in his naïveté, but he apparently does not know with whom he is actually dealing." Ratzinger went on, "My predecessor was Sacharov. Havel was received with me. Adenauer, Churchill, Einstein were members."'

Once again the interviewer said he didn't feel impressed. Ratzinger added, '"Just so you get some idea of what kind of people are members."'

So there was this tendency in the man, what Karol Wojtyla called the visibility of the invisible, a certain sense of superiority, as well as of snobbery. It was evident when elected pope that on his face there was a little smile of triumph, a smirk, almost, of self-satisfaction., Michael Holroyd, the English biographer, commented on how this had struck him seeing it on TV – as if to say – 'I've done it!'

The unsuspecting lack of awareness – or was it lack of self-knowledge? – which were leading to these unfortunate dominating and damning headlines (the Regensburg address, soon the lifting of excommunication on Bishop Williamson, the Holocaust denier, the tepid condemnation of the Irish clergy abuse cases, with their systemic cover-ups by the hierarchy) again seemed endemic and stemming from his background.

When asked how he kept informed, Ratzinger at that earlier time had answered, 'The *Mittelbayerische* is the only newspaper I truly read completely – otherwise I read press reviews. The *Mittelbayerische*, of course, always gets here late, often two weeks late, and often all mixed up.' This seemed to confirm Küng's acid comment about the Pope's narrow background, for a local newspaper arriving late hardly could keep a prince of the universal Church up to date, especially one who was policing the theology and practice of the faith.

When again challenged Ratzinger had confirmed his disdain for the world's reactions, and quickly added, 'I look at *Telegiornale* every day'.

This kind of answer only rarely happened when the guard was down.

† † †

John Paul II had been most keen to reach out to the Muslim faith and world. He had appointed Archbishop Michael Fitzgerald as President of the Pontifical Council for Interreligious Dialogue. Born in Walsall, Fitzgerald was the highest ranking Englishman in the Curia, and as its most skilled Arab specialist he saw eye to eye with John Paul's admiration for aspects of Mohammadonism, especially its fidelity to prayer, and the beauty of the language ('some of the most beautiful names in the language are given to the God of the Koran'). When he had visited Morocco, Fitzgerald told me, the Pope had asked him, 'Well how can I, a Christian, speak to young Moroccans?'

John Paul had invited Muslim delegates to his assembly of world religious leaders in Assisi in 1986 and 1991, and on a trip to Damascus, Syria, was the first pope to visit a mosque.

In 2006, Benedict dismissed Fitzgerald from his post summarily (without his expected promotion to cardinal) and gave him a less important role as ambassador to the Arab League. The dismissal was carried out coldly by Secretary of State Sodano in the manner a newspaper proprietor might sack an editor –

Fitzgerald's Pontifical Council was in effect, according to the London *Daily Telegraph*, 'decapitated'. Fitzgerald had considerable tolerance and understanding of other religions, and the ability to engage in constructive dialogue with their leaders. It appeared his approach was too liberal for Benedict.

In July 2007, following this, the absolute primacy of jurisdiction of the Roman Catholic Church was asserted by the Doctrinal Congregation. 'Roman glorification and alienation of the world,' Küng called it, 'contrary to the explicit desire of the Second Vatican Council'. According to this the Orthodox churches of the east are 'defective churches and the Reformation churches aren't churches at all'. He was becoming, from that softer beginning, more ultra-reactionary.

21

Year Three

Benedict only visited Brazil in South America for the first time from 9 to 14 May 2007, confirming those critics who said that first and foremost his concerns centred on European Catholicism. While he decried in public homilies and addresses the large number of people in the region leaving the Church, the fact that he had left it so long to travel west could hardly be called inspiring – again in contrast to John Paul II, who in his first year as pope made a point of beginning with the third world Latin American country of Mexico, of travelling to the four points of the compass.

Again Benedict took up the superior Catholic role of warning against the evangelical Protestant churches, and condemned Marxism and globalisation, which was unlikely to stem the outflow, for these other churches had something to offer that the Church under his leadership was failing to provide.

Describing himself once again audaciously as a 'pilgrim' pope, he made a two-day trip in September to Austria to the sites of Mariazelli and Heiligenkreuz Abbey in the Vienna Woods, but given the meagreness of his foreign forays, he could better be described as a 'stay-at-home' pope. The concept that travel broadens the mind had not made much impression, for he again deplored the disorientation of Western society and underscored the Christian roots of Europe. The last thing he was able to do, it seemed, was blaze forth to the world a positive message.

Benedict visited the United States from 15 to 20 April 2008. The last papal visit to the United States, by John Paul II, had been in 1986. There were now 61 million Catholics there, some 6 per cent of the world's total. For the first time in history, Muslims, with 1.25 billion adherents and 17.4 per cent of the world's population, outnumbered Roman Catholics, with 1.13 billion followers, and 17.4 per cent of the total.

The pope visited Washington and New York, where there was the greatest concentration of Catholics. The Church in the USA still reeled from the scandal of sexual abuse by over four thousand priests since 1950, while over a billion dollars had been paid out in compensation. The *Boston Globe* had won a Pulitzer Prize in 2002 for its investigative reporting of this sexual abuse of minors by priests. One of the first things Benedict voiced, admitting his deep shame at the abuse, was how he was unable to understand how priests could 'betray their mission... to give the love of God to these children'.

He met with the victims of sexual abuse, and offered a model of pastoral sensitivity, which impressed Americans – according to a poll more than 75 per cent registered approval. But was it enough? In the long term, given the scale of the abuse, and that revelations and scandals were likely to continue, probably not. 'We do have a big dirty bubble in the center of the Church over here, and yet no official is screaming,' says a character in the ex-Jesuit Malachi Martin's 1996 novel *Windswept House*. 'Are all the baddies in charge? And are all the good ones blind?'

Another character takes this up:

There's the matter of all those paedophiliac priests who are moved about by their bishops, and a constant refusal to laicise known offenders. There's the special fund the bishops have set up to pay hundreds of millions of dollars in out-of-court settlements... I think the question to ask from here on out is whether there's an effort to transform the Church into a safe sanctuary for known paedophiles. And, in the process, to create a perfect fields of harvest for Satanic cults.'
(Martin, 1986)

This was 1996. The Church, and with it the Pope at its head, had
been sleeping.

† † †

By now Benedict's message had become clear: he didn't believe in
'horizontal evaluation, or in statistics and marketing approaches,
calculating gains and losses'. 'The Church doesn't exist for itself
but is God's instrument', was one of his memorable phrases; and
he repeated what was now his considered resolve over Church
governance, namely that he didn't believe in imposition: 'The
Church must evolve organically.' But how could he say this when
he so firmly believed it could only evolve along strictly authoritative lines, as in the rigorous overseeing of the appointment of
bishops? Or did 'organically' mean something else: 'selectively for
the few', or 'protecting the Magisterium'?

On his return to Rome he ruffled feathers by baptising
publicly a former Muslim journalist, who described Islam as
characterised by intolerance.

In this third year he issued his second encyclical, *Spe Salvi*, 'on
Christian Hope', laying down better than he had done before,
in a concise and accessible style, his challenge to the scientific
outlook, and emphasising how Christian faith-hope needs transformation in the modern age.

There were two further trips in 2008, the first to Australia in
July. Having criticised John Paul's inauguration of World Youth
Days in 1986, he now attended the 23rd World Youth Day, the
climax of which was in Sydney, when 400,000 pilgrims enthusi-
astically attended a Mass he celebrated. Here again he overturned
expectations, while the very negative press coverage before he
arrived, had reversed by the end of the visit. He went to France
in September, when he warned against avarice and false idols.
The climax of this second visit was his celebration of Mass on the
150th anniversary of apparitions of the Virgin Mary in Lourdes.

Again the simple appeal of his humility and modesty, and the
direct appeal of his homilies struck a chord in his followers. If
the ambiguity of some of his utterances continued, these unprecedented gestures towards young people revealed yet another side,

dormant since that short spell he served as Archbishop of Vienna, that of Joseph the teacher and pastor. But soon events were to explode which called in question his leadership of what had now become an increasingly centralised and autocratic church.

22

CHILL WINDS: FAMILY MATTERS IN 2009

> The power of the dark is ascending. The light retreats to
> security, so that the dark cannot encroach upon it.
> *I Ching*

Archbishop Michel Lefebvre, formerly from Dakar in French
Senegal, had a wide following in France and a conservative seminary in Econe, Switzerland. He took exception to Vatican II as
heresy, and had been suspended by Pope Paul, but was allowed
scope to practise by the more generous John Paul, who wanted
to avoid schism.

Lefebvre had haughtily dismissed the new pope John Paul
in 1979: 'He didn't seem like a pope to me: he had no character.' Even John Paul, who followed Paul in supporting *Dignitatis
Humanae*, approved of the use of preconciliar rites such as the
Tridentine rite, which Lefebvre maintained should never have
been superseded by Mass in the vernacular tongues.

Lefebrve was out to cause a breach with Rome; he stated
Dignitatis Humanae was heresy, and held that an established church
in an officially Catholic state was the will of Christ. John Paul tried
strenuously to bring the recalcitrant archbishop and his vociferous
following to reconciliation with Rome. Lefebvre was especially
against John Paul's 'spirit of Assisi' (1986) meeting with leaders of
other churches (and so also was Ratzinger), calling it 'interreli-
gous syncretism', a term of contempt for trying to join together

different faiths. Of the 1986 world Day of Peace Ratzinger had also said, disparagingly, 'This cannot be the model,' to which John Paul commented, 'That's his personal opinion.' When Lefebvre ordained four new bishops to implement his principles in June 1988, the Pope had no choice but to excommunicate him.

Fractious, inflexible, stuffed into his 'too-tight suit of doctrinal armour studded with anathemas', Lefebvre found many followers on France's extreme right, the National Front led by Philippe le Pen, which polled 11 per cent of the vote in the 1984 European elections. This schism was a symptom of the split between the traditionalists and the liberals, while those who supported Vatican II believed it had freed Catholics from the Jansenist pessimism that had made religion a chore for three centuries, an attitude that turned the faithful into dour pilgrims marching fearfully towards salvation while ignoring the beauty of creation, and while the rest of humanity went to hell.

You might have thought Benedict would see the danger of bringing back this neo-fascist movement, which many dismissed as minimal, into mainstream Catholicism, but he clearly felt sympathetic to certain aspects of it. This campaign of his became obsessive, and you might well ask why. Lifting virtually all restrictions on celebrating the Tridentine rite was a measure taken in defiance of Vatican II's spirit of reform.

On 24 January 2009 he rescinded the excommunication of those four bishops, restoring them into full communion with the Church. Lefebvre by now had died.

One of the four, Bishop Richard Williamson, an old boy of Winchester College and a Catholic convert of Malcolm Muggeridge, denied the Holocaust had taken place. Another, Bishop Bernard Tissier de Mallerais, had once accused Benedict of apostasy, while they and all Lefebvrists expressed, in public, loathing of homosexuals and the equal status of women (and their wearing of trousers or jeans). They were opposed to the Vatican II document that absolved present-day Jews of responsibility for the crucifixion of Jesus. They were, it goes without saying, supporters of the move to canonise Pius XII and his anti-modernism.

They remained, even upon re-instatement, in many ways defiant, for example reinstating in the Good Friday Prayers reference to Jews as 'deicides' which Benedict had reformed by removing references to the 'blindness' of the Jews, as well as the appeal that 'they be delivered from darkness', and that God 'may take their the veil from their hearts'. Their extreme view was that this was doing a disservice to the Jews' eternal salvation and that therefore Benedict was anti-Semitic. Their leader, Bishop Bernard Fellay, said they would stick to the unchanged prayer. By implication, then, they still held Jews as the deicides of Christ.

But, for Benedict, the reinstatement of the holocaust denier Williamson was a public relations disaster on an epic scale, and it immediately hit the world headlines. Again it was disingenuous of him or his followers to claim the Pope did not know Williamson's views. To claim that nobody had told him was simply not good enough for a leader in his position, especially for one famed as a 'micro-manager'. Holocaust denial is a crime that carries a prison sentence of five years in Germany. Angela Merkel, once so proud of her German pope, expressed outrage and demanded 'clarification' from the Vatican. German cardinals criticised the Pope, as did shocked Jewish leaders.

That Williamson also denied al Qaeda's involvement in the World Trade Center attacks of 9/11 only reinforced the anti-Semitic and revisionist implications of his Holocaust denial. David Willey the BBC Vatican correspondent wrote, 'in all my thirty years in Rome I have never seen a communications debacle comparable to this'. The London *Financial Times* called it 'a solipsism of cosmic proportions'. One can only assume the reinstatement of Williamson, although later redressed when the outcry became too great to resist, was a deliberate move: either Benedict did not care, or he was fishing to see how far he could go in playing once again the game of deniability. When he conferred a bishopric on an Austrian priest who publicly preached Hurricane Katrina was retribution for the abortionists, prostitutes and homosexuals of New Orleans, and then, just before Christmas, preached gay lifestyle choices were as much a threat to God's creation as global warning, he seemed more of a reactionary than ever.

The unpopular move to canonise Pius XII, too, taken up in late 2008, was untimely and provocative. Jewish leaders complained, especially as the Pope refused to open up the Vatican secret files so everyone could examine the record for themselves.

The good that he was doing now, more and more was likely to be interred with his bones. The foreign visits he made in 2009 hardly made up for the increasing pessimism he created and felt himself. It took him four years to travel to Africa for the first time, and here again his visit to Angola and Cameroon was overshadowed by his pessimistic and reductive utterances as he inveighed against the spread of esoteric sects and cults, African corruption, and condoms.

Of the AIDS epidemic affecting 22 million in sub-Saharan Africa he said, 'You can't reduce it with the distribution of condoms. On the contrary it increases the problem.' Sexual behaviour was the issue, 'and the solution must be found in spiritual and human awakening'. Abortion in the case of incest or rape, legal in 45 African countries, 'should not be an option'. Outrage in Europe swiftly followed, condoms were scattered on the ground in front of Notre Dame, and unusual protests issued from government ministers in France, Belgium, and from the German Health Minister, Ulla Schmidt. It seemed there were more and more of these backward steps as his pontificate wore on, followed by Vatican back-pedalling.

† † †

When the Vatican Council's first session had finished, Ratzinger had summed up a central issue: 'Was the old policy of exclusiveness, condemnation and defence to be continued?' he said. 'Or would the Church... turn over a new leaf and move on into a new and positive encounter with its own origins, with its brothers and with the world of today?' And when in the 1964 session there was talk of excommunicating Communists for their beliefs and the bishops decreed not to do so, he commented, 'The weapon of condemnation has been tried to the limit... it is no longer possible to deal with the problem in that way now.'

Now, 46 years later, it seemed he had recourse to little else, with the increasingly easy and common denunciation of 'relativism', 'historicism', 'Marxist influences' and liberal academic attitudes.

† † †

A lot of this disfavour came from a sense that Benedict was out
of touch, which he, and not the Curia or Vatican press office,
was responsible for. The steep rise in the number of Catholics
in Austria leaving the Church over the appointment to bishop
of a right-wing priest, Father Gerhard Wagner, the delayed and
tepid response to the outcry over the lifting of excommunication of four Lefebvrist bishops, continued to suggest the block in
the pope closely connected with his upbringing was deepening.
There was also that strong tendency in Benedict to place the
human family on a pedestal.

Given the rarified and unusually holy family in which he was
raised, with its rather contradictory ethos and example of non-
perpetuation, for none of the three children ever married and
had children, Benedict's championship of family values did strike
an odd note.

John Paul had gained deep experience of married life from
the confessional, was fussed over and looked after by Polish nuns,
formed close friendships with women, and reached out to men,
women and children in such a way that the whole human race
was his family. But for Benedict the family was a theory, while
his closest relationships were with music, with theology and with
Church liturgy.

There is no doubt that Ratzinger behaved with perfect deco-
rum, a well-balanced trustee and museum director of the faith.
But every now and again he let slip something that suggested
there was another Ratzinger inside who is not allowed to emerge.
There were virtues in this, as there were shortcomings in his cus-
todianship, and the gain in Benedict's case was an unusual quality
or power of dispassionate reasoning. His thought never changed,
remaining inductive and empirical rather than deductive, flexible
and free from dogma.

But it was when he enters the field of ethics that he seems
short on experience. No one who has had direct experience of
family life could believe, while both loving and advocating it,
there weren't also violent and destructive aspects, or potential for
them, in every family or marriage. The family can be a force for

good or for bad, and it was more able to resist the evils of society and the human person than any individual, institution, grouping by sex or material circumstance, nation, or race.

Benedict's utterances on family life in *Caritas in Veritate* reflected a romanticised fantasy engendered by his own upbringing, and it would seem especially that it cut out too close a contact with anything outside its religious comfort zone. Few people in today's world would be able to romanticise about this in a similar way. He left out how difficult it must have been, for example, for his sister to remain harnessed to working to support her parents, then her brothers, through all her life, ending up as Joseph's housekeeper, typist, cook and cleaner. Had she resented her role? No, said her brothers, she renounced the chance of marriage for service; but did they ever encourage her to marry? Did anyone ever want to marry her?

The Ratzinger's basic family attitude was that you did not grumble or complain, but here, from the one objective account we have of her, her relationship with Joseph was not untroubled, and it was not unusual for there to be 'a heavy atmosphere in the household they shared'. Reading between the lines, it seems she was quite a burden to Joseph, and had ended up querulous and withdrawn, or 'retiring' – by which one infers surly. However, in that airy way we associate with the Ratzinger family, from what her brother said, she was an 'eternal reminder to protect the faith of simple people... against professors who take refuge in know-it-all hypotheses'.

She had died in 1991. The comment on her was that at her funeral, in 1991, 'there had probably never been so many nuncios, cardinals, archbishops, and politicians at a secretary's funeral as there were for that of Maria Ratzinger'. They were not there, it seemed, for her but for Joseph. It did suggest she had little life of her own outside that of her brother.

Benedict's predecessor did not preach a Utopian view about love, marriage, and the family, while it is a platitude but important to point out that Cain was Abel's brother. Some commentators pointed out that Catholic teaching, especially that in nineteenth- and twentieth-century Ireland, for example, was to blame for the many crimes of sex abuse which were hidden away and only recently uncovered; then also, as well as the scandal itself, there was much evidence of careful 'equivocation' or double-think in the cover-up.

Yet while he was now in his early eighties he continued to draw in crowds in their hundreds of thousands, in Angola, for example, although in the stampede in the football stadium where Mass was held two people died. His next trip in May 2009 was to Jordan, Israel and the Palestinian territories or Holy Land, where he called for dialogue and reconciliation between Christians and Muslims. The world did not feel any great vigour or commitment behind such initiatives. In September he visited the Czech Republic, and celebrated open-air masses in Brno and Stara Boleslav. But by now a cyclone was quickly heading in the direction of the Vatican.

23

If You Keep Quiet
I Won't Say Anything

The duty of a good leader is to foresee dissatisfaction and to remedy injustice before complaints are made.
André Maurois

Sin is a personal act. Moreover we have a responsibility for the sins committed by others *when we cooperate in them*
– by participating directly and voluntarily in them;
– by ordering, advising, praising or approving them;
– by not disclosing or not hindering them when we have an obligation to do so, by protecting evil doers.
Catechism of the Catholic Church (editorially overseen by Ratzinger)

Mainly, cases of clerical sexual abuse, if we may pick on the Hullermann case of 1980 as the first, have remained unknown and in the dark until March 2010. As a result this priest was still practising until his case came to light and was taken up widely and reported across the globe.

Hullermann, on being discovered to have sexually abused boys in his diocese had been, with Ratzinger's agreement, moved from far-away Münster to Munich.

Instead of handing over Hullermann to civil jurisdiction, Ratzinger was in charge of and kept him within the canonical process by which Hullermann was given a few days' treatment (and presumably absolved in confession), and then returned to parish work in Munich. In March 2010 the Munich archdiocese, when this case came to light, claimed 'bad mistakes had been made, but that officials subordinate to Ratzinger had made them'. This was, it emerged, clearly not what happened.

A memo in the possession of the *New York Times,* its contents reported on 24 March 2010, showed that Ratzinger not only led a meeting on 15 January 1980, approving of the transfer of Hullermann to his district, but that he was kept informed about his later treatment. Six years later Hullermann was convicted of molesting boys in Munich, but still left free to transfer and continue offending.

Here, it could be claimed, a moral relativism was at work: a clamping down with theological rectitude on dissident views which would impress Church hierarchy, but laxity or failure of scrutiny in relation to clerical sex civil misdemeanour of a kind looking very similar to that operating in the BBC television hierarchy 2012–13.

On 15 March 2010 the news of Benedict's involvement as Munich primate on his home ground, and then, after 1981, as papal watchdog in the Vatican with the specific task of dealing with child rape, widened world media attention on the case.

It followed on many other cases brought or dragged to light (some 300 in all in Germany, as well as Ireland, Austria, Belgium, the Netherlands and the United States). The most horrific of these was that of the deaf Father Lawrence Murphy, the Milwaukee priest accused of molesting some 200 helpless deaf boys from 1950 to 1975. Two Wisconsin bishops urged the Vatican to prosecute Murphy, but this never happened. Eventually, years later, the deaf community demanded justice. The trial went ahead in 1997, but Ratzinger halted it on compassionate grounds because Murphy had fallen ill. He died in 1998. This new case of abuse emerged in sensational headlines, such as 'Infallible Pope turns blind eye to deaf boy molestation.'

In this and the Hullermann case the point made against the Church was that the pope and the hierarchy of his choice, which surrounded and protected him, believed that the crime of bringing these repeated crimes into the public domain was actually worse than the acts committed by the perpetrators against the minors. Effective compassion towards the victims had been missing, and the heads of senior figures involved had failed to roll.

Ratzinger, as Vatican prefect for the Congregation for the Doctrine of the Faith, had sent, in May 2001, to every Catholic bishop the directive to keep inquiries into child abuse behind closed doors, and secrete the evidence of such abuse perpetrated by a cleric on a minor as confidential for up to twelve years after the victim reached the age of 18. To insist upon such a closed system of jurisdiction, to be enforced upon pain of excommunication, was only too evocative of the system of justice operated and supported by professed Catholics in his youth too. His later, much quoted phrase, ran thus: 'Cases of this kind are subject to the pontifical secret'. It seemed therefore that disclosure of the offence was actually worse than the offence itself.

At this same time, in 2001, Ratzinger's letter was co-signed by Archbishop Tarcisio Bertone, now Ratzinger's deputy, who in early 2003 said in an interview, 'In my opinion, the demand that a bishop be obligated to contact the police in order to denounce [*sic*] a priest who had admitted the offence of paedophilia is unfounded.' Bertone had particularly claimed there was a link between homosexuality and sexual abuse, while the Vatican compared media critics of the pope to the Nazi persecution of the Jews.

Gruber and Huth's subsequent claims that Ratzinger knew nothing of Hullermann's swift return to pastoral duties were unlikely to be true. The Rev Thomas Doyle, former employee of the Vatican nunciature in Washington and an early critic of the slow response dismissed these as 'Nonsense. Pope Benedict is a micro-manager. He's the old style. Anything like that would necessarily have been brought to his attention. Tell the Vicar General to find a better line. What he's trying to do, obviously, is protect the pope.'

This was far from being an isolated view. Meticulous attention to detail, as well as form, had always been the hallmark of Ratzinger the man. Bishop Kevin Dowling of Rustenburg commented in a talk in 2009 in Cape Town. 'The minutiae of Church life and prayer at the lower level are subject to authentification and examination [by Ratzinger] being given by the highest level.'

Not only was he copied in on the memo, but Huth tells us he chaired the meeting at which therapy was decided upon. Sexual abuse by a junior priest on his watch should have been of burning concern to someone who had been present during the whole-scale massacre of innocence in his own childhood. Why did he not identify with the raped children in the three Essen families and say, 'I want to know everything that happens to this priest and his victims. At all costs keep me informed'? Given the toxic nature of such crimes in the long term, and an awareness of the harm they cause to victims, he should have been haunted forever by what had happened to make sure it could never happen again.

The chorus of defence of the Pope over Easter 2010 led by Secretary of State Bertone, maintaining that Ratzinger did not know, that he was later assigned to Rome and that, when future allegations were made, he had been in the Vatican for years, was as weak as any defence put forward by a secular governments to cover scandal and corruption. In the United Kingdom we were by now only too aware of such whitewash and how its users operate.

The Vatican's defence predictably turned into accusations that the press was waging a campaign against the Pope, that the wave of attacks on the Church was like anti-Semitism, and that the Vatican was 'trying to turn the persecutors into victims', as an eminent rabbi noticed. Again, wasn't this all too reminiscent of German 'revision-ism' over the responsibility for Nazi crimes? And even, faintly, of the cries of the accused Nazi leaders during the Nuremburg Trials, who would always try to put the blame onto someone else in the chain of command, and, failing that, the Allied powers.

Now, as so many of these cases came to light at the same time Benedict was no longer on probation. But of what, exactly, could the Pope be personally held guilty or accountable? In his first years since his election in April 2005 he had trodden very carefully to give an impression that he was not the reactionary churchman that everyone expected. But, in his expressions of sorrow and regret, and his treatment of other explosive issues he said too little, using 'situational' excuses, suggesting the fault did not always lie with the guilty.

Those who vehemently supported him at first belonged to the right-wing, conservative axis of Bavarians and Italians whom he advanced during his reign. One of these, Walter Mixa, Bishop of Augsburg, blamed the scandals 'at least partly [on] the sexual revolutions of the 1960s', as had Bertone, a patently absurd assertion. Mixa ultimately was forced to resign, but Benedict registered displeasure at this.

He also complained at the treatment Cardinal Godfried Danneels of Belgium received when being suspected of being involved in a cover-up of sexual crimes committed earlier by the Bishop of Bruges. He publicly reprimanded a senior cardinal who accused a colleague of failing to act in another important case.

Mixa, himself, was being investigated by the *Suedeutsche Zeitung* for the allegedly brutal beating of inmates of both sexes, in Catholic institutions he visited, with carpet beaters, balled fists and sticks, in places where the bruising could be hidden. One victim, an Augsburg sales assistant, claimed she was struck at least ten times; five accusers officially notarised their statements.

In a further, related revelation, Benedict's brother Georg, often described as the only person the pope was close to, admitted repeatedly slapping the pupils in the Bavarian choir school he directed. 'I had a bad conscience about it,' he said in an interview. Before they hastily withdrew him from public view, lest he say the wrong thing and embarrass his brother further, the old monsignor, reputedly fond of a tipple, said, 'The problem of sexual abuse that has now come to light was never spoken of... Of course today one condemns such affairs.' A further phrase he used eerily echoed what Ratzinger had written about his family's reaction to the Nazi takeover of Germany in the 1930s: 'These things were never discussed.'

Ms Wankerl, aged 61, a pensioner in Bad Tölz, said in 2010 of the Father Hullermann case, 'If you get divorced and remarry you can't take holy communion, but someone convicted of molesting children can celebrate Mass for the rest of his life'.

† † †

Nietzsche once declared that the degree and kind of a person's sexuality had repercussions on the very apex of his or her spirituality. In their incontinent outbursts of confession and bickering in Nuremberg prior and during the 1945–46 trial, the German war criminals not only fluctuated in the ambivalent feelings they accused each other of, but Hans Frank, now caught and on trial, revealed at a very deep level how deeply his 'soul' had been 'seduced' in the years of his manhood.

'I quoted from Goethe's *Faust*, "*Zwei Seelen wohnen, ach! in meiner Brust*" ("Two souls dwell, alas, in my breast!")' he told Dr Gustav Gilbert, the US Army psychologist assigned to watch and investigate the prisoners.

He finished the quotation, and went off on the desired theme of split-personality in one of his expansive, introspective monologues:

'Yes, we do have evil in us – but do not forget that there is always a Mephistopheles who brings it out. He says, "Behold! The world is wide and full of temptation – behold! I will show you the world!" – There is just a little triviality of handing over your soul!'

He became more and more expansive, dramatising his speech with all the appropriate gestures, waving his arms to behold the world, and rubbing his fingers like a miser asking for the triviality of a soul in payment. 'And so it was. – Hitler was the devil. He seduced us all that way.'

He harped on the theme of surrender, seeing himself as paradymic:

'You know, the [German] people [*Volk*] are really feminine. – In its totality, it is female. One should not say *das Volk* [neuter], one should say *die Volk* [fem]. – It is so emotional, so fickle, so dependent, on mood and environment, so suggestible – it idolises virility so – that is it.'

'And it is so ready to obey?' [Gilbert interpolated].

'That, yes – but not merely obedience – surrender [*Hingabe*] – like a woman. You see? Isn't that amazing?' He burst into explosive laughter as though tickled by projection into a lewd joke. The identification was unmistakable. 'And that was the secret of Hitler's power. He stood up and pounded his body shape, he was the man!' – and he shouted about his strength and determination '– and so the public just surrendered to him with hysterical enthusiasm. – One must not say that Hitler violated the German people – he seduced them! They followed him with a mad jubilation, the like of which you have never seen in your life! It is unfortunate that you did not experience those feverish days, *Herr Doktor* – you would have a better conception of what happened to us. – It was a madness – a drunkenness.'

Here Frank would have been in full accord with Mann's *Doktor Faustus.*

In their bickering and recrimination the old North–South German antipathy (Prussia versus Bavaria) also surfaced again among the war criminals: with Arthur Seyss-Inquart Dr Gilbert questioned why Admiral Dönitz and Hermann Göring said Rudoph Höss, the commandant at Auschwitz, was a southern German, while a Prussian could never do what he had done. Gilbert mentioned the popular notion that Austrians and Bavarians were very similar people.

Seyss-Inquart launched into an interesting distinction:

Yes, as I told you, the southern German has the imagination and emotionality to subscribe to a fanatic ideology, but he is ordinarily inhibited from excesses by his natural humaneness. The Prussian, on the other hand, does not have the imagination to conceive in terms of the abstract racial and political theories, but if he is told to do something, he does it. When he has an order, he doesn't have to think. – That is the categorical imperative; orders are orders. In Höss you have an example of how Nazism combined the two. Hitler would never have gotten anywhere if he had remained in Bavaria, because while the people would have followed him fanatically they never would have gone to such excesses. But the system took over the Prussian tradition as well and amalgamated the southern emotional anti-Semitism with the Prussian thoughtless obedience. – Besides, the Catholic authoritarianism achieves the same effect as Prussian militarism – you need only look to the

Jesuits for an example of that. When fanatic ideology is combined with authoritarianism, there is no limit to the excesses it
can go to – just as in the Inquisition.

Frank made to Gilbert some interesting and prophetic statements
about 'old Europe', and how barbarism was a strong German
racial characteristic. He was terrified, he said, at the thought that
Hitler was only the first stage of a new type of human being in
evolution, which would end in destroying itself. 'Europe is finished,' was his verdict.

For Benedict it was the Catholic Church, smaller, leaner, more
committed to dogmatic faith, which was responding to the mass
hysteria and barbarous mass culture, to lead the purification to
a better world of very different values from the ones it had. At
that time Benedict said he did not read 'any secondary literature', for it was 'important to be in conversation only with the
greats... Perhaps the possibilities of our Western culture have
been exhausted,' he mused, 'as in the ancient world.' He saw 'a
violent change, with great losses...'

† † †

By March 2010 it seemed rather that it was the possibilities of his
papacy and himself that had been exhausted, as the revelations of
the further child abuse cases weakened his authority, and virtually destroyed his credibility. The case of Peter Hullermann was
the most glaring one directly connected to Ratzinger.

Bishop Mixa, the pope's Bavarian ally, after his blustering and
blundering efforts to excuse himself, resigned in April 2010, but
still maintained he was innocent. The Pope took strong measures to make sure these abuses would not happen again, and his
expressions of regret to the victims deepened: 'You have suffered
grievously and I am truly sorry. I know that nothing can undo
the wrong you have enduring' – but the timing was bad, and it
was too late to make an impression. The horse had already bolted
and it was on the late side to close the stable door.

At the very moment when the cover-up of abuse cases in
Ireland was first revealed he should at once have summoned the

Vatican jet, and flown to Dublin to talk to the victims, expressed his horror and sorrow, said he was sorry, and offered '*mea culpas*'.

Presidents and heads of state make a point of flying instantly to the scenes of natural disaster; he was a head of state, and on the spiritual plane the religious institutions where the victims had been abused were his territory. He could have at once made himself a witness to the abuse, and a penitent pilgrim.

He did, late in the day, meet victims in an orphanage when he made a trip to Malta in mid-April 2010. By then the harm was done, it was too little too late, and the world media had vented their anger and disappointment. 'I believe you've killed the Church, Holy Father' was one headline in the authoritative London *Sunday Times*: 'he carries on as if nothing has changed, as if nothing in these revelations about his life really matters', was the essence of many of these responses.

In Malta he had shed tears, he had talked of his 'shame and sorrow'. Joseph Magro, one of the victims, asked Benedict why his abusers had done such things to him. Benedict answered, 'I do not know... I do not know why they did this to you. It is too great a horror, too great a horror even for God.'

This once again was a response clouded by ambiguity, hardly very comforting although undoubtedly very sincere. What Benedict did not say was, one reason why the abusers had been able to do such things to their victims was that the abusers comfortably thought that it was not that uncommon in the Church, and, as his brother Georg said, before he was carefully removed from saying anything, 'We did not talk about such things.'

Moreover the abusers could be sure if found out to avoid criminal proceedings and punishment, and not lose their jobs. The reputation of the Church came first, and if the crime came out it had to be kept within Church jurisdiction as a 'pontifical secret'.

Benedict did not seem to acknowledge was that it was a culture of cover-up that worked both from top down, and from the base upwards. For many years it was complete. It was not as if the crisis had suddenly happened without warning, so the hierarchy could claim it was unprepared, or did not know the dangers. But now there were significant signs that from the beginning of

Benedict's papacy were not heeded even then, that from then on
it shouldn't have been allowed to go on.

The reporting of it, and the accompanying shocked and outraged
comment, was demonised by Vatican officials as a media conspiracy.

More and more it would seem apparent now that Benedict
had simply blanked on the whole issue, put to one side the difficulties of his past and his background, retreated away from them,
using his religion as safeguard and protection, which is what it
should never be.

But then, when the abuse was found out and revealed to the
world, the lawyer's observation at Nuremberg to the US army
psychiatrist on German ambivalence and for the abuse of power
generally, still sadly had some relevance, this time for the Catholic
Church, and in a very different context: 'To tell you the truth, they
think whatever you want them to think. If they know you are still
pro-Nazi, they say, "Isn't it a shame the way our conquerors are
taking revenge on our leaders! – Just wait!" If they know you are
disgusted with Nazism, the misery and destruction it brought to
Germany, they say, "It serves those dirty pigs right! Death is too
good for them!" You see, *Herr Doktor*, I am afraid that 12 years of
Hitlerism has destroyed the moral fibre of our people.' Surely that
influence of an august, proud, 'doublethink' culture, which on the
one hand wanted to please and excuse, on the other hand condemn
and win approval for being tough, needed to be eradicated for ever.

The Irish victims in particular criticised Benedict for hollow
affirmations of faith and belief instead of connection with their
suffering. Again what was missing was the heart, for it was the
head finding reasons, looking for excuses. One recalls Juno's emotional outburst in the atheist Sean O'Casey's play, *Juno and the
Paycock* at the horrors of the: Irish civil war: 'Sacred Heart o' Jesus,
take away your hearts o' stone, and give us hearts o' flesh! Take
away this murderin' hate, an' give us Thine own eternal love!'

The counter-attack of the Vatican apologists, those who analysed the causes, the Pope's dismissal of the 'petty gossip', excuses
from the time the crimes took place, historical causes (situ-
ationism), or the prevalence of changing and different mentality
(relativism) carried little weight in a world where even the young
or the ill-informed no longer respected authority, and could

straight away spot the hypocrisy of the Church's use of methods which it and its leaders were quick to attack in the secular world. The murder of innocence was an eternal crime or sin.

The *Catechism* made it clear, 'Sin is a personal act,' and cooperation or protection of sinners was also sinful. 'Thus sin makes men accomplices of one another and causes concupiscence, violence and injustice to reign among them..."Structures of sin" are the expression and effect of personal sins. They lead their victims to do evil in their turn. In an analogous sense they constitute a "social sin".'

How otherwise were we to view the most recent episodes, which continue into 2013 with two high-ranking American clerics being accused and questioned over cover-up, and the most senior UK priest Cardinal Keith O'Brien with his coruscating attacks on gay marriage at last, and when he could not longer escape , pleading guilty to sexual misdemeanour – after his massive denial. Unnoticed here was that the cardinal, just before accepting his red hat, had solemnly promised to obey Church teaching, but now, before news of his improper behaviour surfaced and he was preparing to go to Rome for the conclave, positioning himself to question the Benedict line on mandatory celibacy.

In May 2010 Cardinal Christopher Schönborn of Vienna told Austrian newspaper editors that Cardinal Angelo Sodano, dean of the College of Cardinals, 'deeply wronged the victims of sexual abuse when dismissing media reports of the scandal as "petty gossip"'. Schönborn also said the Roman Curia was 'urgently in need of reform', that lasting gay relationships deserved respect, and the Church needed to think again about its position on remarried divorcees. He told the editors that when Sodano was the previous pope's Secretary of State he blocked an inquiry into sexual abuse allegations against Cardinal Hans Hermann Groër, his predecessor, that were proven true, forcing him to step down in 1995. As Benedict was then Prefect he must have known the facts of the case.

The Pope wrote Schönborn a letter, then rebuked him in person, saying 'competency falls exclusively to the pope' to make accusations against a cardinal. Again it was a question of authority not truth, which was the issue, and to fulfil his own motto, 'Co-workers or co-operators in the truth' he would have had to dispense with the services of Sodano, who in 2010 also came under scrutiny for receiving large sums from Legionaries of Christ officials seeking to buy influence in Rome.

When we add to the above the Italian police's investigations into the property and financial dealings of the Archbishop of Naples, Cardinal Crescenzia Sepe, head of the Vatican Propaganda Fide 2001–2006, as part of a huge corruption investigation involving bribery and sexual favours, it now seemed that cardinals were at war, hurling allegations at one another when not actually being under investigation. Many warned of implosion within the Church's structure. One humourous solution suggested sending half of the Curia to man understaffed parishes. When asked many years before how many people worked in the Vatican, John XXIII quipped, 'About half'!

Benedict reshuffled his hierarchy and in these fraught times replaced three high-ranking diplomats with trusted theologians, and therefore incurred more criticism that he was on the retreat into his theological safe house.

Bishop Kieron Conry of Arundel and Brighton questioned Benedict's decision to set up a new 'Pontifical Council for New Evangelisation' to try and re-evangelise secular Europe. The Church, he stated, was declining quite radically, and had become 'simply irrelevant to many... It's authoritative. It's intolerant. It's demanding. It's exclusive.'

In January 2010, in Rome, Conry revealed, he had discussed the rise of Islam in Europe with the Pope, mentioning that in his part of England there were increasing numbers of Muslims wanting to get in to Catholic schools.

The Pope's only question was, 'Is there fundamentalism?' Conry replied, 'No. Muslims want the same as us: they want schools; they want housing; they want jobs.' The Pope just had not connected.

† † †

2010, Benedict's *annus terribilis*, brought out more than any other year of his pontificate the impression of a man trapped by his past. However much his intention was opposite to this Benedict projected the idea that the Church and its members were above all the fuss, somehow it was not his business, there was a higher purpose, the sight of which must not be lost. And why should he, as pope, be involved? His exact contemporary Küng was convinced that he had the answer, namely that the Pope was complicit in the whole cover-up.

'No one in the whole of the Catholic Church,' he said on Swiss television in April 2010, 'knows so much about abuse cases scandals in the Roman Catholic Church. The situation is largely, or in large part, that of his own making.'

Küng wrote an open letter to all Catholic bishops published in the *Irish Times* on 16 April 2010, holding the Pope responsible for the handling of the abuse cases leading to the leadership crisis and collapse of trust in Church leadership.

'There is no denying,' he wrote, 'that the worldwide system of covering up cases of sexual crimes committed by clerics was engineered by the Roman Congregation for the Doctrine of the Faith under Cardinal Ratzinger (1981–2005)'. Küng also accused the Pope of missing opportunities for rapprochement with the Protestant Church and with Jews, to hold dialogue with Muslims, to help the poor of Africa with birth control and to embrace modern science.

Küng's letter provoked a vehement, accusatory response from George Weigel, a leading right-wing theologian and ex-adviser of President Bush, who had supported Bush's Iraqi invasion as a just war, and even claimed earlier that John Paul II had voiced approval of the first Gulf War. His online response, published on 21 April, sought to exonerate (along the usual lines) Ratzinger, then cardinal, and now as pope, from all blame. He claimed he had himself had been critical of the way bishops handled abuse cases. He called Kung's attack 'a piece of vitriol...utterly unbecoming a priest', while there were only 'a small minority of abusers...the bishops took the promise of psychotherapy far more seriously than they ought, or lacked the moral courage to confront what had to be confronted'.

Again this unprecedented high drama caused by the 'Pope of Suprises', showed how personal the mudslinging had become in the highest theological circles. It is hard to understand why Weigel, a biographer of John Paul II, should be in denial about how the spiritual capital of the Church had been diminished since the death of John Paul. Latterly his praise for Benedict knew no bounds.

In March 2010 an opinion poll had revealed that a favourable view of Benedict in the USA had fallen from 63 per cent to 43 per cent while among Catholics those viewing him critically had doubled. His approval rating among Catholics had fallen to 63 per cent: John Paul's rating in 2005 was 93 per cent. These were mere statistics, but the main decline was in morale and spirit. 'If the leadership is unable to speak truth and deal with the fall-out they should have enough integrity to step aside,' was a commonly voiced feeling. But still there was the warning, 'Only God can fire a pope.'

In the previous year, on 17 July 2009, the English *Catholic Herald* had published figures from a poll conducted among British Christians, which indicated only 38 per cent agreed that 'Catholic popes are true representative of the Christian faith'. Significantly too, admiration for Benedict fell from just over two-thirds of respondents saying they admired John Paul II, 'greatly', or 'somewhat', to 47 per cent.

The arguments continued to rage to and fro. Specific Catholic admiration for Benedict in other polls that confirmed each other fell from 85 per cent who 'greatly' admired John Paul, to 65 per cent, while among Baptists the comparable figures were 24 per cent compared with almost half for John Paul.

This decline accelerated dramatically in the first five months of 2010. The German *Stern* Magazine in late March 2010 showed that trust in Pope Benedict fell from 62 per cent in late January to 39 per cent among German Catholics. 39 per cent now trusted the Catholic Church as a whole as opposed to 56 per cent in January. Since then the figures continued into further free fall. In Marktl am Inn hooligans defaced the wall of his birthplace with obscene and abusive graffiti.

Few, outside the Catholic community in Great Britain, which was divided in its view, but was at least polite, could hear his name without voicing anger or outrage. The fiasco when UK Whitehall officials in April 2010 suggested as their 'think-tank' or 'brainstorming' proposals that the Pope on his forthcoming September visit should open an abortion clinic, launch a range of Benedict condoms, and 'Bless a Gay Marriage' T-shirts, indicated a general contempt.

24

The Mimetic Double of Celestine V

On 4 July 2010 in Sulmona, an Abruzzan town near Rome hit by an earthquake in 2009, paradoxically also the birthplace of the erotic poet Ovid, the Pope celebrated an open-air Mass for the 800th anniversary of the birth of an obscure pope, Celestine V, who was a monastic hermit.

Gesturing towards the glass coffin of the embalmed saint's body, sweat running down his face in the stifling heat, he preached, 'Let us not be afraid to be silent... Celestine's simple and humble life-style can serve as an example for modern men and women.'

Pope Benedict, like most of his flock, is far from simple. With his red leather sentai suit, scarlet capes, red velvet caps trimmed with white fur, and voted 2009 'accessoriser of the year' by U.S. *Esquire Magazine,* by no stretch of the imagination can his life-style be called humble. Sometimes even the envied icon of gay Catholics whose sexuality he condemns as 'intrinsically evil', the passion he has for the ornate trappings of his office is, in the broader sense, hardly the mark of a celibate priest.

His close aide, Monsignor Gänswein, known for his handsome looks as the 'Adonis from the Black Forest', has said the Vatican is like 'living in a gilded cage'.

This second mysterious trip by a pope who rarely travels to honour an obscure saint has provoked speculation. Elected pope when eighty, Clement V resigned after a few weeks saying he was not up to the task – the only pope ever to do so. Could Benedict be thinking of following his example?

No doubt it will be the politeness, the openness, the intelligence, as described by Father Warnbrough, we shall see next week [when he comes to Great Britain].

I wrote this for an English newspaper in August 2010. I said he should resign. But what had Celestine V actually done, and did it relate to the present Pope?

Pope Celestine V was born Pietro Angelario in Sicily either in 1210 or 1215 (according to one of several sources used here), so he was elected pope either at the age of 79 or 84. He was ordained as a Benedictine in his teens but opted for the solitary existence of a hermit and lived in a cave for several years, near Sulmona in the wild Abruzzi. He retreated even further as a penitent and ascetic into the Maiella range and won renown for his miraculous healing powers and dedicated monasticism. He built a monastery to house his disciples who became known as Celestines, and escaped Episcopal intervention by travelling to Lyon in 1274 and convincing Pope Gregory X to grant him a solemn privilege of continuing in the Benedictine order. Charles I of Anjou later took his church under his protection, although Angelario gave up direction of the community he created to others.

The cardinals elected him pope in reaction to the faction-riven papacy in the hope he would become the 'angel Pope' who would usher in an 'age of the spirit'. He accepted, protesting loudly (Ratzinger followed the example here, although Angelario hadn't been in charge of the 'Congregation' as Cardinal Ratzinger had been – and at 78 still able to vote in the conclave.)

Rapidly he became a puppet or creature of the next Charles, known as Charles II, exercising corrupt papal power from Naples, rather than Rome and appointing the favourites of Charles to benefices (sometimes in his incompetence several to the same office). Once, while he went away to fast, he decreed three cardinals should rule in his place; he spoke no Latin and expanded his own congregation by taking over Monte Cassino.

Deeply tortured and unhappy at the deprivation of his tranquillity, and at his increasing physical weakness, he then passed a decree (after consultation with Cardinal Benedetto Caetani) allowing a pope to resign.

So, after only five months, from 5 July to 12 December 1294 he stepped down, becoming once more 'brother Pietro' and was replaced by – guess who? – Caetani who became Boniface VIII.

The new pope, fearing schism, would not allow him to retreat to the Abruzzi, and kept him under guard in Rome, from where he managed to escape to the woods for several months, then was recaptured and imprisoned in Castel Fumone, Ferentino in Campagna, where he eventually died from an infected abscess in 1296, and became canonised out of revenge by the next pope, Clement pursuing his vendetta against his predecessor Boniface on 15 May 1313 (exactly 700 years ago).

Dante, it is alleged, spotted without naming him Celestine V in an ante-chamber of Hell:

> *Poscia ch'io v'ebbi alcun riconosciuto,*
> *vidi e conobbi l'ombra di colui*
> *che fece per viltate il gran rifiuto*
> ('After I had recognised some amongst them, I saw and knew the shadow of him whom from cowardice made the great refusal.' Inferno, III, 58–60)

Dan Brown cites him as an example of a murdered pope in *Angels & Demons*, which was untrue – 'there is no proof he was treated with harshness', according to the *Oxford Dictionary of Popes*.

Was this a scenario to be followed by other popes? Pope Paul VI had visited Ferentino in 1966, for he, like Benedict, had contemplated retirement, while Benedict must have had the same idea in mind when he visited Sulmona again a little after the scandal broke on 4 July 2010, to mark the observance of what had been proclaimed the Celestine year 800 years after his birth. Benedict recorded in Latin in the *Martyrologium Romanum* the following tribute (19 May 2010) to the saint:

At Castrum Fumorense near Alatri in Lazio, the birth of Saint
Peter Celestine, who, when leading the life of a hermit in
Abruzzo, having become famous for his sanctity and his miracles, was elected *Pontifex Romanus* when eighty, taking the
name Celestine V, and abdicated from his office the same year
out of his preference to retire into solitude.

† † †

Given this identification with the former pope (and again hardly
calling attention to the real life of Celestine, his corruption
and incompetence) why did Benedict not step down in 2010?
Feeling, surely, some degree of guilt and responsibility, he clearly
must have thought very hard about doing this. What made him
feel he would be better at clearing up the mess than his successor? Did God order him to stay on?

He was trusting his own will, not God's, in making this decision, which, it would seem, had in it more than an element of
saving face, for wouldn't stepping down be an admission that he
was guilty? Yet why keeping himself in power should have been
described as it was, as an act of courage, I cannot understand,
especially as he now, which was very important to him, had a
precedent, had an enablement to step down.

Let us do what Fr Ronald Rolheiser does in one of his End
Columns in the *Catholic Herald*: play *What if*?

What if Pope Benedict had resigned in April or May 2010,
which was the opportune moment to do so?

What if …

1 his elected successor would have been completely outside any
   taint of scandal?
2 his successor had immediately put in place overdue reforms
   discussed at length and even by many churchmen agreed in
   Paul VI's papacy vis-à-vis contraception, married priests, and
   other issues (I am not taking sides here, but the form these
   took could have been worked out)?
3 his successor had cleaned up and decisively reorganised the
   Curia, devolving greater authority to local churches, and

decentralising the stifling and unpopular (outside the boundaries of the Vatican) power-orientated clerical class, who had become similar in their sense of self-entitlement to the political class in the UK and the Eurozone?

4 instead of expressing his sorrow and contrition eloquently and in beautifully cadenced and nuanced language, carefully avoiding direct and personal culpability, Benedict had actually stepped down? He had become, as John Allen put it, like the headmaster writing great essays in his room while all around him the school buildings were on fire. This one action would have had a much great effect than the humble, faltering utterances that ensued, the pious and weak photo shots, kissing of victims and so on.

The results would have been spectacular, for at a stroke the Catholic Church would have regained credibility, respect, and spiritual authority. More than this, it would have gained love from ordinary people, who would have agreed the Pope had done the right thing.

1 He would have avoided, as would happen from now on, an endless and acrimonious debate over guilt and blame, and why the Church has got itself into such disrepute (which as I write still goes on).

2 He would have cleaned up by removing himself from the murky, in-fighting half-lit followers and Vatican hierarchy intent on entitlement and self-advancement.

3 He would have gained greater authority for his brilliant theological expertise, instead of the vapid branding of 'by the pope'.

4   He would have genuinely embraced humility, from the point of view of his own avowed position (created by his intellect, not by his life example). In this context I cite some relevant lines of Yeats:

> The intellect of man is forced to choose,
> Perfection of the life, or of the work.

Which had he chosen? It was a terrible irony that the paedophile priest abuse crisis should surface so explosively during the Pope's 'Celestine year, 2009–10'. No one noticed the eerie coincidence.

† † †

Considering the early life of Benedict and his alleged behaviour as Bishop of Munich, and certainly his utterances confirming the closed nature of the Church in the matter of Father Peter Hullermann, it is not so surprising on balance that he decided to stay on, even given Celestine's example after only five months (and without undue scandal) to step down.

Shy people, John Powell, the American Jesuit writer, points out, 'have been taught that others will accept them only on certain conditions, their basic reaction to people is fear … their person and their worth are always on trial'. In Benedict's case the apparent shyness and retiring nature may have been a myth, mainly used as protection and the avoidance of unpleasantness. We have heard how he wove a spell as Archbishop of Munich. How also he has been called 'baroque' and 'unfathomable':

> As a thoroughly Bavarian man, Ratzinger himself finds no problem in bringing together things that his overly strict contemporaries regard as irreconcilable. He lacks, as he quite openly admits, 'the instinct for any kind of purism'. That, he says, comes from his having 'from childhood, read an atmosphere of the baroque'... In this respect, Ratzinger is not one of the really earthy and powerful representatives of his race, but one of those subtle and cryptic types, brilliant and perverse – men like Bert Brecht and Karl Valentin. Yet that does not mean that he detests company or that at any minute in a tavern would be torture for him. He's even familiar with the proverbial pugnacity of the Bavarians – at least in verbal form – and his passions to go far enough to employ a feint in conflict, and, then, secretly rejoice to have downed his opponent in elegant style. (Seewald, 2008)

Tougher measures to be taken by the Church were prescribed to deal with abuse, and overturned was the reluctance in the Church to report such crime to civil authority.

25

Is the Light Dark Enough?

A moment arrives when theory becomes a personal enemy.
Witold Gombrowicz

The combination of Benedict's introversion, his reserved personality, with the Vatican's secrecy and refusal to be accountable, cumulatively had, during 2010, produced a negative effect. He still seemed keen to use the 'weapon of destruction' he once referred to so disparagingly.

Back in Rome on 15 July he elevated the ordination of women to the same level as sexual abuse in 'new substantive norms' or 'delicts against the faith'. Again there was outcry against what was called as 'the shameful sexism which lies at the heart of Catholic doctrine' although to suggest that women had no moral capacity for spiritual leadership was not the point of the rule against woman being ordained – just that Jesus Christ and subsequent apostles had laid down that the priesthood was a closed order for men.

To deem female priests as 'sinful as child abuse' was a counterproductive measure. Much better, surely, to say the rule was the rule, and the Church was sticking to it, as all structures and hierarchies, from games to governments are obliged to stick to rules, such as, for instance, the off-side rule in football – also open to interpretation and much contested.

But why the new measure? It was completely unnecessary and only served to inflame and provoke opposition. Ordination of women was already forbidden in the Catholic Catechism. (Articles 1577, 1578, 1579): 'The college of bishops, with whom the priests are united in the priesthood, makes the college of the twelve an ever-present and ever-active reality until Christ's return. The Church recognises herself to be bound by this choice made by the Lord himself. For this reason the ordination of women is not possible.' Many rules can be called foolish, but this was the rule, and its restriction did not actually harm anyone. If the rule was changed this was perfectly feasible and should be followed too.

To emphasise this just as the Anglican Synod voted to consecrate female bishops, was a further proovocative measure, as it only (as shown by a photograph in *The Times* of the 'illicitly ordained' attractive singer Sinead O'Connor – no relation!) heightened the romance and popularity of such rebellion. In contrast to the radiant-looking O'Connor, the Pope in making these pronouncements appeared on BBC television to be suffering marked physical deterioration. His shoulders were round and hunched, his posture stooping. The face and features had taken on a dark foreboding and aggressive thrust. In sum he had the angry and ugly look of a leader at bay, as if making his last stand towards a hostile world.

What of his health and will to continue? Officials were now curtailing his daily schedule – 'He's very careful of his health,' said a visiting American priest. In 1991 he had had a minor stroke and took medication regularly for circulatory ailments. Some time later he had a pacemaker fitted so his pulse, as Hamlet says, would 'temperately keep time and make as healthful music'.

Like Hamlet, Benedict alluded to the heart problem in musical terms: 'Like [*sic*] in a concerto there have been a few discords in my heart; but now it is resolved.' Fr Daniel O'Connell, President of the Catholic University of America in Washington met him at this time and said he was 'harried', feeling the burden of the abuse cases deeply and personally. The pressures did not decrease. On 13 June 2010 the Pope described priests as gifts to the world on the very day five clergy in Italy, one aged 51, the other four in their sixties, were suspended after allegations of sex abuse.

The world could only wait to see what he would do next, having not stepped down. At the very Bavarian centre of the man, there was still the unresolved ambiguity beneath the dazzling 'Paradise Regained' of concepts. But it was not the whole story, and we should perhaps remember what Blake noted of

Milton: 'The reason Milton wrote in fetters perhaps when he wrote of Angels and God and at liberty when of Devils and Hell, is because he was a true Poet, and of the Devil's party without knowing it...'

Invoking the cliché of the iceberg, nine-tenths of Benedict remained hidden from sight: even more of a strained cliché, had the Catholic Church, with an iceberg as captain at the helm, hit the rocks? As the young Wojtyla wrote in his play *Jeremiah*:

> When the ship is sinking
> everyone counts and clings to his bundles,
> unmindful of the water that fills and sinks it.
> Fools! What will you do then with your bundles?
> When the ship is sinking, what is private?

Should he abandon ship, or go down with the vessel? Which was the better option, and if the first, when should this happen?

The first phase of what was clearly a conscious effort at restoring credibility and moral standing in the eyes of the world was the much praised and fêted visit to the United Kingdom in September 2010. In the *Catholic Herald* issue of April 30, with more accounts of abuse, notably with the headline and picture of Bishop Vangheluwe of Bruges confessing 'I abused a boy 25 years ago', the paper's leader proposed, ' There is one relatively simple way out of this minefield, and that is to make the Pope's visit a pastoral rather than a state one.' This was what John Paul's visit had been in 1982, and it would have meant the British taxpayer would not have had to foot the bill, reckoned at 10 million.

The Catholic, well-seasoned conciliator John Patten was called in to paper over the cracks and ensure that as a public demonstration of state hospitality and warmth nothing untoward happened. Benedict, no doubt, fired by adrenaline and every possible ambition and need to create a good impression, reached out at every level in his inimical urbane and polished way to make contact, and got as near as he ever got to being a populist pope. Temperamentally he felt affinity with the traditional British spirit, its essentially Anglo-Saxon and Norman institutions, and its understated love and celebration of ritual and hierarchy.

The desire to court popularity had taken a slightly absurd form earlier in 2010 when, at the papal weekly audience in the Vatican Paul VI Hall, a pyramid of acrobatic male bodies towered over Pope Benedict XVI's slight presence on the stage. A ten-man troupe from Italy's American circus performed and shared his limelight, and then brought him a lion cub to pat. John Paul II, his heroic predecessor, may have been a great actor, but this was theatre of the absurd. You might be forgiven for thinking you were at a Tom Stoppard play.

On John Paul's 1982 visit to Britain, Paisleyite hardliners along his papal route had displayed placards with the words, 'Anyone blessed by the pope will go straight to hell,' John Paul had promptly made the sign of the Cross and blessed them.

'Lord, will Poland regain her independence some day?' he once asked God, before Poland did so. 'Yes,' said God, 'but not in your lifetime.' Then he asked, 'Lord, after I'm gone, will there be another Polish pope?' 'Not in my lifetime,' said God.

Although Benedict never rose to make a self-deprecating joke about a German pope, he again showed his capacity to surprise, and completely overturned gloomy expectations from the moment of his arrival in the United Kingdom. He came here as leader of the Vatican state, and before his arrival all three party leaders expressed disagreement with some aspects of his Church's teaching. He flew first to Scotland, celebrating Mass in Bellahouston Park, Glasgow, then to London where he made an address in Westminster Hall to invited guests in the place where St Thomas More was condemned for high treason in 1535, and subsequently died a martyr's death, refusing to put service to the king of England before service to God.

The anomaly, underlining the ambiguity more than evident in this pope's rule was the highlight of the visit: his beatification of the former Anglican Cardinal John Henry Newman in Birmingham on the final day of his visit. This was a particular plus for British Catholics, given Newman's influence and his greatness as a Catholic writer and apologist. Yet at a personal level it provoked fierce controversy, led by Peter Tatchell, the gay rights campaigner, as it was clear to scholars and biographers of Newman that the latter had had a long-term mental and spiritual love relationship with his friend Father Ambrose St John, the priest with whom he lived for over 30 years, and about whom he said, 'from the first he loved me with an intensity of love, which was unaccountable...[and that] I was his first and last.'

This suggested that the same sex love, although generally held to be platonic, was both very deep and long-lasting, and deserving of respect. Again we have here both a paradox, and also clearly an ambiguity in Benedict's own love and respect for Newman, hailed by James Joyce as the greatest prose stylist of the Victorian age, and the most eminent Christian thinker of recent times. It sat uneasily alongside the Pope's previous public utterances on homosexuality and indeed his own same-sex friendships. A gay orientation can be as happily rich and if not physically expressed as perfectly well sublimated as a heterosexual one; Matthew says, 'Judge not, that ye be not judged', but it is not my intention to take sides on this issue, apart from noting that it has a relevance to this portrait.

Newman and St John were buried side-by-side in the same grave in 1890 when Newman died, while in 2009, before the beatification, the Vatican requested that this grave should be dug up to separate the two men, and use Newman's bones as holy relics, and also presumably to separate the two men's remains. This proved impossible, as these had fully decomposed, but it is an eerie echo (in reverse?) of Ratzinger dealing with his parents' graves in Pentling.

There was a personal agenda in Benedict's devout attention to Newman: a deep homage to his thought and writings, and a sense of the affinity he shared with him. Perhaps, as with Celestine, this may have been a primary reason for the British visit, for Benedict's ambition still remained that of the academic and writer. If so, then it could hardly be said that he was here on a state visit, but more as universal religious thinker and teacher on a private act of homage.

Legally, if Mussolini had not made the Vatican an independent state in 1929 in return for the scandalous Concordat the Roman Church signed, there would have been no question of it being other than a pastoral visit. It is surely this rather bizarre temporal power the Catholic Church still held which was in large part responsible for the leadership crisis and collapse of trust. The irony is that it should have conferred legal protection on

Benedict as a head of state, over actions over the abuse cases brought against him in the US courts.

† † †

The wily Ratzinger side was patently evident in the next public action or defence he undertook of his position, and of his inner self (granted to the world as the privilege of allowing them to share the private views and thoughts of the pontiff). This was the six-hour interview he gave in October 2010, which rapidly emerged in print and onto the bestseller list under his own authorship as *Light of the World*.

One cannot but admire his skill, his connected thought, the coherence of his replies. Clearly he was making a fight-back against all the adverse comment and attack of the past few months, and we could call it as near to a personal confession as we would ever get, and therefore not surprisingly this old contested issue of speaking as a private persona, as opposed to speaking as an infallible pope, quickly came into prominence and gained wide publicity.

He asserted the old axiom of the Catholic Church, first formulated by St Augustine, 'It goes without saying that the Pope can have private opinions that are wrong.' But when he spoke as supreme pastor 'then he no longer says something that is personally his, whatever happens to him... Then conscious of the Lord's protection he knows that he is not misleading the Church...'

But then, one might ask, 'Who is it, exactly, who has decided to be pope, to step or not to step down: is it the private person, or the infallible pope?

This was the difficulty, and the ambiguity of 'human person' divided from pope that Benedict so perfectly exemplified. To be more clear, was it the private person who was beyond his control who became pope, and remained pope? If he was a private person, and not acting with, and as, the will of God, surely he should have now seen his duty was to step down?

Celestine, it cannot have escaped Benedict, stood down as pope as a private person, in accordance with his personal conscience, not as an infallible pope.

In his answer to this and many other issues in the interview the same ambiguity of thought pervaded that we have noted before. For instance, when he talked of the victims of abuse and how it was difficult for them to believe the Church was a source of light, he said, 'I can understand that.'

But then he left this and spoke about others 'that have these negative precepts, and 'can no longer see the overall picture'. At that moment of extreme crisis there was no overall picture. It was the theologian moving into his comfort zone. He argued that 'the Church must strive to make this vitality and greatness visible again, despite all that is negative'.

Here he would seem to confuse or sow confusion, or split hairs, as to whether it was the way people looked at the Church that was negative, or the Church itself. He didn't start from, and hold on to, the basic premise that it was the Church itself which had been negative and negligent. He further, and completely unnecessarily, said the abuse was not something specific to the Catholic priesthood or the Catholic Church, 'but unfortunately rooted in man's sinful situation'. He then emphasised as he had so many times, all the good the Church did.

Surely, it was not for him to either make the Church assume the mantle of victimhood, or to excuse itself. (Jimmy Savile raised millions for charity, but that did not excuse him; nor that Hitler built autobahns and sponsored the Volkswagen.)

So as well as regret, still evident throughout was the familiar instinct to whitewash, to paper over the cracks, quoting statistics to show how small a percentage priests who abuse actually were of the total (while of course decrying other 'false' statistics to show how many might have been saved from AIDS-related deaths if they had used condoms).

Then he gave himself the carefully prepared exit strategy, after his visit to Sulmona, again couched in an elaborate wrapping of humility: 'If a pope realises that he is not longer physically, psychologically, and spiritually capable of handling the duties of his office, then he has a right, and under some circumstances and obligation, to resign.'

Here he was saying quite a number of things, one among which was that he saw he had no obligation to resign at that moment (which would have been wise). That it had crossed his mind to resign was also implicit here, but he was not going to (as many said he should), because he still thought he was better equipped and still more able to lead the Church than anyone else.

So now the counter-offence in his favour championed the idea that far from being brave and courageous in stepping down (and accepting responsibility as other leaders could and did, such as Harold Macmillan over the Christine Keeler scandal in 1963, and Lord Carrington over the unpreparedness of the UK to meet the Falklands invasion in 1982), he was not fleeing for fear of the wolves (these being the world press) who were trying to 'force' his resignation.

He 'held firm', or rather clung on, implementing sensible and firm measures to stop the abuse ever happening again, showing in public a not very convincing face of contrition for the Church's sins. Whether he did or did not know was now longer relevant. He was not setting a good example to follow.

BBC Radio 4 asked him to broadcast a 'Thought for the Day' on Christmas Eve, 2012. This time he reversed high expectations, delivering a polite message, 'recalling with great fondness my four-day visit... I am glad to have the opportunity to greet you once again', that was altogether flat and humdrum, full of sermon phrases. 2010 was a very bad year for the Pope and the Church, and he must have grown very tired by the end of it, and not felt he had much to say.

26

The Interpretation of the Time

So our virtues
Lie in the interpretation of the time:
And power, unto itself most commendable,
Hath not a tomb so evident as a chair
To extol what it hath done.
One fire drives out one fire; one nail, one nail;
Rights by rights falter, strengths by strengths do fail.
William Shakespeare, *Coriolanus*, IV, vii.

In Shakespeare's plays the self-destruction of authority in all its forms is fundamentally exposed: he shows power teetering on the edge of its own collapse, and most of the leaders he depicts, as he is a dramatist, have a fatal taste for self-dramatisation.

Light of the World marked the next phase of Benedict's self-rehabilitation and the doctoring of his self-image.

There is no record of a joke about what God might have said about a German pope. Many thought Benedict XVI was a pope without humour, although he has quite frequently told us what God has told him to do, as if this empowered him. Did God need conscious attention from believers in the way leaders do all the time from their voters? The ordinary consciousness of most people on this planet, for most of the time, was for the greater part agnostic. Many people could function and live with honesty, warmth, generosity, goodness, intelligence, and humour, and be altogether life-giving and immersed in this life and everything it brought, without any necessity of having God at the centre of their being.

To rant, rail, to point out deficiencies in their material concerns, was not the way to engage or convert them to taking seriously the workings of the Holy Spirit. A further concession, or cause for worldwide attention, in the Seewald interview over the use of condoms begged the question was this a genuine change of heart, or just a ploy to save face in view of the hostility:

> People can buy condoms if they want them anyway... the secular realm itself has developed the so-called ABC Theory: Abstinence – Be – Faithful – Condom where the condom is understood only as a last resort... the fight against the banalization of sexuality is also a part of the struggle to see that sexuality is treated as a positive value...

This was part of the rambling lead-up to, again, the much-quoted:

> There may be a basis in the case of some individuals, as perhaps when a male prostitute uses a condom, where this can be the first step in the direction of a moralisation, a first assumption of responsibility, on the way toward recovering an awareness that not everything is allowed and that one cannot do whatever one wants. But it s not really the way to deal with HIV infection. That can really lie only in a humanisation of sexuality. (Benedict XVI, 2010)

The next question asked was: 'Are you saying that the Catholic Church is actually not opposed in principle to the use of condoms?'

Benedict's answer was, 'She of course does not regard it as a real or moral solution, but, in this or that case, there can be nonetheless, in the intention of reducing the risk of infection, a first step in a movement toward a different way, a more human way, of living sexually.'

Did this signify, as the *Daily Telegraph* wondered, the end of the absolute ban on contraception, or as others grew wild with excitement in exclaiming, 'Pope endorses condoms for gays.' This situational change was highly welcomed everywhere, but what did it tell us about Benedict, except that he had once adamantly refused to believe condoms saved lives (and similarly woman having too many babies they couldn't support), and now, given the Church's unpopularity, here was a climb-down. Wasn't this an example of the relativism he so often condemned, and if not, what was it?

Even authorisation in certain circumstances, and in gay sex to avoid the spread of AIDS, did little to heighten the ratings. Yet the Courtyard of the Gentiles, as it was known, was one positive initiative undertaken, specifically to encourage dialogue between believers and non-believers, a measure inconceivable earlier on in the papacy. This was led by Cardinal Gianfranco Ravasi, President of the Pontifical Council for Culture, launched in Paris in early 2011 to grant 'symbolic status to the French Enlightenment' – hitherto much frowned on in Catholic thought.

The thaw or broadening of perspective was genuine, suggesting that the shock of the abuse scandal was at last reversing, or freeing Benedict, from that previous trauma which had triggered a reactionary response in Tübingen, and that a new side of him was emerging, one of atonement and an increased and deep-felt humility. Truly he could embody better the notion that 'God gives us authority in giving it away' and the great importance, as Canon John Udris, spiritual director of the Oscott Seminary, Birmingham, which the Pope visited in 2012, applauded: 'listening to the other in the otherness of their thinking'.

Significantly in these last years, there were no gaffes which had been so visible in the first years. Kissing the casket of John Paul II provided a genuine opportunity to identify Benedict with the previous pope, while fast-tracking his beatification on 1 May 2011 brought out a crowd of over a million in St Peter's Square.

Why he should want to speak to eleven astronauts aboard an International Space Station was puzzling, except that someone clearly thought it would be a good idea for him to do so, and show he could push buttons and was on the side of scientific progress. In August of the same year he hosted another packed World Youth Day in Madrid, but here the headlines were grabbed more during his visit by rioters starting fires to protest again the impoverished Spanish Government spending money on his visit.

Late 2011 saw age beginning to take more of its toll. Arthritis in his knee joints was now affecting him to the degree that he took to using the mobile platform to progress down the aisle of St Peter's. Early in 2012 he started using a cane to walk in public and to those who attended the public audiences he looked very frail.

On 12 December 2012 he began personal Twittering @ Pontifex, sending out his first message, and immediately engaged three million followers from 14 posts in different languages. This could be characterised as the expense of spirit not so much in a waste of shame as triviality. What could he say of any significance in 140 characters? The 'predictable lacking in substance', commented Bishop Conry, which put it in perspective. It was a gesture in vain by a great intellect to engage the media, taking a few very little steps to engage the spirit of the age.

The last years gave the impression of a pontificate gradually grinding to a halt in effectiveness, not without its quota of good works and thoughtful reforms in liturgy, and other areas of the Church, but nothing sweeping, striking and in depth in the way of restoring Church morale and confidence in the hierarchy. The last years were fragmenting into small plans and insignificant gestures. On the other hand, as if successful layers of the onion had been peeled away, it showed at core, the centre of being, that final side of Benedict by which he will probably be most remembered.

27

The Greatest Drama
of the Pontificate

Reality is designed in such a way that even the improbable is essentially possible. The first swallow from the cup of the natural sciences makes atheists – but at the bottom of the cup God is waiting.

Werner Heisenberg, Nobel Prize-winning nuclear physicist

So this was by no means the whole story, and we can't leave it there. Benedict had, when Archbishop of Munich for a short spell, impressed one priest in particular. His former Vicar-General, Fr Gerhart Gruber, attested to his modesty and warmth, and how his first and last words 'concerned the peace of Christ, and it would seem that this will also be the main theme of his pontificate'.

This was true. He explained constantly his relationship with Jesus had always been in the nature of an encounter, a love story, but essentially of a different kind from that of John Paul II. John Paul's had been centred on the figure of the Virgin Mary in a very Polish way, mystically, mythically, and miraculously, and was deepened by his early loss of his mother.

That of Benedict was centred firmly, more exclusively, on Jesus, with whom he identified closely. In his spare moments, and in the spirit of free theological enquiry Ratzinger had set out before he became pope, and not stopped in his mission to render the figure of Jesus, 'based on my personal research into the face of the Lord'.

This book has from the start been a quest or search to find and connect with the inner man, to discover for myself and for my readers what made this extraordinary man tick. Some may object (and some of my family have) that you should never separate the pope as the head of the Catholic Church from the man who embodies the Church and fulfils the office of running it by imprinting on this his own decisions and personality. But there were two distinct figures in, or sides to, this one man, possibly sometimes in a surreal way, as if in a Salvador Dali portrait. Often they had not been entirely consistent with one another. They didn't, or haven't exactly held together.

Joachim Navarro-Valls, the former Madrid Professor of Psychiatry, who was John Paul's press secretary, summed up in an interview he gave me the papal colossus he served for 27 years as follows: '*Tout se tient*' – 'Everything holds together.'

Not less true was the definition he made of his successor: 'There are many ways of communicating,' began Navarro-Valls on this subject, 'There is not just one way.'

So what about Benedict's method of communicating? Navarro-Valls answered with just one word – 'Concepts!'

† † †

Philosophy distinguishes broadly two main methods of reasoning; the first is *a priori* or deductive, which starts from a general premise or theory, forms a hypothesis, and then moves on to observe and find examples, which prove or illustrate its truth; the second is *a posteriori* or inductive reasoning, when the mind is led from particular instances, or observation, towards a pattern, then a tentative hypothesis from which is formed a general theory.

Benedict's reasoning followed the second path. Not only did it do this, but as a theologian he had begun long before and continued even though he was pope, that most difficult of biographical challenges – to write at the present time, using an inductive method, a life of Jesus Christ. Some theologians claimed this approach bordered on heresy.

'The greatest drama of the pontificate – greater than the drama of relations with secular humanism or Islam, greater even than the drama of the scandals of the Church – is the drama occurring within Pope Benedict himself', wrote Dr Robert Moynihan in *Inside the Vatican*. In such terms it was presented, this was the build-up.

It should have been this first volume of his *Jesus of Nazareth* (Bloomsbury, 2007) fulfilling this long-cherished aim, which could have told us a great deal more about the remoteness of Ratzinger, the man, as well as his nearness to his subject. He was at pains to make it clear that *Jesus of Nazareth* was a private book, gestated over a long period, and as yet incomplete. It was written, he made it clear, not in his capacity as Pope Benedict, but as Joseph Ratzinger, and the idea was to show, through his encounter with his subject at many levels, that the greatest drama of his pontificate was the drama which had been, and was perhaps even still, taking place inside Ratzinger himself. But even here there was ambiguity, as both the Pope's name and that of Ratzinger appeared boldly on the jacket, one above the other, and on the title page.

Ratzinger thought he stood up to pronounce simply and nakedly, not as pope, but rather like St Francis in his defining moment of taking Lady Poverty as his bride, that he was publishing a work of a private nature which was itself a *proposal* –and here was the defining word, and sign of his humility – that the historical Jesus was the same as the Jesus of faith. What he wrote in his preface shows how seriously he took his position as pope, showing how far he was prepared to step down from his entitlement: 'This work is not an absolute act of magisterial teaching, but merely an expression of my personal research into the face of the Lord. Therefore everyone is free to contradict me!'

He stated that as a biographer he was setting out to answer the question, the central question, that Jesus put to his disciples, 'Who do men say that I am?'

The critic Desmond McCarthy once said, in a memorable image, that trying to work out William Shakespeare's personality was like looking at a very dark picture under glass. 'At first you see nothing, then you begin to recognise features and then you recognise them as your own.'

Writing about the Jesus of flesh and blood was similar in some ways to writing about Shakespeare the man, with the obvious difference that Shakespeare was a prolific playwright who hid himself very successfully in his plays, while Jesus wrote down nothing.

In ten chapters Ratzinger covered Jesus's career from his baptism to Peter's confession and the Transfiguration. Mainly the text consisted of lengthy meditations of a largely personal nature on parables, the Lord's Prayer, the Sermon on the Mount, the Gospel of the Kingdom. These, the reader is constrained constantly to believe, at the same time while unrelated to academic research or historical criticism, came from true and correct understanding, and that we must trust Ratzinger's traditional convictions. He made little or no reference to texts which went against his theological answers.

Did the other side of his *proposal* stand? That the Gospels were not fables was hardly new, but that they were historical documents which in each case had very different contexts and driving forces?

In spite of the bold assertions my perception was that the reader encounters not so much the Jesus of flesh and blood, but the spiritual Jesus of the Gospels and of subsequent commentators and theologians. No one could deny the force and fluency of these meditations, yet his reiterated papal claim, which gained credibility from the fact that he was pope and not exactly writing just as Ratzinger the theologian, was that 'the divine Christ of faith', i.e. the product of Ratzinger's musings and meditation – and the historical Jesus, the Galilean itinerant, healer, exorcist and preacher – were one and the same. So what should have come into play here? Successful suspension of disbelief, or confirmation of traditional Catholic thinking?

The Pope was fiercely challenged by one critic, the Oxford biblical scholar Geza Vermes. I was pointed in Vermes' direction by Fr Peter Hackett SJ, a former editor of *The Month*. Vermes found it disturbing that Ratzinger made no reference to texts that in some way contradicted his cherished beliefs. Vermes failed to find the authentic Jesus in the book, and declared Ratzinger's appeal to 'canonical exegesis' groundless. His exercise in biblical theology, 'whereby any text from the Old or New Testament can serve to explain any other biblical text' was an approach to biblical studies that would 'force back Catholic Bible experts, already the objects of frequent papal disapproval in *Jesus of Nazareth*, to a pre-Copernican stage of history.' This may be harsh, but it confirmed that Ratzinger's approach was very personal.

† † †

If *Jesus of Nazareth* was written, as Ratzinger said, not as Milton wrote *Paradise Lost* to 'justify the ways of God to man' – a patriarchal, deductive endeavour – but as the opposite inductive search of Jesus ('Who do men say I am?), then his main task was revealed as not really biographical at all! Instead he wanted to *show* how Jesus Christ brought God into the world, to bring to man the truth about his origin and destiny. As he eschewed historical fact and investigations, he fell rather short of this, and ended up like St Paul more an advocate of Jesus' truth – telling us who he was, rather than showing it.

Even so, using his inductive method of reasoning, he did demonstrate a quite extraordinary range of intellectual understanding of the subject of Christology and his wide exhaustive research, often illuminating, sometimes of a dogmatic, unappealing kind. Yet where was the drama of the life? It should have been, if he followed his own description in this respect, in every way also a flesh-and- blood encounter. The drama could have been that he was showing in answering that question about Jesus, that he was at the same time attempting to answer the same question of himself: 'Who am I?'

As he was revealing for the reader the life of Jesus, in his actions and in his parables, so also could he be revealing his own innermost feelings about life, family, brothers, followers, what his likes and dislikes were? But unfortunately, even tragically, he did not do this. (Likewise he could have written a much clearer, more illuminating memoir of his life as Prefect, but writing *Milestones* in 1999 he stopped short at 1977).

The method he adopted in his intellectual 'verifying' of Jesus of Nazareth began with a subtle and commanding concept – 'Only if something extraordinary happened, if the figure and words of

Jesus radically exceeded all the hopes and expectations of his age, can his crucifixion and effectiveness be explained.'

This was moving. Yet it began and ended as only concept. It didn't go on to command, affect, move or have much mimetic power. Where were the doubts, the temptations, the falterings of faith, the conflicts, the true flesh and blood Jesus? Perhaps only justice could be done to these, better than we find in the synoptic Gospels, in fiction or faction. We must turn to Nikos Kazantzakis's *The Last Temptation,* or *He Who Must Die* for a vividly realised flesh and blood figure, in which the writer's primitive earth and blood imagination catches fire and captures us in a visceral way. A very different, wonderfully balanced 'faction' of Jesus, grounded in biblical scholarship and applying consummate dramatic skill is *The Man Born to be King*, Dorothy Sayers' 1940s sequence of twelve radio plays.

In attempting to show the historical Jesus was the same as the Jesus of faith, and that the gospels were not fables, Ratzinger threw us back on Goethe's expression of man's dual nature, and possibly his own sidestepping of his own. In this first volume the face of the Lord that dimly emerges from the opaque mystery of Galilean times, and citations of biblical authority came to resemble, in its haphazard mixture of life and doctrine, that of the theologian Ratzinger. He was, like the Shakespearian biographer, looking into a mirror, valiantly seeking the face of the Lord, but in the end finding his own. This is often the fate, I have to add, of biographers.

† † †

If he wrote much of the first volume before he became pope, Benedict brought out the second volume: *Holy Week from the Entrance into Jerusalem to the Resurrection*, in early 2011. The date of the foreword, 25 April 2010, is when he was in the thick of child abuse scandal, and when his own reputation and that of the Church was at its lowest ebb. The foreword dealt with some criticism of the first volume again and encouragement he received from the praise, with that constant ambivalence of thought and ambiguity of statement which was now a settled habit. He disclaimed ever having set out to write a 'Life of Jesus', saying that a

Catholic theologian has labelled his book 'together with Romano Guardini's masterpiece, *The Lord*, as an example of "Christology from above", not without issuing a warning a danger inherent in that approach'. While being pleased to have his work coupled with a masterpiece, in restating his intentions, expressed with characteristic modesty, he does again say he has set out 'to discover the real Jesus', hedging his comments to the extent that he loses in this foreword most average readers like myself.

What, for example, does he mean exactly by the following: 'The quest for the "historical Jesus" as conducted in mainstream critical exegesis in accordance with its hermeneutical presupposition, lacks sufficient content to exert any significant historical impact. It is focused too much on the past for it to make possible a personal relationship with Jesus.'?

Some of that personal relationship does exert an impact in presenting what he calls 'the figure and the message of Jesus' (what is that but part of 'a life of Jesus'?) when he writes about Jesus who before the Sanhedrin said he was the Son of Man:

> There now erupts over Jesus, who had prophesied his coming in glory, the brutal mockery of those who know they are in a position of strength: they make him feel their power, their utter contempt. He whom they had feared only days before was now in their hands. The cowardly conformity of weak souls feels strong in attacking him who now seems utterly powerless.

Clearly he identifies strongly here with Jesus, perhaps conscious of his own plight at the Vatican, and what greater glory or mockery might accrue from it.

The next sentence is pure biographical speculation: 'It does not occur to them that by mocking and striking Jesus, they are causing the destiny of the Suffering Servant to be literally fulfilled in him.' Nothing wrong of course in that, except that Ratzinger thought and claimed he wasn't doing that.

The central tenet of Catholic and Christian faith is belief in the truth of the resurrection of Jesus. Joseph Ratzinger, Benedict XVI as he signed the foreword, creates in his lengthy coverage a hypnotic spell over the reader, a mixture of theological reference, speculation and detail: consider this, for instance when the resurrected figure of Jesus stood on the beach at Gennesaret. Peter recognises him:

> It is, as it were, an inward recognition, which nevertheless remains shrouded in mystery. For after the catch of fish, when Jesus invited them to eat, there is still a strange quality about him...This dialectic of recognition and non-recognition corresponds to the manner of the apparitions. Jesus comes through a closed door; he suddenly stands in their midst. And in the same way he suddenly withdraws again, as at the end of the Emmaus encounter. His presence is entirely physical, yet he is not bound by physical laws, but the laws of space and time. In this remarkable dialectic of identity and otherness, of real physicality and freedom from the constraints of the body, we see the special mysterious nature of the risen Lord's new existence. (Benedict, 2011)

Here I have to confess that while the flow of understanding, justification or proof of truth, biblical quotation used as factual evidence, carries me along in a strange, hypnotic and enjoyable rhythm, I remain completely mystified. Except that it does say to me, 'Yes, this is him, distinctly him, Joseph Ratzinger, Benedict XV – as the saying goes, '*Le style, c'est l'homme même.*'

Vermes, in keeping with his response to Volume 1, felt the tone of this longer, more complicated book remained unchanged, and it continued as an 'extended sermon', shying away from an awareness of problematic issues. One of these was the concatenation of events: the arrest, trial and sentencing to death of Jesus occur all on the same day, that of the Passover Festival, to which the first three Gospels (Mark, Matthew and Luke) add Jesus's Passover meal, the Last Supper. Dramatic though it was, this timetable could not be historically accurate.

Benedict followed John's Gospel in ante-dating the trial twenty-four hours. But then, claimed Vermes, he wanted to have it both ways. He took the liberty of transferring the synoptic details missing from John's Gospel, including the Jewish trial, to the day before Passover. 'It clashes with the reference that Jesus and his party had sung the halleluiah psalms, 'the hymn' concluding the Passover dinner before they departed to Gethsemane.'

Sayers was much more forthright. She explained that in her play she disregarded John's chronology and assumed that the Last Supper was the Passover. 'I have supposed that the actual cooking was done in the courtyard by the women, and that the Disciples, as they passed through, brought up the dishes as they were ready.'

She then detailed the order of the Passover:

> The first cup of wine; the bitter herbs (eaten with sauce); the unleavened bread; the second cup – at which point the eldest son has to ask the head of the household the ritual questions: 'What mean you by this service?'... The Institution fits very well into this frame with the explanation, 'This is my blood of the New Covenant' taking the place of the usual ritual answer, and suggesting, by association with that answer, the 'sacrificial' nature of the Eucharist, without the use of the controversial word. (Sayers, 1943)

The hypnotic spell of his ingredients apart, the harder problem for the Pope was justifying the truth of the resurrection testimonies to the bible scholar. Again Vermes found the vaunted historical-critical approach fell rather flat when Benedict simply asserted it was 'a historical event that bursts open the dimensions of history and transcends it... the last and highest evolutionary leap' (by whom and where?) This somewhat confirms Peter Ackroyd's simple assertion at a lecture I once attended that 'biography is a convenient fiction'.

'The evidence, he said, was twofold: confessional (the apostles and Paul profess that Jesus was resurrected) and narrative (the reports of the empty tomb and apparitions). The confessional traditions were certain, whereas the narrative (on which I would suggest, the confessions rely) is "not binding in every detail". In scholarly language this means that the records do not tally and are sometimes irreconcilable.' (Vermes)

Sayers' approach in the notes to her twelfth play was more down-to-earth: she goes convincingly into the mechanics of the resurrection, saying it was unnecessary to have any fixed ideas. 'The operative elements in the problem are (1) the open sepulchre, (2) the undisturbed grave-clothes.' Her examination of all this, fascinating though it is, is too long to print, but she dealt in her no-nonsense attitude so eloquently and realistically with the reactions of the disciples and the women – the dejection and depression of the men, the practical measures taken by the women – that you feel she was more on the wavelength of Jesus and the original Gospels, than Benedict who, a theological bird of prey, hovered above his subject, then pounced and created through, in, and around it a wonderful complex palace of baroque, romantic mystery.

She was deeply concerned to present the resurrection (and by extension the whole synoptic coverage of the nine supernatural appearances) 'without suggesting either Surrey melodrama or the more lily-livered kind of Easter card'. She pointed out the narrative 'contains a good deal about doors, and knocking at doors. It is, in fact, a play about the door between two worlds.'

Sayers brought the whole event alive, while Benedict did something very different, wielding a mixture of gilded, scholarly disciplines some of which were at odds – those of theological musing and inexact detail, and the rigorous interpretation or questioning of facts.

† † †

The Pope showed much greater skill in his much shorter *Paul of Tarsus*, published in 2009. He passed in half a sentence over Paul's persecution of Christians, and his anti-Christian attitude. Whether he personally tortured Christians and felt they, as godless inferiors, were to be exterminated, was a point he didn't address.

Paul confesses, in *The Letter to the Galatians* (1. 13–14) that having studied with a rabbi in Jerusalem he violently persecuted the Church of God and tried to destroy it. In *The Acts of the Apostles*, (7. 57–8 and 9. 1–2) we learn he set out to arrest Christians in Damascus and bring them back to Jerusalem, have them thrown into prison, and get them to blaspheme the name of YHWH. He had also been highly visible at the trial of Stephen, the first recorded Christian martyr, where he watched over the robes of those who were stoning Stephen.

Paul's true life began, Ratzinger maintained, with his conversion on the road to Damascus, when he met and experienced the risen Christ. There is only this one confession in all Paul's letters, and no regret such as John Paul made for the 'sins of the Catholic Church', for his earlier misdeeds and association with what were presumably gangs who murdered and terrorised Christians, or Jewish courts who summarily passed death sentences on them. In terms of his future reputation St Paul left mention of these out. He cut down any reference to this to the very minimum. It is interesting that Ratzinger had no comment on this or on how little Paul dealt with the actual life of Jesus.

With such an encounter with Jesus, real or to non-believers imagined, Paul chose to make his conversion very public. By contrast, the English actor Alec Guinness, who took the role of Hitler in a film of his last days, and compassionately impersonated him, felt the privacy of his own conversion, like that of T.S. Eliot, should be respected. As Teilhard de Chardin wrote, 'The incommunicable part of us is the pasture of God.' On the path to his conversion, while serving in the British navy in 1944, and on leave in Rome just after its liberation, Guinness met Pius XII, whom he found gentle and decisive, and blessed with a ravishing smile. To Guinness the pope spoke of God, at the same time raising his eyes and arms, which made the actor realise how simple and beautiful such a movement could be. For the first time in his life he felt he had met a saint. It was Hitler, not T.S. Eliot nor Alec Guinness, who followed St Paul in the blinding light and dramatic power of the conversion that came to him, although in Hitler's case it was not Jesus that appeared to him, but a wronged and betrayed fatherland, with himself cast as prophet for its rebirth.

Not withstanding this, Benedict got right inside Paul's skin, closely and positively identifying with a figure, who, for twenty-first-century tastes, is held to be bigoted about women, homophobic and anti-semitic.

Inevitably, to begin with, Paul provoked suspicion from his background and persecution of Christians (as did, it might be claimed, by Benedict by virtue of his own historical context).

The disciples were suspicious of his conversion, but not surprisingly, as in keeping with the man we know, the Pope never described this but takes it as a given: 'although it is not easy to imagine in what his persecution actually consisted, his attitude was intolerant'.

Surely it should have been very easy, given how much present-day graphic evidence of persecution there is around us, to imagine what it was. Again, as in his treatment of the unpalatable, Benedict distanced himself. He didn't want to know.

More tellingly he hardly questioned the great event, the 'irresistible presence of the Risen One whom subsequently he would never be able to doubt, so powerful had been the event of his encounter.' This became the foundation of Paul's apostolate and of his new life.

So it was the resonance, the event in Paul's life which illuminated the book – not only a conversion, something affecting his life, but a death and a resurrection. Not, as Benedict noted, even with a touch of self-deprecation, just 'the fruit of his thought'.

This extreme shock, as far as one can tell, never happened to Benedict: the life-changing positive encounter never happened. Only the narrowing, horrendous shock. So was he unconsciously still hoping it would, something that would prepare him to escape from 'the fruits of his thought' – his concepts.

In his eloquent, fast-moving passion of his writing about Paul he even quoted Martin Luther (then, with this proviso, 'an Augustinian monk') on Paul's paradoxical words: 'This is that mystery which is rich in divine grace to sinners, wherein by a wonderful exchange our sins are no longer ours but Christ's, and the righteousness of Christ is not Christ's; but ours.'

There's a dynamic thrust in *Paul of Tarsus*, something of the zest and spirit you feel in Chesterton's Life of St Francis and his Thomas Aquinas, as if he delights in the disputes and controversy whipped up, and identified with his outbursts. It might mischievously be suggested that Benedict was really a closet St Paul. And that he embraced more wholeheartedly than he ever showed Paul's effortless embrace of faith which makes most Christians feel lily-livered and cowardly.

Yet on balance Benedict's own religious fires were very subdued and contained, and though like Paul he too remains an enigma, also like Paul his legacy will not be able to be sensibly or simply dismissed: it will be more complicated than that.

† † †

Just before announcing his abdication in February 2013 Benedict, again in private person mode, published the final part of *Jesus of Nazareth: The Infancy Narratives*. This tender short book is easily my, and I am sure everyone's, preferred volume of the three – more readable, more direct and accessible than the other two. He sets the tone with 'The ordinariness of Jesus, the provincial carpenter, seems not to conceal a mystery of any kind. His origin marks him out as one like any other.'

The single new Covenant, he goes on, is 'humility, hiddenness – the sign of the mustard-seed'. The book has an inner continuity which reflects some change or lowering of high theological expectation in its author, who perhaps can now allow the simple truths of the biblical narrative to come through with little analysis and intervention: let the story speak for itself, he avers, and he is especially moving about, and empathetic towards, the anguish Jesus's parents suffer when they lose him for three days.

He includes this as an epilogue. The sketch of Joseph and Mary taking Jesus on the pilgrimage to the Temple in Jerusalem for one of the great feasts of the Jewish year, as a means of accustoming him gradually to the commandments, to confirm his own identity in the encounter with God, is the best part of the book.

Jesus is twelve and on the journey back from the visit, at the end of the first day his parents realise that Jesus is no longer with them but has stayed behind in Jerusalem. Joseph and Mary pass three days in fear and anxiety before, on their return to the Temple they find Jesus sitting quietly among the teachers, listening to them, and asking them questions.

Benedict explains, and you can see behind this that he has returned to the quiet and piety of his early days with his own Joseph and Mary, recapturing the safety and security – at the same time the anxiety that the bond is to be fractured, only to give way to a greater binding:

These are days spent suffering the absence of Jesus, days of darkness, whose heaviness can be sensed in the mother's words: 'Child, why have you treated us so? Behold your father and I have been looking for your anxiously' (Lk 2: 48) Thus an arc extends from this first Passover of Jesus to his last, the Passover of the Cross.

Jesus' divine mission bursts through the boundaries of all human criteria and repeatedly comes, in human terms, a dark mystery. Something of the sword of sorrow of which Simeon had spoke (cf. Lk 2:35) becomes palpable for Mary at this hour. The closer one comes to Jesus, the more one is drawn into the mystery of his Passion. (Benedict, 2012)

It is clear that, in order to be able to write this, he has gone through fire, through suffering, to be able to arrive at such simple expressions of luminous faith: the intellect, the conceptual scaffolding with its hoardings of exegesis (a favourite Benedict word) has been taken down to reveal the graceful presence of the new temple: its stonework blasted free of the encrusted grime of centuries.

The Infancy Narratives and his stepping down as pope, which we will come to next, taken together are Ratzinger and Benedict's last great gesture of resolving that ambiguity and unfathomability. Both show what Dorothy Sayers expressed in a nutshell: 'The history and the theology of Christ are one thing: His life is theology in action, and the drama of His Life is dogma shown as dramatic action.'

Jesus' reply to his mother is astounding: How so? You were looking for me? Did you not know where a child must be? That he must be in his father's house, literally 'in the things of the Father' (Lk 2:49)? Jesus tells his parents: I am in the very place where I belong – with the Father, in his house.

There are two principal elements to note in this reply. Mary had said: 'Your father and I have been looking for you anxiously...' Jesus corrects her: I *am* with my father. My father is not Joseph but another – God himself. It is to him that I belong, and here I am with him. Could Jesus' divine son ship be presented any more clearly?

The second element is directly linked with this. Jesus uses the word 'must,' and acts in accordance with what *must* be. The Son, the child, *must* be with his father. The Greek word *deï*, which Luke uses here, reappears in the Gospels whenever mention is made of Jesus' readiness to submit to God's will. He must suffer greatly, be rejected, be killed, and rise again, as he says to his disciples after Peter's confession (cf Mk 8:31) (Benedict, 2012)

† † †

So did *Jesus of Nazareth* turn out to be by the end a work of personal discovery? In the first two volumes there was little to reveal the man Jesus behind the theological methodology to convince us that Benedict had an existential concern in writing his life of a genius, instead of producing a distinguished work of scholarship.

Packed with comparative theology and exegetical claims, *Jesus of Nazareth* undoubtedly benefited from the papal insignia, although its author declared it to be the work of a private man. It sold millions of copies worldwide. 'Nor was it fortuitous, reported Küng in a devil's advocate comment, 'that he condemned the liberation theologian Jon Sobrino, whose Jesus book, unlike his own, cannot be discussed freely in public.'

As for 'proof' that the historical Jesus was the same as the Jesus of faith and the Son of God, the final question perhaps to be asked is, did we need it? Or, does it need to be answered? Piers Paul Read's essay entitled 'Jesus as a Character in Fiction' demonstrates, albeit sketchily, how Jesus was unique as a character in both history *and* fiction. Read quotes from Gabriel Josopovici's *The Book of God* that what makes Jesus challenging was not the working of miracles, but his extraordinary air of authority.

He seems utterly sure of the ideas he puts forward, [writes Read, paraphrasing Josopovici] even though they are met with incredulity by his contemporaries quite as much as they are by sceptics today. Little by little, he gets across that he is not a mere prophet but the Son of God. When he says it too clearly, some of his audience try to stone him.

When he goes on to say that his flesh is real food and his blood real drink, and that only those who eat this flesh and blood will live forever, many of his followers said 'This is intolerable language. How could anyone accept it?' (Read, 2008)

Read then quotes Chesterton, who recognised it was precisely this insistence that he was God that makes Jesus unique both in history and fiction: 'Normally speaking, the greater a man is, the less likely he is to make the very greatest claim. Outside the unique case we are considering, the only man who ever does make this claim is a very small man; a secretive or self-centred maniac... [Jesus however] was exactly what a man with a delusion never is, he was wise.'

Read adds a further thought: 'If the gospels were fiction, said Jean-Jacques Rousseau, then the authors would be more extraordinary than their hero.'

28

Il Grand Refiuto

Know then thyself, presume not God to scan,
The proper study of mankind is Man.
Alexander Pope

It must be said, and here is the catch, that the impact of one pope can never be the whole story, that the Church goes on and will forever go on, with hundreds of millions of faithful and hundreds of thousands of devoted clergy, the religious and leaders, while whoever is at the apex of the broad-based pyramid can only affect its survival in the short term, for in the long term it will survive. Macaulay wrote in his *Essay on Ranke* over 150 years ago:

Her spiritual ascendancy... Her acquisitions in the New World have more than compensated for what she has lost in the Old... She was great and respected before the Saxon had set foot in Britain, before the Frank had passed the Rhine, when Grecian eloquence still flourished at Antioch, when idols were still worshipped in the temple of Mecca. And she may still exist in undiminished vigour when some traveller from New Zealand shall, in the midst of a vast solitude, take his stand on a broken arch of London Bridge to sketch the ruins of St Paul.

So how are we to interpret Benedict's last act, his refusal, or resignation, which happened in February 2013, during the morning

of the 11th, when he announced to the world that he was stepping down? He quoted as his previous exemplar of retirement
Celestine V, who passed the decree making this possible over 700
years before. The world and the Church were shocked by the
news in the main. According to tradition, the Vicar of Christ did
not give up his throne: was Benedict overriding God's will?

There was no doubt he was getting weaker and his long-term
health problems, beginning with the slight stroke, were complicated by worsening sight and mobility. But people asked if it
was not also political, for Church reasons – for the 'good of the
Church', as he told a crowd of 100,00 in St Peter's Square on
17 February: 'I'm an old man and the strength is ebbing.' One
explanation that sprung to mind was that he had decided he no
longer wanted that power and influence the Church conferred
on him, and which came about largely through his own volition
and intention. He had simply had enough.

But Paul VI had seen himself, as Vicar of Christ, in a mystical relationship with God, which he could never break off. John
Paul II saw the office as Peter as something he embodied as an
apostle. Here again, Benedict was nearer to those detractors of
his, by defining the papacy as a term of office. He demystified the
apostle aspect of being pope, demoting himself to a functionary.
Cardinal George Pell of Melbourne saw a danger here; he told an
Australian TV network the resignation set a worrying precedent,
for those who might disagree with a future pope would 'mount a
campaign to get him to resign'.

The English *Catholic Herald* listed ten reasons to 'thank God'
for Benedict, at the head of which was the special affection he
held for Great Britain, according it the patronage of his visit in
2010, when many other countries with a far superior numbers of
Catholics perhaps deserved greater attention.

The 'ordinariate' he created for former Anglicans the *Herald*
called 'one of his greatest legacies'. Important as it may be for
a few thousand former Anglicans and their followers, it hardly
rated highly on the effect it had on the world's 1.2 billion
Catholics. But as many of those Anglicans who became Catholics
had spouses, perhaps it was setting a precedent of married priests
in the Church.

Championing his 'great resolve to resist secular atheism', in a Europe building pluralistic societies devoted to interdependence of faiths and communities, was a weak reason to applaud him. Becoming so bothered over the 'dictatorship of relativism' in fact represented a big sell-out to relativism, playing into the hands of so-called relativists – first and foremost by identifying and calling them enemies. People do not see themselves as relativist and can switch many times, even in a single day, between various states of mind and feeling, and even opinions. To brand people by their opinions and by the labels attached to these goes wholly against the Catholic ethos of condemning the 'sin' and not the sinner. Someone may hold an atheistic view, as someone might suffer from schizophrenia or cancer, but it by no means defines them as a person. The Catholic Church on the defensive was beginning to sound like King Lear: 'I have been more sinned against than sinning.'

Example, not censure, was surely the better way to engage people in following Christian values. John Paul II grew old and weak in the public view, allowing his weakness to give value to the value and power of weakness. This carried a very potent message to a society which shied away from any expression or sign of declining strength. He lived out his pontificate from peaks to troughs on the world stage and there was nothing concealed or hidden about him. 'Many' averred Graham Greene, 'have become aware of the papacy as a point of suffering, a needle of pain, and a certain love always arises for the man who suffers.' Paul Claudel had a similar view: 'It is not by our virtues, but by our infirmities, that we have a right to God's intention.'

Benedict promised 'unconditional reverence and obedience' for his successor, but to some degree obfuscated that succession and the reasons for it, by not expressing who he was, displaying himself as usual only partly in the limelight, still applying to himself the papal secrecy life code. He kept what knee-jerk reactions he may have felt to himself, and as he departed he radiated that vibration ultimately of ambiguous self-projection (again related to his early years), not of the sinful protestations of a saint.

† † †

When Ratzinger was elected pope, his old antagonist Küng had expressed disappointment at the election, but this was not unmixed with a generous hope that he would enjoy a period of grace and change: he wrote down his hopes.

> The name Benedict XVI leaves open the possibility of a more moderate policy. Let us therefore give him a chance... At every turn he faces tremendous tasks which have been piling up for a long time and which were not tackled by his predecessor:
>
> 1. The active advancement of ecumenical relations between the Christian churches;
> 2. The realisation of the collegiality of the Pope with the bishops and the decentralisation of Church leadership, which is desired on all sides, in favour of greater autonomy of the local churches;
> 3. The guarantee of an equal footing for men and women in the Church and the implementation of the full participation of women at all levels in the Church.
>
> (Küng, 2008)

Küng, like many others, believed he did not tackle these tremendous tasks successfully. Küng knew the Vatican II doctrine had advocated the college of bishops should have more say in governing the Church, and that the Pope could have called the presidents of bishops conferences to work out a shared response. It was Ratzinger's own *Apostolus Suos* decree of 1998, which earlier had rendered the principle of collegiality ineffective. He appointed cardinals, nearly half of whom would be voting for the next pope, who on the face of it would elect another like-minded cardinal to follow him in the footsteps of St Peter. Yet those footprints were of one who hardly ever behaved like a cardinal:

> Headlong, impulsive, self-confident, blundering into error and then quickly humble and repentant – and then exactly the same thing all over again. All his instincts are generous – and he is really humble, and instantly sorry and quick to confess when he is wrong. He is confident about the Washing (of feet)

— then in a moment sees his mistake, rushes into the other extreme and has to be checked again. He is loud and positive that he would die, that he would never disown Jesus; when swords are mentioned he rushes to the conclusion that the Kingdom is (after all) going to be conquered by force; in the garden he is prepared to do it single-handed if necessary. No warning shakes his confidence in himself; prayer is lavished on him, but he takes no notice. Only when that ghastly cock-crow comes will he really get the shock that brings him to himself… But he still has the vision. Peter can always see the angels. And when he does finally know the extent of his own weakness, his real generosity and humility will save him from the despair that overtakes Judas, who has no humility, and no real generosity at all.

(Sayers, 1943)

The period of grace, or the gesture of grace, his stepping down, did have a very different impact on the Church itself, and its influence remains there, together with his enriching of the narrative of Jesus of Nazareth. He talked often of how Jesus brought a new awareness into the world, a new spirit and understanding, as well as approach to life, which had never been there before his arrival on earth. Perhaps a new awareness and approach to governing the Church will have been stimulated in his successor by Benedict's stepping down.

The Catholic Church in Bavaria was unable to stand up to and defeat Hitler because his vision and his magic were broader and greater in appeal than the rigid and narrow schematisation of Catholic thought and the hierarchy of Church governance. That there were, just as Benedict left, yet more new cases of sexual abuse or cover-ups by senior clergy points back to the stifling conformity and power play of the earlier Church and its return in the last few years. Cardinal Keith O'Brien, by preaching against homosexual love (while practising it) made things worse by denial, until forced to confess in public and resign. That his case of abuse should be revealed just as Benedict was stepping down was a microcosmic reminder of how the macrocosm of the Church had become its own worst enemy.

† † †

One of Jung's most famous cases was of a theologian, described in *Archetypes of the Collective Unconscious*. This theologian described to Jung that he dreamt that he stood on a slope commanding a beautiful view of a low valley covered with dense woods. It sounds just like Bavaria. There was, he knew, in the middle of these woods, a lake, but somehow he had been prevented on previous occasions from going there. This time he was determined to visit it, and as he got near the lake the atmosphere 'grew uncanny, and suddenly a light gust of wind passed over the surface of the water, which rippled darkly. He awoke with a cry of terror.' Jung ultimately interpreted this as the theologian's 'flight' at the prospect of reaching down into the nucleus of personality, a process, he says, especially difficult for theologians who are 'closer to religions, but on the other hand... more bound by church and dogma'.

They are especially prone to become victims of the psychic dichotomy of our time. No one, Jung asserts, has any objection to a concept. For what is so agreeable about conceptuality is that it promises protection from experience. 'There are many ways of communicating, there is not just one way,' Dr Navarro-Valls had replied. 'Concepts!' was the overriding, single word he had pointed out that summed up Benedict.

Jung claimed that his most difficult and most ungrateful patients (habitual liars aside) were the so-called intellectuals, for with them 'one hand never knows what the other hand is doing'. They cultivated a 'compartment psychology'. The reality of that 'compartment psychology' of the 1930s and 1940s in Nazi Germany was only too evident during Ratzinger's early years. He could not be blamed for it, and it became part of him. Self-awareness and self-knowledge, as well as sense of historical perspective, would have been one way to avoid its influence over him. Jung expresses it so well: 'The spirit does not dwell in concepts, but in deeds and facts.'

It was these deeds and facts which had come out of the woodshed to haunt the Pope and his entourage in these final years of his papacy. Ratzinger and the Catholic Church, with his liturgical reforms, his flow of tender homily and gracious admonition from his superior intellect appealed mainly to his intellectual following, and those who wanted simple direct commands and unquestioned answers. It did much to consolidate orthodox Church teaching.

In so doing he placed himself and in the long run a much smaller church, 'a little flock' Karl Rahner anticipated by foreseeing it in the 1960s, at a safe distance from real experience, and substituted in its place 'an apparently secure, artificial, but merely two-dimensional conceptual world in which the reality of life is well covered by so called clear concepts'. But did the Catholic Church need any way to be smaller? With Benedict's departure there remained, as Küng has expressed it,

> above all the question of the leadership of our Catholic Church: where is it taking our church? On the way of the First Vatican Council back into an authoritarian ghetto?
> I would still like to hope that in the end the spirit of true evangelical catholicity will triumph over the pernicious ideology of a legalistically narrow, doctrinally fossilised dogmatic and triumphalistically, fear-filled Catholicism.

In his book *Mimesis* Erich Auerbach describes what happened to St Augustine, who wrote up in his *Confessions*, which had been such an inspiration to the young priest Joseph, his experience on going to a brutal gladiatorial games, at first determinedly resistant witnessing the gruesome spectacle, and then succumbing to enjoyment and bloodlust:

> The about face is complete. And such an about-face from one extreme to the very opposite is also characteristically Christian. Like Peter in the denial scene (and inversely Paul on his way to Damascus), he falls the more deeply the higher he stood before. And, like Peter, he will rise again. For his defeat is not final. When God has taught him to rely on Him instead of on himself – and his very defeat is the first step towards that knowledge – he will triumph. For in the fight against magical intoxication, Christianity commands other weapons than that

of the rational and individualistic ideal of antique culture; it is, after all, itself a movement from the depths, from the depths of the multitude as from the depths of immediate emotion; it can fight the enemy with his own weapons. In witnessing the gruesome spectacle its magic is no less a magic than is bloodlust, and it is stronger because it is more ordered, a more human magic, filled with more hope. (Auerbach, 1953)

The last two popes will prove a very hard act to follow: John Paul II, the heroic pope who led from the front and put his person on the line; Benedict XVI, the teacher who could inspire the faithful to look again, and find new and stimulating reasons and ideas to recharge their faith. At the heart of Benedict, when the onion was peeled to the centre in these last years, what we found was the teacher, with the inspiration to renew the theology of the Church, rather than the leader. We must now leave 'the incommunicable part' of Pope Emeritus Benedict, in that wonderful phrase of de Chardin, in 'the pasture of God' (in his case, without wishing any disrespect, one would hope a Bavarian one), to enjoy his retirement.

† † †

Seventy-six-year-old Cardinal Jorge Mario Bergoglio, an Argentinian of Italian extraction, the first ever Jesuit to be elected pope, emerged as the Pope Francis I at 19.10 pm on 13 March 2013 after the fifth ballot – as big a surprise and shock, if not bigger, than Benedict's resignation. Because the conclave was over so quickly, most expected an Italian cardinal, the front-runner being Angelo Scola, Archbishop of Milan.

The reason Bergoglio was elected was that he had run second to Benedict at his election with forty votes, and to these had now been added those of the rest of the Americas, plus Italians who valued his immigrant origins; and he spoke their language. Francis, the first time this name was ever taken by a pope, was a popular choice – that of the founder of the Jesuit movement, St Francis Ignatius Loyola, and St Francis of Assisi, the most popular Italian saint of all, who appealed across every class, rich and poor, across every national frontier, and across the whole political spectrum (even Communists).

As Chesterton wrote of St Francis (and if true of Bergoglio this makes him the opposite of Benedict):

> He is what he is. Not only by what he has, but in some degree by what he has not… [He] is a very strong example of this quality in the man of genius, that in him even what is negative is positive, because it is part of a character. An excellent example of what I mean may be found in his attitude toward learning and scholarship. He ignored and in some degree discouraged books and book-learning… The whole point of his message was to be so simple that the village idiot could understand it.

Pope Francis I, with his example of appearing in a plain white cassock on the Vatican balcony, his calm, unfussed words spoken as if one to one, although before thousands, his reputation in Buenos Aires of eschewing all privilege, of travelling on buses and cooking his own meals, looks set to overturn the triumphalistic and combative image of the Church, and change the tenor of the conversation about its thorny issues, at the same time not running away from them.

He looks ready to address first of all the problem of the world's poor, of social justice, for which it seems he will give out the right message, for his words and example will be of a piece: again, as Chesterton says of St Francis; 'The dominant detail was the interpretation of the vow of poverty, or the refusal of all possessions.' Governance of the Church is potentially a strong point of his too. Most important of all, for the Church, if he can follow St Francis in the following respect, not provoking those for and those against, and heal divisions, he will prove an excellent pontiff:

> [He] does not compare himself with his followers, towards whom he might appear as a master; he compares himself more and more with his Master, towards whom he appears only as a servant … the saint is never supercilious, for he is always by hypothesis in the presence of a superior. The objection to an aristocracy is that it is a priesthood without a god.

We can only hope that Pope Francis sees or takes from Benedict that sense of a new beginning of consciousness, initiates a new phase that is now so necessary in the narrative of mankind in this utterly different context in which the Catholic Church finds itself during the second decade of the twenty-first century.

Cardinal Carlo Martini, former Archbishop of Milan and Jesuit scriptural scholar, before he died in 2012, said that the Church was '200 years behind the times', weighed down by pompous liturgies and vestments, and behaving in a 'fearful instead of courageous' way. A new approach started by Francis I, grounded in the changed circumstances, should be able to enable heart to speak to heart in the freedom of love (defined by John Paul as the extent to which one is capable of giving love).

The largely forgotten potentialities of Roman Catholicism, its mixture of lifestyles, the comprehensive penetration of the processes of existence which you find for example (a tiny list from the great range) in the works of Rabelais, Chesterton, Kazantzakis, C.S Lewis, Tolkien, the paintings and sculpture of Michelangelo, Caravaggio, Barroci, need rebirth and revitalisation, and new implementation. They must be imbued with sensuality, magic, and above all passion and vigour: a Christianity with a magnanimity of surrender, an integrity of faith and hope, an open reasonableness unencumbered by theory. Above all, a Christianity that might appeal to everyone.

Select Bibliography

Accattoli, Luigi (2000) *Karol Wojtyla: L'uomo di fine millennio (Man of the Millennium)*. Pauline Books.

Allen, John L., Jr (2002), *Conclave*. Doubleday.

Allen, John L., Jr (2005) *The Rise of Benedict XVI*. Penguin.

Auerbach, Erich (1953) *Mimesis: The Representation of Reality in Western Literature*. Princeton University Press.

Benedict XVI (2007) Pope, *Jesus of Nazareth, Volume 1*. Bloomsbury.

Benedict XVI (2010) *Light of the World: The Pope, the Church and the Signs of the Times*. Ignatius Press.

Benedict XVI (2011) *Jesus of Nazareth, Volume 2*. Catholic Truth Society.

Benedict XVI (2012) *Jesus of Nazareth: The Infancy Narratives*. Bloomsbury.

Cavell, Stanley (1996) *Must We Mean What We Say?* Cambridge University Press.

Chesterton, G.K. (1937) *Collected Poems*. Methuen.

Chesterton, G.K. (1952) *St Thomas Aquinas*. Hodder & Stoughton.

Chesterton, G.K. (1960) *St Francis of Assisi*. Hodder & Stoughton.

Chesterton, G.K. (1994) *What's Wrong with the World*. Ignatius Press.

Clare, George (1989) *Berlin Days 1946–7*. Macmillan.

Cornwell, John A. (1989) *A Thief in the Night*. Viking.

Cornwell, John A. (1999) *Hitler's Pope*. Viking.

Cornwell, John A. (2004) *The Pope in Winter*. Viking.

Cornwell, John A. (2010) *Newman's Unquiet Grave*. Continuum.

Craig, Mary (1982) *Man from a Far Country*. Hodder & Stoughton.

Crankshaw, Edward (1963) *The Fall of the House of Hapsburg*. Longmans, Green & Co.

Evans, Richard J. (2005) *The Third Reich in Power*. Allen Lane.

Erlandson, Gregory and Matthew Bunson (2010) *Benedict XVI and the Sexual Abuse Crisis*. Our Sunday Visitor.

Falconi, Carlo (1970) *The Silence of Pius XII*. Faber.

Frank, Niklas (1991) *In the Shadow of the Reich*. Alfred A Knopf.

Freud, Sigmund (1985) *The Origins of Religion*. Pelican.

Frossard, André (1990) *Portrait of John Paul II*. Ignatius Press.

Girard, René (1987) *Things Hidden since the Foundation of the World*. Standford University Press.

Gombrowicz, Witold (1988) *Diaries, Volume 1 & 2*. Northwestern University Press.

Grass, Gunter (2007) *Peeling the Onion*. Harvill Secker.

Hebblethwaite, Peter (1994a) *John XXIII: Pope of the Council*. Fount.

Hebblethwaite, Peter (1994b) *Paul VI: The First Modern Pope*. Fount.

Hebblethwaite, Peter (2000) *The Next Pope*. Fount.

John Paul II, Pope (1997) *The Theology of the Body: Human Love in the Divine Plan*. Pauline Books and Media.

John Paul II, Pope (2005) *Memory and Identity*. Weidenfield & Nicolson.

Kazantzakis, Nikos (1995) *Last Temptation*. Faber & Faber.

Kelly, J.N.D. (1986) *Oxford Dictionary of Popes*. Oxford University Press.

Küng, Hans (2003) *My Struggle for Freedo: Memoirs I*. Continuum.

Küng, Hans (2008) *Disputed Truths: Memoirs II*. Continuum.

Lewis, C.S. (2002) *The Screwtape Letters*. HarperCollins.

Longley, Clifford (2000) *The Worlock Archive*. G. Chapman.

Mann, Thomas (1968) *Doctor Faustus*. Penguin.

Martin, Malachi (1996) *Windswept House*. Doubleday.

Moore, Sebastian (1977) *The Crucified Is No Stranger*. Darton, Longman & Todd.

Moore, Sebastian (1985) *Let This Mind Be In You*. Darton, Longman & Todd.

Nichols, Peter (1982) *The Pope's Divisions: The Roman Catholic Church Today*. Penguin Books.

O'Connor, Garry (2006) *Universal Father, A Life of John Paul II*. Bloomsbury.

O'Connor, Garry (2007) *The Darlings of Downing Street*. Politico's.

Oddie, William (ed.) (2003) *John Paul the Great*. The Catholic Herald and the Catholic Truth Society.

Pagels, Elaine (1996) *The Origin of Satan*. Allen Lane.

Peperdy, Alison (ed.) (1988) *Women Priests.* Marshal Morgan and Scott.

Rahner, Karl (1966) *Visions and Prophecies.* Burns & Oates.

Ratzinger, Cardinal Joseph (1998) *Milestones: Memoirs 1927–1977.* Ignatius Press.

Ratzinger, Cardinal Joseph, and Messori, Vittorio (1985) *The Ratzinger Report.* Fowler Wright.

Read, Piers Paul (2008) *Heaven and Other Destinations.* Darton, Longman & Todd.

Sachs, Jonathan (2002) *The Dignity of Difference: How to Avoid the Clash of Civilizations.* Continuum.

Sayers, Dorothy L. (1943) *The Man Born to be King.* Gollancz.

Schenk, Dieter (2008) *Hans Frank: Hitler's Kronjurist und Generalgouverneur.* Fischer Tascherbuch Verlag.

Scruton, Roger (2002) *The West and the Rest.* Continuum.

Seewald, Peter (1997) *Salt of the Earth.* Ignatius Press.

Seewald, Peter (2008) *Benendict XVI.* Ignatius Press.

Shirer, William L. (1959) *The Rise and Fall of the Third Reich.* Simon & Schuster.

Sinclair, Upton (1940) *World's End.* T. Werner Laurie.

Sinclair, Upton (1941) *Between Two Worlds End.* T. Werner Laurie.

Sinclair, Upton (1942) *Dragon's Teeth.* T. Werner Laurie.

Sinclair, Upton (1944) *Wide is the Gate.* T. Werner Laurie.

Sinclair, Upton (1945) *Presidential Agent End.* T. Werner Laurie.

Shortt, Rupert (2005) *Benedict XVI.* Hodder & Stoughton.

Speer, Albert (1970) *Inside the Third Reich.* Weidenfeld & Nicolson.

Spong, John Shelby (1942) *The Black Book, Vol. 2, The German New Order in Poland, 1939-41.* Hutchinson.

Spong, John Shelby (1999) *Why Christianity Must Change or Die.* HarperCollins.

Thompson, Damian (1996) *The End of Time.* Sinclair-Stevenson.

Walsh, Michael (1995) *John Paul II: A Biography.* Fount.

Weigel, George (2004) *Letters to a Young Catholic.* Gracewing.

Willey, David (1992) *God's Politician: Pope John Paul II, The Catholic Church and the New World Order.* Faber & Faber.

Williams, George Huntston (1982) *The Mind of John Paul II: Origins of His Thought and Action.* Seabury.

Wills, Garry (2000) *Papal Sin: Structures of Deceit.* Darton, Longman & Todd.

Acknowledgements

I have to be brief. I have been writing parts of this book from the time in 2005 I finished *Universal Father*. I must acknowledge with deep gratitude all those who have helped or contributed to its writing and production. It was only commissioned in mid-February 2013, and went to press on 15 March. First of all, I thank my friends in, and members of, the Church, as well as other friends of a definitely non-religious 'denomination', too numerous to list at the present time. Without their comments and opinions, as well as information about Pope Benedict over the years, I would have got nowhere. I thank Michael Holroyd, for reading a draft; my agents Julian Friedmann and Tom Witcomb, and their German reader Julia Reuter, who commented on drafts and some early chapters, and to Jackie Bradley for help in various ways. My thanks are due to the Press Association for pictures and their captions.

I thank the many writers of source material I have drawn on, especially Peter Seewald for his interviews with the Pope; as far as possible, I have referred to as many sources as I could in the text, and listed them in the Bibliography. I must stress that the opinions and interpretations I place upon them are entirely my own.

I must especially thank all those involved in this extraordinary effort of publishing. My good fortune was to have Martin Noble edit the final text over an extremely short time, which he did with his usual enhancing and perceptive skill. At The History Press, most of all I thank Shaun Barrington, who has engaged with the book at every stage of its development with boundless enthusiasm and energy, and with whom I have enjoyed working enormously.

Last, but not in any way least – and really they should be first – to Vicky and my family, whose opinions and attitudes I have done my best to incorporate.

Index